An Appeal in Favor
of That Class of Americans
Called Africans

AN APPEAL

IN FAVOR OF

THAT CLASS OF AMERICANS

Called Africans

LYDIA MARIA CHILD

Edited with an introduction by

CAROLYN L. KARCHER

UNIVERSITY OF MASSACHUSETTS PRESS

AMHERST

Copyright © 1996 by The University of Massachusetts Press
All rights reserved
Printed in the United States of America
LC 95-21667
ISBN 1-55849-006-X (cloth); 1-55849-007-8 (pbk.)
Designed by Susan Bishop
Set in Adobe Garamond by Keystone Typesetting, Inc.
Printed and bound by Thomson-Shore, Inc.

Library of Congress Cataloging-in-Publication Data
Child, Lydia Maria Francis, 1802–1880.
An appeal in favor of that class of Americans called
Africans / Lydia Maria Child ; edited with an introduction
by Carolyn L. Karcher.
p.   cm.
Includes bibliographical references (p.   ).
ISBN 1–55849–006–X (cloth : alk. paper). — ISBN 1–55849–007–8
(paper : alk. paper)
1. Slavery—United States. 2. Antislavery movements—United
States. I. Karcher, Carolyn L., 1945– . II. Title.
E449.C532   1996
305.896'073—dc20   95-21667

This book is published with the support and cooperation
of the University of Massachusetts Boston.

The introduction to this book is adapted from Chapter 8 of
Carolyn L. Karcher, *The First Woman in the Republic: A Cultural
Biography of Lydia Maria Child* (Durham, N.C.: Duke University
Press, 1994) with the permission of Duke University Press.

The text of *An Appeal* here reprinted is that of the first
edition (Boston: Allen and Ticknor, 1833). It has been compared
with the second edition (New York: John S. Taylor, 1836) and
emended to include new material from that edition and to
indicate material from the 1833 edition omitted in the 1836
edition. Obvious errata have been silently corrected.

*To Joyce Sparer Adler
and Irving Adler*

Contents

Preface and Acknowledgments

LYDIA Maria Child's *Appeal in Favor of That Class of Americans Called Africans* (1833) fittingly made its initial comeback at the height of the Civil Rights movement, when direct action against racism by masses of African Americans and whites revived memories of the interracial struggle against slavery that had culminated a century earlier in the passage of the nation's first civil rights legislation. Published in 1963, the year of Martin Luther King's March on Washington, *The Abolitionists: A Collection of Their Writings,* edited by Louis Ruchames, included a long extract from the final chapter of the *Appeal*: "Prejudices Against People of Color, and Our Duties in Relation to This Subject." That extract, with its bold call for ending all forms of racial discrimination, from employment bans and segregated schools to antimiscegenation laws, introduced me to Lydia Maria Child. Soon afterward, the *Appeal* became available to the public in its entirety, along with many other abolitionist works in the Arno Press and *New York Times* reprint series.

Though most of the legal and extralegal discriminatory practices cataloged by Child—still prevalent at the start of the Civil Rights movement—have now gone the way of slavery, the *Appeal* remains as timely today as in the 1960s. Institutional racism and socioeconomic barriers continue to operate against the advancement of African Americans, keeping the number in poverty (and in prison) disproportionately high, the number in college and in the liberal professions disproportionately low. Antiblack violence of the type Child observed in northern cities persists. The myths of black intellectual inferiority that Child refuted so incisively a century and a half ago re-emerge in pseudoscientific garb with depressing regularity, hailed by an avid public in each incarnation, as the best-seller status achieved by *The Bell Curve* in 1994 testifies.

The enduring relevance of Child's *Appeal* lies not merely in the tenacious social ills the book exposes, but in the inspiring model it provides of how those ills can be cured—through an interracial solidarity movement committed to translating the ideals of freedom, democracy, justice, and equality into reality for all human beings. The example of Child and her abolitionist comrades, both white and

African American, proves that racism is neither universal nor insurmountable. The battles these activists won in their lifetime—the abolition of chattel slavery, the passage of a black suffrage amendment, the elimination of Jim Crow transportation in many parts of the country, the launching of university education for African Americans—confirm that joint struggle can indeed transform society.

The *Appeal* deserves republication on grounds that go beyond its significance as a memento of the abolitionist movement, however. It also claims recognition as a pioneering work of historical scholarship. Its comprehensive scope, encompassing legal, economic, and political analysis of the peculiar institution, as well as the moral and religious arguments against slavery de rigueur for an abolitionist tract, foreshadows the interdisciplinary approaches that have enriched the study of history over the past few decades. Its mode of setting the slave system of the antebellum South in a broad historical context and examining it in relation to the slave systems of other cultures and epochs anticipates the comparative methodology that has shed new light on the study of slavery and race since the 1970s, informing such classics as George M. Fredrickson's *White Supremacy: A Comparative Study in American and South African History,* Carl N. Degler's *Neither Black Nor White: Slavery and Race Relations in Brazil and the United States,* and David Brion Davis's triptych *The Problem of Slavery in Western Culture, The Problem of Slavery in the Age of Revolution, 1770–1823,* and *Slavery and Human Progress.* Even Child's assertions about the role the slave trade played in retarding the economic development of Africa and about the tendency of democratic countries to produce the harshest slave systems have been substantiated by recent scholars. In sum, the *Appeal* may have as much to teach readers at the approach of the twenty-first century as it did those who experienced the throes of the antislavery controversy.

Inaugurating a new edition of Child's *Appeal*—the first oriented toward the college classroom—presents an occasion for paying tribute to the late Sidney Kaplan, who suggested this project years before it became feasible and who also sponsored the reprinting of Child's collected correspondence. One of the rare literary scholars cognizant of Child's writings and aware of her importance in that early era, Professor Kaplan kept the study of abolitionism—and of the African American legacy—alive in the white academic world during the long reign of New Criticism.

In dedicating this edition to Joyce Sparer Adler and Irving Adler, I wish both to acknowledge their own contributions to the struggle against racism over the last fifty years and to highlight the links connecting the abolitionists of Child's day to later generations of activists. The Adlers' encouragement of my work on Child, which Joyce read and critiqued in its entirety, makes the dedication doubly appropriate.

Paul M. Wright of the University of Massachusetts Press, who resurrected and carried through the idea of reprinting the *Appeal* after Sidney Kaplan's death, has been equally supportive. I am especially grateful for his careful reading of the introduction. I am grateful, too, to Reynolds Smith and Duke University Press for permission to adapt the introduction virtually in toto from Chapter 8 of *The First Woman of the Republic: A Cultural Biography of Lydia Maria Child.*

Patricia G. Holland, coeditor of Child's *Collected Correspondence* and *Selected Letters,* collated the 1833 and 1836 editions of the *Appeal,* advised the Press on how to produce a text combining the important features of both versions, and undertook the editorial preparation and proofreading.

Milton Meltzer, the other editor of the Child correspondence, likewise gave this project his enthusiastic support, as did H. Bruce Franklin, Jane Morgan Franklin, and above all my husband, Martin. To all of them my heartfelt thanks.

Chronology of Lydia Maria Child

1802

February 11: Lydia Francis is born to Convers Francis and Susannah Rand Francis in Medford, Massachusetts, the youngest of five surviving children.

1814

May: Susannah Rand Francis (mother) dies of tuberculosis after a three-year illness.

1815

Summer: Lydia Francis is sent to Norridgewock, Maine (still a province of Massachusetts), to live with her married sister, Mary Francis Preston. During her six-year sojourn in Maine she comes in contact with Abenaki and Penobscot Indians and educates herself in English literature.

1821

Late summer: Moves in with her brother Convers Francis, Jr., now pastor of First Church (Unitarian) of Watertown, Massachusetts; takes the name Lydia Maria.

1824

Summer: Writes her first novel, *Hobomok, A Tale of Early Times*, featuring an interracial marriage between a Puritan woman and an Indian.

December: Publishes *Evenings in New England*, a children's book containing her first statement about the slavery issue; meets David Lee Child (DLC).

1826

September: Starts publication of *The Juvenile Miscellany*, the nation's first successful children's magazine, which she edits until 1834.

1828

October 19: Marries DLC; begins helping him edit his newspaper, the *Massachusetts Journal*, in which she publishes many stories and articles over the next few years.

1829

Early January (or late December 1828): Has privately printed a revisionist history for children of the Puritans' Indian wars, *The First Settlers of New-England*, in which she suggests interracial marriage as a solution to the Indian problem and advances theories of racial equality later amplified in *An Appeal in Favor of That Class of Americans Called Africans*.

October–November: William Lloyd Garrison reprints Child's "Comparative Strength of Male and Female Intellect" in the *Genius of Universal Emancipation* and hails her as "*the first woman in the republic.*"

November 12: Publishes *The Frugal Housewife*, a domestic advice book that goes through thirty-three editions in the United States, twelve in England and Scotland, and nine in Germany.

1830

June or July: Meets William Lloyd Garrison.

September: Publishes her first antislavery story in *The Juvenile Miscellany*, "The St. Domingo Orphans"; thereafter every number of the magazine contains antislavery commentary.

1831

January 1: Garrison founds the *Liberator*.

June: LMC publishes *The Mother's Book*, the first American manual covering all aspects of childrearing from the sensory development of infants to the sex education of teenagers; it goes through eight editions.

August: Editorializes against racial prejudice in the *Massachusetts Journal*; Garrison praises Child's "Noble Commentary"; DLC responds to the Nat Turner revolt by defending the right of the oppressed to rebel.

1832

January: DLC attends founding meeting of New England Anti-Slavery Society.

1833

August 5: Publishes *An Appeal in Favor of That Class of Americans Called Africans*; second edition published in 1836.

December: American Anti-Slavery Society founded in Philadelphia.

1834

January: Joins Boston Female Anti-Slavery Society (BFASS).

May: Mass cancellation of subscriptions forces LMC to give up editorship of *Juvenile Miscellany*.

October: Publishes *The Oasis,* an antislavery gift book.

December: Organizes first Anti-Slavery Fair with Louisa Loring.

1835

May: Boston Athenaeum cancels LMC's free library privileges.

August 1: Helps save the British abolitionist George Thompson from an antiabolitionist mob.

Fall: The Childs attend a meeting of the Philadelphia Female Anti-Slavery Society, where they make the acquaintance of Angelina Grimké; LMC publishes *History of the Condition of Women* and *Authentic Anecdotes of American Slavery*; Boston mob attacks BFASS and nearly lynches Garrison.

1836

January: Publishes *The Evils of Slavery, and the Cure of Slavery* and *Anti-Slavery Catechism*.

Fall: LMC collects evidence that helps Ellis Loring win the case of the slave child Med, establishing that a slave voluntarily brought into a free state by his or her owner automatically becomes free.

1837

May 9–12: Represents BFASS at first Anti-Slavery Convention of American Women (New York).

1838

The Childs move to Northampton to start producing beet sugar as an alternative to slave-grown cane sugar; they circulate antislavery petitions.

1839

May: LMC participates in New England Anti-Slavery Convention, serves on the Business Committee; opponents of women's full membership found rival Massachusetts Abolition Society.

LMC serves as president pro tem of BFASS during schism between pro- and anti-Garrisonian members; attends Margaret Fuller's Conversations and Emerson's lectures; publishes four pieces, including "Charity Bowery" (interview with an ex-slave) in inaugural issue of the abolitionist gift book, *The Liberty Bell*.

1840

May: DLC attends New York meeting of American Anti-Slavery Society, which splits over appointment of women as officers and committee members.

December: LMC publishes "The Black Saxons" in *Liberty Bell* for 1841.

1841

May: LMC moves to New York to edit *National Anti-Slavery Standard* for two years; boards with the Quaker Underground Railroad agent Isaac T. Hopper.

August 19: Inaugurates "Letters from New-York" ("LNY") column in *Standard*.

December: Publishes "The Quadroons" in *Liberty Bell* for 1842.

1842

December: Publishes "Slavery's Pleasant Homes" in *Liberty Bell* for 1843.

1843

May: Resigns from editorship of *Standard* after months of dissension over editorial policy and factionalism; resumes her literary career; DLC replaces her as editor in August, but resigns the following May.

Late August: Publishes *Letters from New-York*; first edition sold out by December, book goes through eleven editions.

December: Inaugurates new "LNY" column in the *Boston Courier*.

1844–55

LMC ceases to work with antislavery societies, but continues to help fugitive slaves and to write for the cause. Publishes *Fact and Fiction: A Collection of Stories* (1846); several children's books; *Isaac T. Hopper* (1853), a biography of her Quaker host in New York, highlighting his Underground Railroad and prison reform activities; *The Progress of Religious Ideas* (1855), a three-volume comparative history of religion; and "Jan and Zaida" in the *Liberty Bell* for 1856.

1856

May 22: Charles Sumner caned in the U.S. Senate by Preston Brooks; civil war rages in Kansas between anti- and proslavery settlers.

October–November: LMC serializes "The Kansas Emigrants" in *New York Tribune* during last week of 1856 electoral campaign; writes "Song for the Free Soil Men"; organizes sewing circle in Wayland for antislavery settlers in Kansas; DLC campaigns for Republican presidential candidate, John C. Frémont, who loses to Democrat James Buchanan; LMC publishes *Autumnal Leaves,* her last collection of short stories.

1857

December: Publishes "The Stars and Stripes. A Melo-Drama" in *Liberty Bell* for 1858.

1859

May: The Childs attend New England Anti-Slavery Convention; John Brown walks out of it.

October 16–18: John Brown and his men raid Harpers Ferry, Virginia.

October 26: LMC writes to John Brown and Virginia governor Henry Wise, asking permission to nurse Brown in prison.

November–December: Publishes exchanges with Brown, Governor Wise, and Margaretta Mason, wife of Virginia senator James M. Mason, in *New York Tribune*; raises funds for the families of Brown and his men; helps Garrison organize Tremont Temple ceremony to commemorate Brown's hanging.

1860

January: Publishes *Correspondence between Lydia Maria Child and Gov. Wise and Mrs. Mason*; 300,000 copies sold.

February: Completes *The Right Way the Safe Way, Proved by Emancipation in the British West Indies, and Elsewhere*; personally addresses and mails more than a thousand copies over the next year.

Late summer: Edits Harriet Jacobs's *Incidents in the Life of a Slave Girl.*

October: Publishes *The Patriarchal Institution* and mails out hundreds of copies; publishes *The Duty of Disobedience to the Fugitive Slave Law,* sending copies to newly elected Massachusetts legislators; raises funds to free Thomas Sims, a fugitive slave sent back to his master by Chief Justice Lemuel Shaw of the Massachusetts Supreme Court.

November: Lincoln elected.

December: The Childs attend two antislavery meetings mobbed by conservatives; South Carolina secedes.

1861

January 24: The Childs attend another antislavery meeting mobbed by conservatives.

April: Civil War breaks out with capture of Fort Sumter by Confederacy.

July: Union defeat at Battle of Bull Run.

Writes anonymous pro-emancipation articles for newspapers, sends relief supplies to "contrabands," knits for abolitionist-led regiments.

1862

August–September: Publishes "Emancipation and Amalgamation" and "L. Maria Child to the President of the United States," in which she calls for an Emancipation Proclamation and the enrollment of African American soldiers in the Union Army and answers fears of race-mixing.

1864

Lobbies for education and training programs for freedpeople, redistribution of confiscated plantations to freedpeople and poor whites, and reelection of Lincoln.

1865

January 31: House of Representatives passes Thirteenth Amendment, abolishing slavery.

April: Lee surrenders to Grant at Appomattox, ending Civil War; Lincoln assassinated.

November: Publishes *The Freedman's Book,* a reader for the ex-slaves featuring selections by or about people of African descent, stressing their achievements.

1866

Publishes articles in the *Independent* criticizing Andrew Johnson's Reconstruction policies.

1867

July: Publishes *A Romance of the Republic,* her last novel, offering interracial marriage as the solution to the problem of the nation's future.

1868

Publishes *An Appeal for the Indians.*

Writes many articles over the next few years for the *Standard,* the *Independent,* the *Woman's Advocate,* and the *Woman's Journal* advocating black suffrage, land redistribution, protection against Ku Klux Klan terrorism for the freedpeople, woman suffrage, Indian rights.

1870

January 27: The Childs attend closing meeting of Massachusetts Anti-Slavery Society and last Anti-Slavery Festival.

April 16: *National Anti-Slavery Standard* ceases publication after ratification of Fifteenth Amendment, enfranchising black men.

1874

September 17: DLC dies in Wayland.

November: Democrats recapture Congress, ushering in end of Reconstruction.

1879

May: Shortly after a visit with LMC, Garrison dies.

August: Publishes tribute to Garrison in *Atlantic* (her last article).

1880

October 20: Dies in Wayland.

INTRODUCTION

Let me say, then, that—taking her for all in all—
she is the first woman in the republic.

THIS encomium appeared in an article of 20 November 1829, head-lined "MRS. CHILD" in bold capitals and featured prominently in the editorial column of the *Genius of Universal Emancipation,* an anti-slavery newspaper issued from Baltimore by the Quaker Benjamin Lundy. Its author was William Lloyd Garrison, who at age twenty-four had recently joined Lundy as coeditor of the *Genius,* having previously edited several ephemeral newspapers and worked briefly as a journeyman printer at the offices of David Lee Child's *Massachusetts Journal.*[1]

The commendation, prefacing an extract from Lydia Maria Child's "Hints to People of Moderate Fortune," was in fact Garrison's second tribute in three weeks to the wife of his quondam employer. On October 30 he had reprinted an article from the *Massachusetts Journal,* "Comparative Strength of Male and Female Intellect," which he had ascribed to "Mrs. Child, (formerly Miss Francis,) a writer who is not surpassed, if equalled, by any other female in this country, and whose genius is as versatile as it is brilliant." Indeed, Garrison had asserted, Child's anonymous contributions to the *Massachusetts Journal* were "worthy of the strongest intellect of the most sagacious politician."[2] Now he pronounced even his earlier "panegyric" inadequate. Not only did Child excel such rivals as Lydia Huntley Sigourney, Sarah Josepha Hale, and Catharine Maria Sedgwick in "depth and expansion of mind," Garrison judged, but she had shown that she could "impart useful hints to the government as well as to the family circle." Through her "Hints to People of Moderate Fortune," published in the *Massachusetts Journal* and currently receiving "extensive circulation" in other newspapers, she was "doing more to reform the manners of the age" and to "restore the simplicity of the good old days of our fathers" than any other writer, "male or female," since Benjamin Franklin. The author of *Poor Richard's Almanac* would be proud to claim Child's "Hints," Garrison added, "for they embody his wisdom, his sagacity, and his wonderful knowledge of human nature." Exhort-ing Child to reissue these essays in book form, he went on to comment that her children's magazine, the *Juvenile Miscellany* (1826–34), likewise deserved a nationwide circulation commensurate with the "admirable" influence it was exerting on the "rising generation." He ended by expressing an intense desire to meet the literary woman who had excited in him a "curiosity . . . greater than toward any other 'north of the Potomac.'"

Clearly, Garrison was already dreaming of enlisting this eloquent and discerning critic of American society in the antislavery cause.[3] Many months would go by before he would find an opportunity to do so, however. At the very moment he was eulogizing Child's talents as a political writer, he was engaged in his first major antislavery battle—the exposé of a Newburyport, Massachusetts, merchant named Francis Todd, who had transported a shipload of slaves from Baltimore to New Orleans. The slave-trading allegation publicly leveled against a wealthy New Englander (though true) would land Garrison in a Baltimore jail for seven weeks on a libel conviction. Not until the New York philanthropist and future abolitionist leader Arthur Tappan paid Garrison's fine would the crusading editor be free to visit Boston in early June 1830.[4]

Meanwhile, the Childs were probably receiving the *Genius of Universal Emancipation* in exchange for the *Massachusetts Journal,* a common practice among editors during a period when local newspapers could not afford to hire correspondents to cover news from distant cities. They were also following the Garrison libel case through other newspapers and hotly debating the advisability of agitating the question of slavery, particularly in the confrontational manner Garrison had adopted. "[I]t was the theme of many of our conversations while Garrison was in prison," Child later recalled, crediting David with being "wide awake before I was."[5] By November 1830, when Garrison was back in Boston for good, David was defending him in the columns of the *Massachusetts Journal.* Rather than censure, he proclaimed, Garrison "deserved praise for 'covering with infamy' as 'thick' as he could any slave-dealer, slave-owner, . . . or slave-agent or driver in the world."[6] David was one of the first to whom Garrison confided his intention of founding the *Liberator,* which would begin publication on 1 January 1831. Yet while David applauded, Child herself pronounced Garrison "too ultra, too rash" for her taste.[7]

David's prior receptivity to Garrison may reflect the similarity of their pugnacious editorial styles. Or it may date back to their earlier acquaintance. In April 1827 both men had participated in an abortive campaign to reelect John Quincy Adams, in the course of which David had spoken at a Faneuil Hall rally that Garrison had covered for the *Newburyport Herald.* During his stint on the *Massachusetts Journal,* the youthful journeyman printer had greatly admired the "vigor and dash" of his employer's writing, as well as the "candor, good sense, and sterling independence" David had shown as editor. Garrison may also have tried to proselytize his employer when he began collecting signatures for antislavery petitions in August 1828, after being spurred into antislavery activism by Benjamin Lundy. He would pay tribute to David half a century later as one of "the very earliest of my anti-slavery friends and co-laborers," though by then he could no longer recollect how much contact he and David had had with each other at the *Journal* office.[8]

It was Maria Child, rather than David, however, whom Garrison most wished to proselytize as he set about building an antislavery movement in June 1830. His extravagant tribute to her as "*the first woman in the republic*" indicates that he considered a meeting with her important enough to attempt arranging it amid a flying visit to Boston on his emergence from prison. Through his former employer and fellow editor, he had a natural entrée to her, as well as a strategic ally in the effort to involve her in the crusade against slavery. Thus, on both sides the stage was set for a catalytic encounter.

Child would remember the event vividly almost fifty years afterward. "I little thought then that the whole pattern of my life-web would be changed by that introduction," she wrote on hearing the news of Garrison's death in May 1879.

I was then all absorbed in poetry and painting,—soaring aloft, on Psyche-wings, into the etherial regions of mysticism. He got hold of the strings of my conscience, and pulled me into Reforms. It is of no use to imagine what might have been, if I had never met him. Old dreams vanished, old associates departed, and all things became new. . . . A new stimulus siezed [*sic*] my whole being, and carried me whithersoever it would. "I could not otherwise, so help me God."[9]

The language inescapably suggests a religious conversion. Like the Old Testament Prophets on whom the word of the Lord descended, commanding them to preach to a recalcitrant people; like the early Christians filled with the spirit of God at Pentecost and empowered to see visions and speak in foreign tongues, Child felt herself possessed and transformed. Inspired by Garrison's ardent fellow feeling for the slaves,[10] impelled by his sense of urgency, and deeply moved by his appeal to her conscience, Child reconsecrated her art to the service of her sisters and brothers in bonds.

Nevertheless, she did not espouse on the spot the doctrines that would come to characterize Garrisonian abolitionism. For one thing, in June 1830 Garrison had scarcely begun to formulate them.[11] More to the point, Child was far too independent minded to embrace a creed she had not thoroughly investigated. Garrison had aroused her sympathy for the slaves and induced her to devote her life to working for their emancipation, but before she could publicly advocate abolition, she had to wrestle with a host of troublesome questions.

For example: Granted that slavery was a gigantic moral evil, was the condition of southern slaves really so intolerable? Wasn't it in the masters' interests to treat their slaves kindly, and didn't simple expediency result in making cruelty the exception rather than the rule? Besides, wasn't it the constitutional prerogative of the slaveholding states to regulate their own internal affairs, and, if so, what right did the North have to meddle with slavery? Wouldn't agitation of the issue anger the South and thereby threaten the Union? Didn't the Colonization Society, founded in 1816, provide a vehicle for gradual emancipation through its program of resettling free blacks in Africa? Was any other means of emancipation safe or feasible? If the slaves were "turned loose," would they go on a rampage against whites? Would emancipation bring economic ruin? What lessons should be drawn from the contrasting precedents offered by the Santo Domingo uprising of the 1790s and the process of gradual abolition by legislative fiat in the northern states? In the event that Colonization should prove unworkable, could blacks and whites coexist in harmony once slavery was abolished? To what extent did racial prejudice on one side and racial hatred or biological inferiority on the other pose insurmountable obstacles to the integration of blacks into the American body politic? Was there evidence that racial prejudice was not universal and that blacks were not inferior?

These questions, and the unresolved issues lurking behind them, had stymied antislavery activism for several decades, ever since the ratification of the Constitution with its fatal compromises tacitly recognizing slavery. In 1830 Child did not have access to a body of antislavery literature to which she could turn for answers. True, protest against slavery had started in the late seventeenth century, and earlier generations of abolitionists had argued persuasively that slavery violated Christian principles and secular doctrines of natural rights.[12] Yet American abolitionists of the pre-Revolutíonary period had not had to face constitutional barriers to legislative action. Nor did British and French antislavery theory always apply to the United States, where slavery was practiced not in distant colonies, but in states that formed an indissoluble part of the nation and benefited from disproportionate political representation in Congress.

In short, to refute the objections that conservative opponents raised to antislavery agitation, Child had to collect facts from a wide variety of sources and synthesize them into a coherent argument addressing all aspects of the slavery controversy—moral, legal, economic, political, and racial. This task amounted to nothing less than writing her own textbook on the subject—the first of its kind. The project would consume three years before reaching fruition in her ambitious *Appeal in Favor of That Class of Americans Called Africans* (1833). During that interval Child would immerse herself in the debates over slavery covered in Garrison's weekly newspaper, *The Liberator*; read a staggering array of scholarly and polemical works; join David in exchanging opinions with Garrison through the editorial columns of the *Massachusetts Journal*; further hone her ideas in discussions with friends who, like David and herself, were gravitating toward Garrison's brand of antislavery activism; and participate vicariously through David in the founding of the New England Anti-Slavery Society. In the process Child would evolve toward the fully developed abolitionist ideology she would articulate in the *Appeal.*

As Child was researching and conceptualizing the *Appeal,* she found Garrison's *Liberator* an invaluable mine of information. The paper not only supplied her with innumerable facts she would use, but directed her toward works to consult for more extensive research. It recorded shocking cases of slave abuse; quoted fugitive slave advertisements from southern newspapers; cited draconian laws against slaves and free blacks, North as well as South; publicized cases of kidnapping involving northern free blacks illicitly sold into southern slavery; and reprinted voluminous extracts from books, tracts, speeches, sermons, congressional debates, and newspaper articles, representing all schools of thought, pro- and antislavery.

The *Liberator* can even be said to have influenced the way in which Child defined the parameters of her subject. Nearly all the issues Child tackled in the *Appeal* can be traced back to articles in Garrison's paper. Probably most important for contextualizing the unparalleled emphasis Child would give to counteracting racial prejudice—a theme that would dominate four of the *Appeal*'s eight chapters—were the *Liberator*'s repudiation of Colonization as a fraudulent, racist substitute for genuine antislavery action; its concerted campaign against all forms of antiblack discrimination in the North, ranging from color bars in schools, jobs, and transportation facilities to laws prohibiting interracial marriage; and its receptiveness to contributions by African American writers, which served both to demonstrate their intellectual capabilities and to expose white sympathizers to the viewpoint of the class they hoped to benefit.

Through the *Liberator*'s African American correspondents, for example, Child learned that blacks categorically opposed repatriation to Africa and cogently defended their right to enjoy the same privileges as other American citizens.[13] Their eloquent protests surely helped sensitize her to the day-to-day indignities and impediments African Americans faced as a result of racial discrimination. The *Liberator* may also have prompted her to read (or reread) the most trenchant analysis an African American writer had thus far produced of his people's oppression—David Walker's 1829 *Appeal to the Coloured Citizens of the World,* which a correspondent signed "V" extensively quoted and reviewed in May 1831. Along with the militant summons to resistance for which it is famous, it presented a searing denunciation of the Colonization scheme that may well have influenced both Garrison and Child. Some have suggested that Child titled her own *Appeal* with Walker's in mind.[14]

While Child was gathering information and forming her opinions, she and David engaged in a journalistic dialogue with Garrison. They felt their way toward new perspectives on the slavery question in their *Massachusetts Journal* editorials, and he responded in the *Liberator* by prodding them toward more radical positions. This dialogue offers fascinating glimpses of Child's evolution toward the *Appeal.*

On 15 January 1831, Garrison reprinted an article from the *Massachusetts Journal,* which sought to defend Colonization without adopting the Colonization Society's postulate that racial antipathies could not be overcome because they were rooted in human nature.[15] Bemusedly, the author of the article (possibly Maria Child, since it appeared underneath one of her own contributions) noted the "very violent prejudices against Colonization to Africa" expressed by blacks. "The Boston negroes have the impression, that the whites care little whether the poor Africans live or die, provided they can get rid of them with safety to themselves," she (or David) reported: "The negroes therefore say, 'the whites brought us here, in a cruel manner and from sordid motives, for their service and pleasure, and now that we . . . are increasing so as to be inconvenient, they would ship us off. We won't go from this continent. If we go anywhere, it shall be to Canada, . . . where we can become respectable, wealthy, and hold offices, as we may under the laws of England.' "·'Though admitting that she had not been "able to reply" to such strictures, Child could not agree with the view that the Colonization scheme veiled a sinister design to annihilate America's free black population through exile to an insalubrious climate. Nor could she relinquish the belief that emigration to Liberia offered blacks an opportunity to escape racial proscriptions and found a "powerful and glorious nation." She did, nevertheless, concede that the "exclusion of negroes of good character and competent qualifications from offices of honor and emolument" in their native land was "wholly indefensible on principles of natural law, religion, or the constitution of the United States." It was an acknowledgment marking a fundamental departure from the Colonizationist ideology of racial separatism and indicating how close the Childs had come, as early as January 1831, to accepting Garrison's premise that blacks could be safely integrated into American society as equal citizens.

Garrison's comments in the footnotes he appended to the article measured the precise distance the couple still needed to travel from Colonizationist to abolitionist ideology. Pointing out that prejudices against Colonization were not confined to Boston blacks, but "pervade[d] the breasts of our free colored population throughout the country," he suggested that blacks could hardly be blamed for distrusting the motives of those who were "anxious to send them to Africa," but "refuse[d] to meliorate their condition here." No people, he insisted, should have to emigrate to improve their status. As for the bright future Child conjured up for the exiles in Liberia, Garrison dismissed it as a "delightful hallucination."

Seven months later, the Childs' dialogue with Garrison had progressed to a point of almost complete accord on the most radical feature of his ideology—his call for an end to racial discrimination. Under the headline "A Noble Commentary," Garrison prefaced another reprint from the *Massachusetts Journal* with the words: "Since we commenced the publication of the Liberator, we have seen noth-

ing in the newspapers which has given us more unfeigned pleasure."
An incisive condemnation of American racial prejudice, the article,
he predicted, would "find a response in the bosom of every true
patriot, and add another rose to the wreath of independence which
crowns the head of its author."[16] Despite its placement on the editorial page of the *Massachusetts Journal,* the style almost surely identified the author as Maria Child. Indeed she would incorporate much
of it virtually unchanged into *An Appeal in Favor of That Class of
Americans Called Africans.*[17]

This is not to say that by August 1831 Child was ready to advocate
immediate abolition, as she would in the *Appeal.* On the contrary, in
a passage of her *Massachusetts Journal* editorial tactfully overlooked by
Garrison, she explicitly disclaimed the intention of entering the controversy over slavery. She even pronounced it "ungenerous to raise an
outcry against the southern states for an evil which their best men
regret as deeply as we do—an evil which it is far more easy to *condemn*
than it is to *remedy.*" Her aim, she specified, was rather to foster a
spirit of self-criticism in the North. "[A]re *we* governed by right
feelings in our deportment towards the negroes?" she asked, urging
northerners to examine their own hearts.

Child proceeded to argue that racial prejudice was not only "contrary to the spirit of the Bible, and contrary to the spirit of the
Declaration of Independence," but indefensible on rational grounds
and politically embarrassing in a republic. "It is a singular fact that we
republicans are abundantly more exclusive" in racial matters "than
our monarchical neighbors," she remarked, playing on American national pride: "In England, it is common to see respectable and genteel
people open their pews when a black stranger enters the church; and
at hotels, nobody thinks it a degradation to have a colored traveller sit
at the same table." A "well authenticated anecdote" about a black
expatriate in London named Prince Saunders served to illustrate
Child's point. Calling on an American family at the breakfast hour,
the gentleman was not invited to join them at the table but was kept
standing while they ate. Only when they had risen did the hostess,
"with an air of sudden recollection," ask if he had had breakfast and
offer him a cup of coffee. His "dignified" reply that he was "engaged
to breakfast with the Prince Regent this morning" drove home the
irony that British aristocrats could treat a black man as an equal while
American republicans made a mockery of their egalitarian creed by
refusing to apply it to their dark-skinned compatriots.

"We are well aware that this is not the popular side of the question—that we shall be called vulgar, and radical," Child went on. Undaunted, she confronted the inevitable challenge: "Would you have us invite negroes to our parties, and give them our daughters in marriage?" The onus, she retorted, was on the prejudiced to supply "a *good* reason why a virtuous, well-educated black should not be invited!" Yet her stand on "mixed marriages" fell short of the one she would take in the *Appeal.* "[T]hey are in bad taste, and are unnatural," she averred. Unconsciously, she was echoing the very words reviewers had used to disparage the plot of her maiden novel *Hobomok* (1824), which had featured a marriage between a Puritan woman and an Indian. She was also contradicting the defense of interracial marriage she had formulated in her revisionist history of Puritan-Indian relations, *The First Settlers of New-England* (1829).[18] It was the sole statement in the article to which Garrison took exception. "We agree with the editor of the Journal & Tribune, that, at the present time, mixed marriages would be in bad taste, but not that 'they are unnatural,' " he demurred, adding that only in the case of different species could amalgamation be termed "unnatural."

Embedded in Child's unfortunate concession to popular prejudice against interracial marriage was a covert critique of antimiscegenation laws, however. They were unnecessary, she intimated, because such marriages "would never take place except in very rare instances." Instead, "we would leave men free to choose their wives, as they are to choose their religion," she concluded. She would expand on this argument in the *Appeal,* where she would openly call for rescinding the Massachusetts antimiscegenation law, couching her plea in nearly identical language, but no longer stigmatizing interracial marriage as "unnatural" or "in bad taste."[19]

Child even anticipated the *Appeal* in the witty peroration of her *Massachusetts Journal* editorial. Pointing out that the Turks, whose "narrow bigotry" had become a byword, had recently passed a law "imposing a fine upon whoever shall call a Christian a dog," she exhorted her readers: "Let us try to keep pace with the Turks in candor and benevolence." In the later work she would suggest that a "residence in Turkey might be profitable to those Christians" who characterized prejudice as eternal and irremediable, for "it would afford an opportunity of testing the goodness of the rule, by showing how it works both ways" (206). Garrison would reprint a long extract from this article in his 1832 *Thoughts on African Colonization.*[20]

The editorial pages of the *Liberator* and the *Massachusetts Journal* once again revealed the increasing ideological convergence between the Childs and Garrison when the Nat Turner revolt burst upon the nation on 21 August 1831. That night a small, powerfully built, thirty-year-old African American from Southampton County, Virginia, who believed he had been commissioned by God to free his people, led a party of his fellow slaves from plantation to plantation, killing every white person they encountered—a total of fifty-five before they were routed by white troops forty-eight hours later. Garrison interpreted the uprising as the fulfillment of his prophecy that death and destruction would rain down on the country until it repented of its sins and freed the slaves. Though "horror-struck" at the bloodbath (which ultimately claimed the lives of some 120 blacks in the gruesome reprisals), he insisted that no one who justified the patriots of the American Revolution for resorting to arms had the right to condemn the slaves. David Child agreed. "[W]e will never swerve from the principle that the oppressed and enslaved of every country, Hayti and Virginia as well as France and Poland, have a right to assert their 'natural and unalienable rights' whenever and wherever they can do it, and that they also have a right to judge of the fitness of the occasion," he maintained, in a statement Garrison reprinted in the *Liberator*.[21]

The only difference between the two men's reactions was that Garrison subscribed to the "pacific precepts of Jesus Christ," which enjoined all believers without exception to return good for evil, whereas David, who had fought in Spain's 1823 war against French domination, feared simply that the odds against the slaves were too heavy for such a revolt to succeed.[22] Under current circumstances, he thought, an attempt like Turner's could accomplish nothing but "to inflict useless misery" on both slaves and masters. "God grant that it may come to good," he apostrophized.

In the midst of these editorial exchanges, the increasing frequency of the *Liberator*'s references to Maria Child suggests that she may already have joined the circle of antislavery friends Garrison was gathering around him. In May 1831 an advertisement in the *Liberator* announced that her latest work, *The Mother's Book*, the first comprehensive childrearing manual published in the United States, was "in the press." A brief extract from *The Mother's Book* appeared in December. Evidently Child did not object to letting Garrison publicize her writings in his reputedly "incendiary" newspaper. More tell-ingly, two sketches with low-key antislavery messages followed in January 1832: "The Moral of an Alarm Watch" and "Stand from Under!"[23]

The first sketch, reprinted anonymously from the *Massachusetts Journal*, drew a lesson from the common experience of sleeping through the ringing of an alarm clock because "the drowsy ear" has become "accustomed to the sound." Child specifically applied the lesson to slavery, citing the case of a "New-England lady," who, after "residing at the South a few years" no longer found herself " 'shocked at the idea of keeping slaves.' " "They who disregard" the alarm clock's warning "soon cease to hear its voice," Child moralized.

The second sketch was a ghost story set on board a slave-trading ship and narrated by a sailor with "misgivings about the business." It symbolically pictured slavery as an evil spirit haunting the ship and warning the crew to "Stand from Under!" Boldly signed "By Mrs. Child," in the format not of a borrowed reprint, but of a voluntary contribution, it represented yet another step toward Child's public identification with Garrison and the antislavery movement.

It is surely no coincidence that Child took this step in January 1832, for during that very month David played a prominent part in the founding of the New England Anti-Slavery Society. Over the previous year he had frequently visited the "dingy," third-story office, with its ink-spattered windows, where Garrison printed the *Liberator* with his own hands, ate at the long editorial table piled high with mail and newspapers, and slept on the floor.[24] The men who congregated there all shared the Childs' growing conviction that "[t]he hour of national expiation had come, and men and women must needs obey the summons."[25] These comrades in struggle included the gentle Unitarian clergyman Samuel J. May, to whom Child would dedicate her *Appeal* "as a mark of gratitude, for his earnest and disinterested efforts in an unpopular but most righteous cause"; May's cousin, the lawyer Samuel E. Sewall, whom David had known since their days at Harvard, where all three had graduated in the class of 1817;[26] May's brother-in-law Bronson Alcott, whose wife, Abba May Alcott, had attracted Child "by her prompt decisions concerning the right and wrong of things" when both were still unattached;[27] the Quaker poet and future laureate of the abolitionist movement, John Greenleaf Whittier, like Child a prize literary recruit; the Congrega-tionalist minister Amos A. Phelps, whose 1834 *Lectures on Slavery and*

Its Remedy would draw heavily on Child's *Appeal*; the printer and editor Oliver Johnson, later Garrison's first biographer; and the lawyer Ellis Gray Loring, who had studied under David at the Boston Latin School, and whose wife, Louisa Gilman Loring, was intimate with Child before either married.[28]

As they prepared to brave social censure, the Childs must have engaged in many soul-searching discussions with their associates, and especially with their closest friends, the Lorings. Sensitive and refined, tenderly attached to each other and to their baby daughter "Nony," naturally inclined toward domestic privacy, and "reluctant to believe in the existence of evil," Ellis and Louisa, like Child, found the "rough work of reform . . . unavoidably distasteful." "The thousand nameless sacrifices to conscience made by such characters are by no means among the smallest offerings laid on the altar of humanity," Child wrote long afterward, speaking as much for herself as for the Lorings.[29] For her part, Child would have much preferred to indulge her propensity toward mysticism and her taste for art and poetry, or at least to devote herself to securing the permanent home she yearned for. Of the four, David was the only one who could claim to relish disputation and combat. But he also aspired to a career in politics that abolitionist advocacy would doom. Soberly, the two couples and their young comrades faced the prospects of revilement, isolation, professional boycott, thwarted ambition, and financial hardship. But none turned back.

By late 1831, no doubt spurred by the Nat Turner revolt, the men in Garrison's circle began laying plans to form an antislavery society and spiritedly debating whether to base it explicitly on the principle of immediate emancipation. According to Oliver Johnson, all of the fifteen men who met in Samuel Sewall's law office on November 13 "admitted the duty and safety of setting the slaves free at once; but six of the number doubted the wisdom of incorporating that principle into the constitution of the society, believing that it would excite popular prejudice, and thus tend to defeat the object in view."[30] Though David and his fellow lawyers Sewall and Loring headed the list of doubters, they joined Garrison and Johnson in drafting the constitution of the New England Anti-Slavery Society. David even presided over the historic meeting of 6 January 1832, at which the constitution was adopted. (Child did not attend because the society had not yet opened its meetings to women, as it soon would.)[31]

Symbolically heralding the obstacles that abolitionists would face, a "fierce north-east storm, combining snow, rain and hail," pelted the crusaders who struggled through the slush on this "dismal night" to seal their commitment to the antislavery cause. The meeting place was equally symbolic. A schoolroom in the basement of the African Baptist Church, located in the black neighborhood known as "Nigger Hill," it betokened the solidarity these early abolitionists felt with African Americans, the ostracism they risked by associating with a pariah class, and the racial uplift they hoped to promote by furnishing blacks with opportunities for higher education. Yet indicative of a paternalism abolitionists would never quite overcome, no African Americans participated in founding the New England Anti-Slavery Society, despite a well-established tradition of black antislavery activism; instead, blacks were invited to join after whites had set the society's initial agenda.[32]

That agenda was spelled out in the second article of the society's constitution: "The objects of the Society shall be, to endeavor, by all means sanctioned by law, humanity and religion, to effect the abolition of slavery in the United States; to improve the character and condition of the free people of color, to inform and correct public opinion in relation to their situation and rights, and obtain for them equal civil and political rights and privileges with the whites."[33] The point of contention between radicals and moderates lay not in this clause, but in the preamble enunciating the "right to immediate freedom from personal bondage." Still unconvinced that it was expedient to alienate potential supporters by making "immediate emancipation" a cardinal doctrine of the new society, David, Sewall, and Loring withheld their signatures from the "apostolic" roster of twelve names making up the original membership. All three quickly changed their minds, however, and by the following year Sewall had accepted a position on the board of managers and David and Loring were serving as counselors.[34]

Concurrently, Child took her final step toward assuming the role of the despised antislavery agitator. In August 1833, when, as Samuel May recalled, "the number, the variety, and the malignity of our opponents had become manifest," she startled friends and foes alike by publishing *An Appeal in Favor of That Class of Americans Called Africans.* "We had seen her often at our meetings," May reminisced. "We knew that she sympathized with her brave husband in his abhorrence of our American system of slavery; but we did not know that she had so carefully studied and thoroughly mastered the subject."[35]

Compounding the "exultation" in antislavery ranks that "such an author—ay, such an *authority*—should espouse our cause just at that crisis" was the stature Child had by now attained. In 1833, some four years after Garrison had hailed her as "*the first woman in the republic,*" she stood at the apex of her literary fame. Only a month earlier, the most prestigious journal of American letters, the *North American Review*, had crowned her with its laurels in a twenty-five-page appraisal of her entire oeuvre. Uncannily echoing Garrison's very words (though attributing the phrase "the first woman in the republic" to a comment Napoleon made to Madame de Staël), the editors of the *North American* reiterated his prophetic judgment: "[W]e are not sure that any woman in our country would outrank Mrs. Child." Like Garrison—but for diametrically opposite reasons—they, too, recognized in Child "just the woman we want for the mothers and daughters of the present generation."[36] It was as if rival camps—one representing social dominance, the other radical egalitarianism and the contumely that went with its advocacy—vied for the privilege of offering her leadership.

Serenely true to the inner convictions she had always exhorted her readers to heed, Child turned her back on the prize laid at her feet by the arbiters of the literary world—a prize she had long coveted—and cast her lot with America's oppressed people of color. "Hardly ever was there a costlier sacrifice," wrote her friend Wendell Phillips. "Narrow means just changing to ease; after a weary struggle, fame and social position in her grasp; every door opening before her; the sweetness of having her genius recognized."[37] Still, Child did not flinch. "I am fully aware of the unpopularity of the task I have undertaken," she avowed in her preface to the *Appeal*; "but though I *expect* ridicule and censure, I cannot *fear* them."

An Appeal in Favor of That Class of Americans Called Africans provided the abolitionist movement with its first full-scale analysis of the slavery question. Indeed so comprehensive was its scope that no other antislavery writer ever attempted to duplicate Child's achievement; all subsequent works would focus on individual aspects of the subject that Child covered in eight thoroughly researched and extensively documented chapters.[38] Even today, the book's wide-ranging scholarship, consummate rhetoric, and signal prescience command attention.

Child's very title is "pregnant with the gist" of her entire argument (as May aptly notes);[39] every word inspires reflection and challenges prejudice. Child simultaneously "appeals" to her readers' human sympathies, subverts their intellectual categories, and redefines the national identity of her subjects and her readers alike. African Americans, she quietly asserts, are Americans, not Africans; compatriots, not foreigners. They can no more be "called" Africans than Americans can be called Britons. They are an assimilable "class," not a biologically separate race.

In her preface Child subtly negotiates the transition from *The Mother's Book* and the *Juvenile Miscellany* to the *Appeal*. Addressing the audience that had hitherto revered her as a model for women and children, and speaking in the familiar tones of nineteenth-century womanhood, she implores it in the name of her past services to grant her a hearing on an admittedly unfeminine topic:

Reader, I beseech you not to throw down this volume as soon as you have glanced at the title. Read it, if your prejudices will allow, for the very truth's sake:—If I have the most trifling claims upon your good will, for an hour's amusement to yourself, or benefit to your children, read it for *my* sake:— Read it, if it be merely to find fresh occasion to sneer at the vulgarity of the cause:—Read it, from sheer curiosity to see what a woman (who had much better attend to her household concerns) will say upon such a subject:— Read it, on *any* terms, and my purpose will be gained.

With her confident allusion to her purpose, however, Child shifts into the "masculine" discourse of political critique that she will use throughout the major portion of the book. "The subject I have chosen admits of no encomiums on my country," she remarks drily, "but as I generally make it an object to supply what is most needed, this circumstance is unimportant; the market is so glutted with flattery, that a little truth may be acceptable, were it only for its rarity." Earlier, her domestic manuals, *The Frugal Housewife* (1829) and *The Mother's Book* (1831), had stormed a market glutted with cookbooks and childhood "education" treatises for wealthy Europeans. Now Child proposes to defy a market glutted with chauvinistic self-congratulation. In her previous ventures she had shrewdly calculated on reaping financial dividends while fulfilling a social need. This time she faces the prospect of financial ruin and public vilification, secure in the knowledge that she is advancing "the inevitable progress of truth and justice." "I would not exchange the consciousness" of performing such a mission "for all Rothchild's wealth, or Sir Walter's fame," she concludes in her valedictory admonition to readers who balk at following her into her new realm.

What is initially most striking about the 230-page treatise this Preface so disarmingly introduces is its solid historical grounding. Organized with flawless logic, the book moves from past to present, from history to political economy, from fact to argument, from problem to solution. It opens with a "Brief History of Negro Slavery.—Its Inevitable Effect upon All Concerned in It" (chapter 1), which is succeeded by a "Comparative View of Slavery, in Different Ages and Nations" (chapter 2). Occupying almost a third of the book, these chapters situate American slavery in a worldwide context that includes ancient Israel, Greece, and Rome, as well as Africa, the Caribbean, and Latin America. Through a detailed analysis of the laws regulating slavery in these various societies, Child shows that "[m]odern slavery . . . in all its particulars, is more odious than the ancient; and . . . that the condition of slaves has always been worse just in proportion to the freedom enjoyed by their masters" (36). As the most democratic society in history, the United States has the most stringent slave codes, she points out. "Slavery is so inconsistent with free institutions, and the spirit of liberty is so contagious under such institutions," Child explains, "that the system must either be given up, or sustained by laws outrageously severe; hence we find that our slave laws have each year been growing more harsh than those of any other nation" (70). In both her comparative approach and her astute insights, Child anticipates twentieth-century scholars who have revolutionized the study of slavery.[40]

After this geohistorical survey, Child proceeds to explore the economics and politics of the slavery controversy. Chapter 3, "Free Labor and Slave Labor.—Possibility of Safe Emancipation," counters fears that emancipation would entail economic disaster and insurrectionary violence. The introduction of a free labor system would improve the economy of the South, she asserts, since slave labor has such serious disadvantages: "*where* slaves are employed, manual industry is a degradation to white people, and indolence becomes the prevailing characteristic" (73). As for the risk of unleashing another Santo Domingo, an "impartial and careful examination" has convinced her that "slavery causes insurrections, while emancipation prevents them" (80). In chapter 4, "Influence of Slavery on the Politics of the United States," Child turns the tables on defenders of the status quo by arguing that the real threat to the Union lies not in agitation of the

slavery question, but in the South's political dominance and commitment to furthering its own interests at all costs. Because of the constitutional clause allowing the slaveholding states to count three-fifths
of their slave population in determining their allotment of congressional seats, the South has acquired "entire control of the national
policy" and has used that control "to protect and extend slave power"
(103–104). The accession of new slave states has already secured "a
renewed and apparently interminable lease to the duration of slavery," and the insatiable thirst for more slave territory portends future
wars of conquest, warns Child, referring to the looming annexation
of Texas (114).

In her pivotal chapter, "Colonization Society, and Anti-Slavery
Society," placed at the center of the book, Child examines the two
parties' opposing solutions to the problem of slavery: gradual emancipation accompanied by repatriation to Africa versus immediate
emancipation followed by the bestowal of "equal civil and political
rights and privileges with the whites" (130). Since the principal point
at issue between Colonizationists and abolitionists is whether prejudice against blacks can and should be overcome, she devotes the rest
of the book to answering that question. Chapters 6 and 7, "Intellect
of Negroes" and "Moral Character of Negroes," demolish the ra-
tionale for prejudice—the myth of the Negro's biological inferiority
and savage past—by resurrecting accounts of Africa's ancient civiliza-
tions and recalling numerous modern instances of blacks who have
distinguished themselves by their talents. The final chapter, "Prejudices against People of Color, and Our Duties in Relation to This
Subject," condemns racial discrimination and urges Americans to
repudiate attitudes and practices inconsistent with their republican
creed.

Although the *Appeal* violates the prevailing norms of feminine
discourse by its very engagement in political controversy, as well as by
its authoritative display of erudition and its preoccupation with such
matters as law, economics, and congressional apportionment, it simultaneously presents a woman's perspective on slavery. Repeatedly,
Child focuses on the special ways in which slavery victimizes women
and makes a mockery of the domestic ideology glorifying "true womanhood." In the process, she pointedly reveals the limitations on her
own freedom as a woman that link her to her sisters in bonds.

"There is another view of this system, which I cannot unveil so
completely as it ought to be," she writes. "I shall be called bold for

saying so much; but the facts are so important, that it is a matter of conscience not to be fastidious" (22). Her ensuing comments on the sexual exploitation of slave women are muffled in circumlocutions:

The negro woman is unprotected either by law or public opinion. She is the property of her master, and her daughters are his property. They are allowed to have no conscientious scruples, no sense of shame, no regard for the feelings of husband, or parent; they must be entirely subservient to the will of their owner, on pain of being whipped as near unto death as will comport with his interest, or quite to death, if it suit his pleasure.

Those who know human nature would be able to conjecture the unavoidable result, even if it were not betrayed by the amount of mixed population. (22)

On the one hand, Child acknowledges, she herself cannot speak as plainly as she ought to because to do so would be to compromise her womanhood by the standards of nineteenth-century ideology. On the other hand, she shows, the slave woman has no right to the "protection" this ideology imposes on the white woman, no right to preserve the sexual purity deemed essential to true womanhood.

Child takes her analysis to a deeper level when she turns to the effects of slavery on the white mistress. "[A]uthentic records of female cruelty" indicate that the slave system perverts the womanhood of the mistress as hideously as it does that of the slave, Child suggests. Significantly, the case she chooses to cite involves a New England woman, thus inculcating the lesson that the system operates on everyone who comes under it. Originally "amiable" and "affectionate," this woman has metamorphosed into a "fiend" since moving South and acquiring slaves: "One faithful negro woman nursed the twins of her mistress, and did all the washing, ironing, and scouring. If, after a sleepless night with the restless babes (driven from the bosom of their own mother,) she performed her toilsome avocations with diminished activity, her mistress, with her own lady-like hands, applied the cow-skin, and the neighborhood resounded with the cries of her victim" (27–28). Having shunted onto the black woman the responsibilities of motherhood and domesticity that supposedly constitute a true woman's glory, the slave mistress has become the mere caricature of a "lady." She has, in fact, become a masculinized brute, Child implies.

The woman's perspective Child brings to bear on slavery determines her choice of supporting illustrations in many other sections of the *Appeal*, as we shall see. Yet she did not originate the female antislavery discourse she so brilliantly manipulates. Rather, she perfected and carried to a new plane of sophistication a discourse initiated by women in the British antislavery movement of the early nineteenth century and pursued by such American pioneers as the Quaker Elizabeth Margaret Chandler, who edited the female department of the *Genius of Universal Emancipation* and helped launch its analogue in the *Liberator*. Child also took many cues from African American women writers she encountered through the *Liberator*—notably Maria Stewart, Sarah Douglass, and Sarah Forten—who developed a parallel discourse.[41]

The distinctiveness of the *Appeal* lies not in the particular arguments it advances, but in its all-encompassing synthesis of facts and arguments from an unprecedented array of sources. Among Child's precursors, the British abolitionist Thomas Clarkson had detailed the horrors of the slave trade. The American legal scholar George Stroud had exhaustively studied southern slave laws and demonstrated their harshness. David Walker and Garrison had dissected Colonizationist ideology and exposed its racism and illogicality. The Abbé Grégoire of the French Amis des Noirs had vindicated blacks against charges of inferiority by amassing examples of their achievements in science, art, and literature. And the American historian Alexander Everett, though a conservative on the slavery question, had promulgated the theory that Africa was the cradle of the civilization Europe had derived from the ancients.[42]

Child not only drew on these prior writers, but she evidently developed her analysis in conjunction with David. At the January 1833 annual meeting of the New England Anti-Slavery Society, he had delivered a marathon speech in support of the proposition that "the free People of Color and Slaves in this land of Liberty and Law, have less liberty, and are less protected by law, than in any other part of the world." Garrison and Whittier would later remember it as "a masterly and exhaustive analysis and exposure of the 'peculiar institution'" and "the best and fullest exposition of our principles and objects" to date.[43] Subsequently expanded for publication, David's speech, *The Despotism of Freedom*, overlaps with the *Appeal* in comparing the southern slave system to its biblical, classical, Caribbean, and Latin American analogues. Shared anecdotes, witticisms, and literary borrowings suggest that the Childs researched their projects simultaneously and pooled their ideas. Yet the *Appeal* is far broader in scope than *The Despotism of Freedom*.[44]

Neither David nor any of Child's predecessors had sought to weave the diverse strands of antislavery thought into a single panoramic tapestry. Nor had anyone sought to combine them with the economic and political analysis she offered in her third and fourth chapters, which constitute an early formulation of the free labor ideology the Republican party preached in the 1850s.[45] One recent historian has even credited Child with having articulated the first major statement of the "slave power" thesis.[46] The most original feature of the *Appeal*, however, distinguishing it from all other antislavery tracts by white Americans, is its concerted refutation of racist ideology.[47] This motif governs four out of eight chapters and recurs elsewhere as a subtheme. It is not too much to say that it motivates Child's rhetorical strategy, which aims at overturning ethnocentric stereotypes and inducing readers to think in unaccustomed ways.

Thus in her history of slavery and the slave trade, Child draws frequent analogies between European Christians and the peoples they denigrate. To illustrate the "bigotry" fostered by the slave trade, she describes how Moors and Arabs base their right to enslave "heathen tribes" on the idolatry of their victims, but refuse to proselytize them for fear of forfeiting the pretext for the lucrative traffic in human flesh. Having decoyed her readers, Child springs her trap: "This is precisely like our own conduct," she notes. "We say the negroes are so ignorant that they must be slaves; and we insist upon keeping them ignorant, lest we spoil them for slaves" (10–11).

Later, Child uses the same technique to puncture the hackneyed claim that the slave trade rescued Africans from "the despotism and wars, which desolate their own continent" (19). Pointing out that "the white man is himself the cause of these wars," and that we have no right to judge for other peoples where they will be best off, she reverses the argument: "If the Turks, or the Algerines saw fit to exercise this right, they might carry away captive all the occupants of our prisons and penitentiaries" (19).

In yet another twist, Child shows that instead of bringing Africans out of savagery and into civilization, the slave trade has actually brought the savagery of African coastal raids to the United States. In American cities, as in African villages, "[a] free man of color is in constant danger of being seized and carried off by . . . slave dealers. . . . Wherever these notorious slave jockeys appear in our Southern States, the free people of color hide themselves, as they are obliged to do on the coast of Africa" (32). David Child would elaborate on this analogy between the African and the American interstate slave trades in a report on the domestic slave trade presented at the New England Anti-Slavery Convention of 1834.[48]

While arguing that the slave trade prevented the economic development of Africa—a thesis upheld by recent scholars[49]—Child takes pains to counteract the stereotype of Africa as the "dark continent." In her chapters "Intellect of Negroes" and "Moral Character of Negroes," she provides a wealth of information about African history and culture, relying on such sources as the travel accounts of Mungo Park and Major Denham, the narrative of the African-born slave Olaudah Equiano, the treatise of the Abbé Grégoire, the *Biographie Universelle,* and the *English Family Library.* She cites the "mechanical skill" displayed by African leather workers, jewelers, and weavers; the eloquence exhibited by minstrels and orators; and the existence of cities presenting "a prospect of civilization and magnificence" (144–45). Most memorable is Child's long account of the Angolan queen Zhinga, who "could neither be subdued by force of arms, nor appeased by presents" (145–48).[50]

Zhinga obviously attracted Child's attention both as a woman and as an African who exemplified outstanding "bravery, intelligence, and perseverance" (145). But Child's admiring portrait also serves another purpose. It is one of many passages in the *Appeal* that defend the resort to armed resistance. A few pages later, Child pays tribute to Toussaint L'Ouverture, describing the Santo Domingo revolution not as an outbreak of barbarism, but as a heroic struggle for freedom (157–60). Just as she had earlier vindicated the right of the Wampanoag chief Philip to lead an uprising against the Puritan settlers who had taken over his people's land,[51] so she now extends the same sympathy to slave rebels like Toussaint and perhaps Nat Turner: "By thousands and thousands, these poor people have died for freedom. They have stabbed themselves for freedom—jumped into the waves for freedom—starved for freedom—fought like very tigers for freedom! But they have been hung, and burned, and shot—and their tyrants have been their historians!" (161).

Recognizing that oppressors monopolize the power to write history, Child predicts that the oppressed will seize it once they liberate themselves: "When the Africans have writers of their own, we shall

hear their efforts for liberty called by the true title of heroism in a
glorious cause" (161–62).

Child's sweeping refutation of racism culminates in her chapter
"Prejudices against People of Color, and Our Duties in Relation to
This Subject." Asserting that northern racial prejudice is "even more
inveterate" than its southern counterpart, she charges: "[O]ur cold-
hearted, ignoble prejudice admits of no exception—no intermission. . . . Those who are kind and liberal on all other subjects, unite
with the selfish and the proud in their unrelenting efforts to keep the
colored population in the lowest state of degradation" (186–87).
Unsparingly, Child catalogs the forms of discrimination practiced
against blacks in schools, churches, jobs, and travel facilities, and she
describes the violence with which whites have enforced them. To
dispel at the outset the bugbear traditionally invoked to justify such
discrimination, she begins with the "unjust law" prohibiting "marriages between persons of different color." In her 1831 *Massachusetts
Journal* editorial, she had attacked antimiscegenation laws under the
cover of anonymity, allowing readers to attribute her views to David.
It took much greater courage to advance in her own name, as a
woman, views that men like Garrison had been anathematized for
expressing. "I am perfectly aware of the gross ridicule to which I may
subject myself . . . ," she writes; "but I have lived too long, and
observed too much, to be disturbed by the world's mockery" (187).

Child's argument boldly equates freedom of marriage with freedom of religion—the principle that had led New England's Puritan
founders to immigrate to America: "A man has at least as good a right
to choose his wife, as he has to choose his religion. His taste may not
suit his neighbors; but so long as his deportment is correct, they have
no right to interfere with his concerns" (187). The equation redefines
as sacred an exercise of individual "taste" that society stigmatizes as
indecent. Revealingly, however, Child here speaks in male accents.
She does not dare couch her defense of interracial marriage in terms
of a woman's sacred right to choose her husband regardless of race.
Still, the examples she cites are white women who have chosen to live
in common-law marriages with black men, and she refers to them in
a manner that implies personal acquaintance: "I know two or three
instances where women of the laboring class have been united to
reputable, industrious colored men. These husbands regularly bring
home their wages, and are kind to their families" (188). Moreover, as

in her analysis of the slave system, Child focuses on the ways in which antimiscegenation laws victimize women:

If by some of the odd chances, which not unfrequently occur in the world, their wives should become heirs to any property, the children may be wronged out of it, because the law pronounces them illegitimate. And while this injustice exists with regard to *honest*, industrious individuals, who are merely guilty of differing from us in a matter of taste, neither the legislation nor customs of slave-holding States exert their influence against *immoral* connexions. (188)

True, Child distances herself from these women by intimating that she does not share their tastes.[52] She does, nevertheless, challenge the sexual and racial double standard, once again focusing on how it oppresses women.

This time Child cites the case of New Orleans' famous quadroon concubines, a class of women as refined as their upper-class white sisters, yet forced by the slave system and the color bar into illicit relations with white men: "White gentlemen of the first rank . . . often become seriously in love with these fascinating but unfortunate beings. Prejudice forbids matrimony, but universal custom sanctions temporary connexions, to which a certain degree of respectability is allowed, on account of the peculiar situation of the parties. These attachments often continue for years—sometimes for life—and instances are not unfrequent of exemplary constancy and great propriety of deportment" (188).

Having anticipated and disposed of the plea that racial discrimination is necessary to prevent intermarriage, Child devotes the rest of the chapter to showing how discrimination functions to prevent blacks from improving their status. Her most telling examples involve the virulent opposition to higher education for African Americans. Not only are blacks systematically excluded from white schools, Child points out, but mobs have repeatedly prevented the founding even of segregated academies and colleges for African Americans.

Among the instances Child cites, one must have resonated with special significance for her, since it dramatized the obloquy a white woman must face if she allied herself with women of color. During the very months when Child was writing the *Appeal,* a Quaker teacher named Prudence Crandall had attempted to open a school for "young ladies and little misses of color" in Canterbury, Connecticut. The irate citizens of Canterbury had smeared her door with filth; poisoned her well with excrement; organized a boycott against her and her students among the town's merchants; served a warrant on one of her students under an obsolete vagrancy law, threatening the young woman with a public whipping on her "*naked body*"; and actually imprisoned Crandall herself for one night in a cell previously occupied by a murderer. The case was going through the courts as the *Appeal* came off the press, and it would climax the following year in the mob destruction of the school.[53] Child acknowledged its role in steeling her own resolve to defy racial prejudice when she dedicated the *Appeal* to Samuel May, who had been leading Crandall's defense.

The explanation that a self-styled "Friend of the Colonization Cause" gave for the vendetta against Crandall's school—an explanation Child paraphrases and rebuts in the *Appeal* (191)—illuminates her reasons for according so much importance to the issue of interracial marriage. What purpose, asks this writer, can an institution like Crandall's serve?

Why, to break down the barriers which God has placed between blacks and whites—to manufacture "*Young Ladies of color*," and to foist upon community a new species of gentility, in the shape of sable belles. They [Crandall and her abolitionist supporters] propose, by softening down the rough features of the African mind, in these wenches, to cook up a palatable morsel for our white bachelors. After this precious concoction is completed, they are then to be taken by the hand, introduced into the best society, and made to aspire to the first matrimonial connections in the country. In a word, they hope to force the two races to amalgamate![54]

Child must have recognized in this scurrilous broadside a foretaste of the public reaction to the *Appeal.* Yet she perceived—and had the courage to maintain publicly—that it was vital to carry the defense of racial integration to its logical conclusion by affirming the right to intermarriage. Since Colonizationists were leading the campaign against efforts to promote African American uplift and integration, Child formulated her most radical statement on interracial marriage in her chapter on Colonization and antislavery:

Perhaps, a hundred years hence, some negro Rothschild may come from Hayti, with his seventy *millions* of pounds, and persuade some white woman to *sacrifice* herself to him. . . . Shall we keep this class of people in everlasting degradation, for fear one of their descendants *may* marry our great-great-great-great-grandchild?

While the prejudice exists, such unions cannot take place; and when the prejudice is melted away, they will cease to be a degradation, and of course cease to be an evil. (125)

Thirty-four years later (well short of the "hundred" envisioned here) Child would translate this prediction into a novel advocating interracial marriage as the ultimate solution to racial prejudice: *A Romance of the Republic* (1867).

As Child had somberly expected, the *Appeal* outraged a public that had just canonized her as a paragon of feminine virtue. No portion of it touched a rawer nerve than her indictment of northern racial prejudice. In a vitriolic ten-page rejoinder a prominent Colonizationist clergyman, Leonard Bacon, indignantly contested the charge that prejudice was more rampant in the North than in the South. Characterizing the Prudence Crandall case as exceptional and blaming abolitionists for having fomented the excitement, he personally denied ever having sought to "discourage or embarrass the people of color, in their struggles after knowledge and respectability." "If Mrs. Child has any confessions [of her own] to make, very well," he sneered; "only . . . let her not attempt to impute the same guilt to the public sentiment of New England."[55]

Negative reviews were the least of the trials Child had to face. Her favorite brother, Convers, to whom she had looked up all her life, dismayed her by counseling prudence and charity toward southerners and by exhibiting the constitutional timidity of a minister dependent on a wealthy congregation for support. Her elder brother, James, who had named his daughters Lydia Maria and Mary Conant (after the heroine of Child's *Hobomok*), turned hostile; a Jacksonian Democrat, he could not stomach either "niggers" or "nigger-lovers." Her father, though he sympathized warmly with her abolitionist principles, did not extend the same sympathy toward David, but instead blamed his son-in-law for the heavy financial price of the couple's antislavery activism. Only David's family backed the couple wholeheartedly (David's sister Lucretia would express her ardent identification with the abolitionist cause by naming her three children for heroes of the movement: George Thompson, William Lloyd Garrison, and Lydia Maria Child).[56]

Friendships, as well as family ties, gave way under the pressure of social disapproval. Lois Curtis, under whose roof David had pro-

posed to Child, now snubbed the couple. Relations grew strained
with morally earnest but conservative Lucy Osgood, who had moth-
ered Child in her lonely youth and applauded her triumphs of au-
thorship. Child herself felt compelled to stop seeing Emily Marshall,
despite the kindness the Marshalls had always shown her; their paths
in life had diverged after Emily's 1831 marriage into one of Boston's
most aristocratic families, and Child had feared both that she would
no longer find in her friend's "spirit an echo to the voice of mine" and
that Emily's father-in-law, Boston mayor Harrison Gray Otis, would
consider it politically embarrassing if she received an abolitionist in
her home. When Emily died giving birth in 1836, Child's remorse
knew no bounds.[57]

Abolition also came between Child and the novelist Catharine
Maria Sedgwick, to whom she had "respectfully and affectionately"
dedicated her collection of short stories, *The Coronal* (1832). Sedgwick noticeably "cooled" after Child sent her a copy of the *Appeal* and
invited her to contribute to her projected antislavery gift book, *The
Oasis*. In her tardy and temporizing reply, Sedgwick accepted only on
condition that she not be viewed as "an advocate of the principles of
the abolitionists." Slavery was "a dark & fearful subject," she ventured, and some abolitionist leaders were "foolish & doubtful zeal-
ots," besides which she could not see why abolitionists and Colonizationists were attacking each other when they had the "same aim." As
Child judged bitterly in retrospect, Sedgwick "sincerely wished well
to the negroes, but she could not bear to *contend* for them, or for
anything else. . . . She was very deficient in moral *courage*" and
"*afraid* of reformers," as well as of the slavery question.[58]

In addition to the pain of broken friendships, Child bore the cost
of professional blacklisting as her erstwhile patrons among the Boston aristocracy mobilized against her. Former admirers like Harvard
professor George Ticknor slammed their doors in her face, cut her
dead in the street, and enforced a policy of ostracism toward anyone
who violated the ban against her. The future attorney general of
Massachusetts, James T. Austin, a political enemy of David's who
several years later would defend the mob killing of an abolitionist
editor as a patriotic act, hurled the *Appeal* out the window with a pair
of tongs. The Boston Athenaeum withdrew the free library privileges
Ticknor had induced the Trustees to confer on Child in a token of es-
teem only one other woman, the religious historian Hannah Adams,
had been accorded (library privileges Child desperately needed for

her research in progress on *The History of the Condition of Women*).
Most damagingly, readers boycotted her writings and parents can-
celed their subscriptions to the *Juvenile Miscellany. The Mother's Book,*
which had been reissued five times in two years, promptly went out of
print; the *Miscellany,* though beloved by its broad juvenile audience,
folded; even sales of her most commercially successful work, *The
Frugal Housewife,* then in its thirteenth printing, plummeted, reducing Child's already meager income to a pittance.[59]

Although the *Appeal* destroyed Child's literary popularity and
evicted her from Boston's salons, it propelled her to the forefront of
the abolitionist movement, elevating her to a position of unparalleled
political influence for a woman. Abolitionists immediately hailed the
Appeal as a "powerful auxiliary to the Anti-Slavery cause." "We were
particularly struck with the appearance of extensive research which
characterizes the work," commented the reviewer for the *Unionist,* a
newspaper founded to support Prudence Crandall: "Written in a
style, easy, simple and elegant; enlivened with occasional flashes of
wit, rich in important facts, happy illustrations and forcible, conclusive reasoning—its satire delicate but keen; its appeals touching and
powerful; its reproofs grave, just and severe, yet couched in a language courteous and dignified—it is altogether one of the most valuable publications which have for a long time fallen under our eye."
Asserting that it was "impossible for any candid mind and unprejudiced person to read this book . . . without becoming a decided
Abolitionist," the reviewer urged that copies be distributed to "every
friend and every enemy of our cause." "[A]n armory well stored with
weapons of approved temper," it would arm friends for combat and
not only disarm enemies, but "enlist [them] under the banner of
justice," he predicted.[60]

Abolitionist reviewers universally echoed his judgment. "[T]hat
heart must be harder than the nether mill-stone, which can remain
unaffected by the solemn truths" the *Appeal* so ably propounded,
Oliver Johnson averred. "[I]t cannot fail to afford incalculable aid to
the cause of universal emancipation," agreed a correspondent who
praised the "noble independence" Child had shown by "hazard[ing]
her glorious reputation" in defense of an "injured people."[61]

Soon, anecdotes bearing these reviewers out began appearing in
the *Liberator.* A prominent Colonizationist and manager of the
American Bible Society complained that his wife and daughter had
gone over to the enemy since reading the *Appeal.* "I will not read the

book," he swore, because "I do not mean to be an abolitionist." The heiress of a large slave estate, induced by friends to read the *Appeal* while on a visit to the North, had "thrown [it] down in anger," only to find herself impelled to take it up again and yield at last to its persuasion. Promising to free her slaves, she had determined to learn how to do her own housework. (One can imagine her being handed *The Frugal Housewife* to help her on her way.)[62]

As these anecdotes indicate, Child played an instrumental role in bringing women into the movement at an early stage. Indeed, reviewers again and again expressed the hope that women would be "provoked to emulation, by the example of Miss Crandall and Mrs. Child." "[W]e need the aid of our virtuous and principled females," they proclaimed. "[N]othing great and good can be accomplished in our country without their assistance. . . . Should *they,* one and all, lend their aid to the cause of emancipation, we might safely predict, that at no distant period, this horrible stain, this humiliating reproach, would be wiped away from our nation forever!"[63]

Child's influence was by no means confined to women. With her calm, rational tone; her method of allowing facts to speak for themselves; and her technique of framing conclusions as rhetorical questions that engaged the reader in a dialogue—she succeeded in converting readers repelled by Garrison's scathing denunciations and alien to the world of religious revivalism out of which Garrison had emerged. Men trained in the discourses of legal argumentation, scholarly induction, and Unitarian-style preaching responded to the *Appeal* in a way that they could not respond to the thunderous accents of the evangelical exhorter summoning sinners to repentance— the rhetoric that was Garrison's forte.

The *Appeal* recruited into abolitionist ranks a new cadre of leaders, who would extend the antislavery movement in many directions. A roll call of those who would credit the *Appeal* with exercising a "formative influence" on their thinking—and often with changing their lives—furnishes a gauge of the political authority Child achieved. It includes the Unitarian minister William Ellery Channing, idol of the Boston aristocracy and a vital mediator between abolitionists and their conservative opponents; his fellow Unitarian John Gorham Palfrey, Massachusetts state legislator and quondam editor of the *North American Review;* the brilliant, Harvard-trained lawyer Wendell Phillips, star orator of the antislavery movement and second only to Garrison in its councils; the Transcendentalist militant Thomas

Wentworth Higginson, who went on to lead the first black regiment in the Civil War, publish the first collection of African American spirituals, write the first biography of Margaret Fuller, and introduce the world to the poetry of Emily Dickinson; the Massachusetts senator and future vice president under Ulysses S. Grant, Henry Wilson; and above all the towering leader of the Radical Republicans, Charles Sumner, largely responsible for the legislative victories of Reconstruction. Over a forty-year period these men would read Child's publications, heed the advice she offered in adroit letters on public policy, and seek her endorsement of the aims and strategies they pursued. Higginson's 1868 testimonial best sums up their considered judgment of the *Appeal*: "As it was the first anti-slavery work ever printed in America in book form, so I have always thought it the ablest; that is, it covered the whole ground better than any other."[64]

The decades following the publication of the *Appeal* would find Child's name blazoned on an editorial masthead and her articles featured prominently in the major newspapers that shaped antislavery and later Radical Republican ideology; her books and pamphlets distributed to members of Congress, as well as to antislavery lecturers, for whom the *Appeal* constituted required reading; her utterances targeted for rebuttal by opinion-makers of the dominant camp. Baptized in the fires of abolitionism and reconsecrated as a proselytizer for the cause of black liberation, she would indeed become what Garrison titled her at the dawn of her career: "*the first woman in the republic.*"

Notes

1. "MRS. CHILD," *Genius of Universal Emancipation* 20 Nov. 1829, p. 85. Garrison joined the paper on September 2, as indicated by his salutatory address "To the Public" of that date. For the details of Garrison's acquaintance with David Lee Child, see *The Letters of William Lloyd Garrison*, ed. Walter M. Merrill and Louis Ruchames (Cambridge, Mass.: Belknap P of Harvard UP, 1971–81) 1:38 and 6:352, hereinafter cited as *GL*; and Wendell Phillips Garrison and Francis Jackson Garrison, *William Lloyd Garrison, 1805–1879: The Story of His Life Told by His Children* (1885–89; New York: Arno, 1969) 1:73, hereinafter cited as *Life*. In future citations of Garrison's letters, his name will be abbreviated as WLG. To avoid confusion, I will refer to Lydia Maria Child as Child and to David Lee Child as David.

2. "Comparative Strength of Male and Female Intellect," from the *Massachusetts Journal*, in *Genius of Universal Emancipation* 30 Oct. 1829, pp. 60–61. The article is reprinted in the "Literary" column. Garrison writes that he had "cut [it] out, in February last, for insertion in the Journal of the Times; but, as the press of other matter prevented its publication at that time, I have hoarded it up ever since for that purpose, and to praise a very meritorious woman."

3. Garrison's efforts to recruit Whittier for the cause provide indirect evidence of the high priority he assigned to enlisting the best writers of the day as propagandists for antislavery. In a letter to Harriott Plummer dated 4 March 1833, he writes: "You excite my curiosity and interest still more, by informing me that my dearly beloved Whittier is a *friend* and townsman of yours. Can we not induce him to devote his brilliant genius more to the advancement of our cause . . . ?" (*GL* 1:209).

4. The ostensible purposes of Garrison's June 1830 trip to Boston and Newburyport, as he explains in a letter to Ebenezer Dole of 14 July 1830 (*GL* 1:104–106), written on his return to Baltimore, were to collect "some essential evidence to be used in the civil action" pending against him and to explore the possibility of obtaining funds to reestablish the *Genius*, which had suspended publication after his imprisonment. *Life* 1:192 reports Garrison as "passing through Boston on the 10th of June, and paying his respects to friendly Mr. Buckingham of the *Courier*," before proceeding to Newburyport. Garrison's letter to Dole implies that he returned to Boston on his way back from Newburyport to Baltimore, however, and suggests that his stay in Boston may have been somewhat longer.

5. Lydia Maria Child to Samuel J. May, 29 Sept. 1867, *Lydia Maria Child: Selected Letters, 1817–1880*, ed. Milton Meltzer, Patricia G. Holland, and Francine Krasno (Amherst: U of Massachusetts P, 1982) 474–75. In future citations of Child's letters, her name will be abbreviated as LMC and this edition will be abbreviated as *SL*.

6. "W.L. Garrison," *Massachusetts Journal and Tribune* 13 Nov. 1830, p. 1.

7. Lydia Maria Child, "The *Liberator* and Its Work," *Independent* 28 Dec. 1865, p. 1, reproduced in *The Collected Correspondence of Lydia Maria Child, 1817–1880*, ed. Patricia G. Holland, Milton Meltzer, and Francine Krasno (Millwood, N.Y.: Kraus Microform, 1980), microfiche card 64, letter 1698. In future citations, this edition will be abbreviated as *CC*, and microfiche card and letter numbers will be indicated as follows: 64/1698.

8. WLG to Editor of *Newburyport Herald* 21 Apr. 1827, *GL* 1:38; WLG to LMC, 25 Oct. 1874, *GL* 6:352. On the chronology of Garrison's involvement with Lundy and antislavery work, see *Life* 1:92–98; *GL* 1:xxvii, 63–65.

9. LMC to Anne Whitney, 25 May 1879, *SL* 558. Child's reminiscences to Whitney and to Samuel J. May (*SL* 473–75) about her first meeting with Garrison, unfortunately supply no dates. The appearance of her first antislavery story in the September 1830 issue of the *Miscellany*, however, and the succession of antislavery pieces that follow on its heels provide strong evidence that the meeting took place before that date. Hence I am assuming that it took place during Garrison's brief visit in June, rather than after his permanent return to Boston in September-October, the other possible date.

10. Garrison's seven-week imprisonment in a jail that served as a depot for apprehended runaways and slaves waiting to be transported south intensified his identification with the slaves. See his letter to Ebenezer Dole, 14 July 1830, *GL* 1:105–106, in which he contrasts his own situation in prison with that of "the poor slave."

11. See *Life* 1:142–48 on the development of Garrison's thinking during this period. Garrison had proclaimed his commitment to immediate rather than gradual abolition in his inaugural editorial for the *Genius* (2 Sept. 1829, rpt. in *Life*), but he had not fully spelled out what that entailed. Nor had he repudiated the Colonization Society or questioned the desirability of reducing the black population through a voluntary emigration program. He began to do so after a black correspondent of the *Genius*, who styled himself "A Colored Baltimorean," pointed out the racist implications of the repatriation scheme in an article of 27 November 1829, reprinted in Garrison's *Thoughts on African Colonization: or an Impartial Exhibition of the Doctrines, Principles and Purposes of the American Colonization Society. Together with the Resolutions, Addresses and Remonstrances of the Free People of Color* (1832; New York: Arno, 1968), Part 2:52–54. Two historians have identified this "Colored Baltimorean" as William Watkins (presumably the uncle of Frances Ellen Watkins Harper); see Floyd J. Miller, *The Search for a Black Nationality: Black Emigration and Colonization, 1787–1863* (Urbana: U of Illinois P, 1975) 84; and R.J.M. Blackett, *Building an Antislavery Wall: Black Americans in the Atlantic Abolitionist Movement, 1830–1860* (Baton Rouge: Louisiana State UP, 1983) 50–51. Herbert Aptheker, however, has suggested Hezekiah Grice as another candidate for the "Colored Baltimorean"; see his *"One Continual Cry": David Walker's Appeal to the Colored Citizens of the World (1829–1830). Its Setting & Its Meaning* (New York: Humanities P, 1965) 35–36. As late as 8 January 1831, Garrison was not yet ready to take a public stand against the Colonization Society. Though he had criticized it in a private letter to Lundy, he was disconcerted when Lundy published the letter in the *Genius* without his authorization. In response, however, Garrison promised on January 8 to "thoroughly sift . . . [the society's] pretensions," and by January 22, he was announcing that "it is time to repudiate all colonization schemes, as visionary and unprofitable" and advocating that blacks be educated and "made useful in society." See "Another Libel," *Liberator* 8 Jan. 1831, p. 7; and "Removal to Texas," 22 Jan. 1831, p. 13.

12. For an excellent history of antislavery protest in England and America, from the colonial period through the Civil War, see Betty Fladeland, *Men and Brothers: Anglo-American Antislavery Cooperation* (Urbana: U of Illinois P, 1972). For a brilliant analysis of early antislavery ideology and the international socioeconomic context in which it developed, see David Brion Davis, *The Problem of Slavery in the Age of Revolution, 1770–1823* (Ithaca: Cornell UP, 1975).

13. For a fascinating account of how early African American leaders who were initially receptive to the idea of selective voluntary repatriation to Africa were induced by the militant opposition of the black masses to change their stand and present a united front against Colonization schemes, see William Loren Katz's introduction to the Arno Press reprint edition of Garrison's *Thoughts on African Colonization*. Katz also details the influence that African Americans exerted on Garrison, prompting him to investigate the subject and change his stand. It should be noted that even those African American leaders who had favored repatriation never supported a program of forced mass emigration; and many of the early supporters of repatriation—Prince Hall and Paul Cuffee, for example—were influenced by African parents. African American interest in repatriation declined in direct correlation with the Colonization Society's ascendancy.

14. Garrison reprinted the anti-Colonization statements he had collected from black correspondents in "Sentiments of the People of Color," Part 2 of *Thoughts on African Colonization*. Surprisingly, he did not include extracts from Walker's *Appeal*, though he had commented on it in both the *Genius* and the *Liberator*; see *Life* 1:159–62. For a modern edition, see David Walker's *Appeal, in Four Articles; Together with a Preamble, to the Coloured Citizens of the World, but in Particular, and Very Expressly, to Those of the United States of America*, ed. Charles M. Wiltse (New York: Hill and Wang, 1965). The comments by Garrison and review by "V" are reprinted in Truman Nelson, ed., *Documents of Upheaval: Selections from William Lloyd Garrison's THE LIBERATOR, 1831–1865* (New York: Hill and Wang, 1966) 4–6, 12–26. "V" may be Garrison's black friend from Pittsburgh, John B. Vashon. Among those who suggest a relationship between Walker's and Child's titles are Thomas Wentworth Higginson, "Lydia Maria Child," *Contemporaries,* Vol. 2 of *Writings of Thomas Wentworth Higginson* (Boston: Houghton Mifflin, 1900) 121; and Jean Fagan Yellin, *Women and Sisters: The Antislavery Feminists in American Culture* (New Haven: Yale UP, 1989) 54. It is possible that David Child, rather than the *Liberator,* first brought Walker's *Appeal* to Child's attention. In an editorial note of 11 December 1830 (p. 3), titled "Walker's Appeal," David comments on Walker's death, refers to having made inquiries about its cause, and invites "our colored friends" to send the *Massachusetts Journal* any evidence they can find of Walker's having been assassinated.

15. See "Liberia Colony," reprinted under the heading "Colonization," *Liberator* 15 Jan. 1831, p. 11. The original article appeared in the *Massachusetts Journal and Tribune* on 1 January 1831 (p. 1).

16. "A Noble Commentary," *Liberator* 13 Aug. 1831, pp. 129–30. The original appeared in the editorial column of the *Massachusetts Journal and Tribune* 6 Aug. 1831, p. 3, under the title "Novel Incident."

17. I have compared this editorial to both David Lee Child's *The Despotism of Freedom; or the Tyranny and Cruelty of American Republican Slave-Masters, Shown to be the Worst in the World; in a Speech, Delivered at the First Anniversary of the New England Anti-Slavery Society, 1833* (Boston: Young Men's Anti-Slavery Association, 1833) and Lydia Maria Child's *An Appeal in Favor of That Class of Americans Called Africans* (Boston: Allen and Ticknor, 1833) and found it much closer in style and content to the latter. For example, although both Childs cite the Prince Saunders anecdote, Lydia Maria Child's version of it in the *Appeal* is stylistically more similar to the version in the *Massachusetts Journal* (see *Appeal* 127; *Despotism* 11). The *Appeal* also cites a second anecdote that appears in the *Massachusetts Journal* article, but not in *The Despotism of Freedom*: the reference to a man who defended his refusal to hire blacks by saying, "I am too great a democrat . . . to have any body in my house, who

don't sit at my table; and I'll be hanged, if I ever eat with the son of an Ethiopian" (*Appeal* 194; *Liberator* 13 Aug. 1831, p. 130). Other close verbal parallels between the *Massachusetts Journal* article and the *Appeal* will be discussed below. Page references are to the present edition of the *Appeal.*

18. See the *North American Review* 19 (1824): 262–63; [Jared Sparks], "Recent American Novels," *NAR* 21 (1825): 87; and *The First Settlers of New-England: or, Conquest of the Pequods, Narragansets and Pokanokets: as Related by a Mother to Her Children, and Designed for the Instruction of Youth.* By a Lady of Massachusetts (Boston: Munroe and Francis, n.d. [1829]) 66. The context makes clear that Child intended the argument to apply to intermarriage with blacks as well as with Indians. For further discussion of this work and its anticipation of the *Appeal,* see Carolyn L. Karcher, *The First Woman in the Republic: A Cultural Biography of Lydia Maria Child* (Durham, N.C.: Duke UP, 1994) chap. 4.

19. See *Appeal* 187–88, quoted and discussed below. Child herself did not use the term *miscegenation,* which was not coined until 1864; on the origins of the word, see Sidney Kaplan, "The Miscegenation Issue in the Election of 1864," in Kaplan, *American Studies in Black and White: Selected Essays, 1949–1989,* ed. Allan D. Austin (Amherst: U of Massachusetts P, 1991) 47–100.

20. Garrison, *Thoughts on African Colonization* 145–46n.

21. For Garrison's reaction, see the editorial "The Insurrection" in the *Liberator* 3 Sept. 1831, reprinted in Nelson, *Documents of Upheaval* 28–31; for David's, see "*Insurrection in Virginia,*" reprinted under the heading "Remarks of Editors," *Liberator* 10 Sept. 1831, pp. 146–47. The issue containing the original is missing from the *Massachusetts Journal and Tribune* file at the American Antiquarian Society. David provided extensive and sympathetic coverage of the Turner rebellion in other issues, however. For example, in an article "The Virginia Slave Insurrection," he comments that "nearly twice as many [blacks] have been put to death as were concerned in it." And in one titled "Gen. Nat," he disputes a Virginia newspaper's claim that Turner had "sold his body for Gingercakes which he ate before his Execution." David retorts: "We think this improbable. In the first place he was a slave and by the laws of Virginia a slave cannot make a bargain nor own anything. In the next place it is the policy of the Southern press to make the black race appear despicable. In the third place the fact is totally in consistent [*sic*] with the heroism with which he met his death, which is described by a witness as follows. . . . " See the *Massachusetts Journal and Tribune* 15 Oct. 1831, p. 1; and 26 Nov. 1831, p. 3. For Turner's own account of the rebellion, though filtered through the judgments of his Virginian interrogator, see Thomas R. Gray, *The Confession, Trial and Execution of Nat Turner, the Negro Insurrectionist; also, a list of persons murdered in the insurrection in Southampton County, Virginia, on the 21st and 22nd of August, 1831, with Introductory Remarks* (1831; New York: AMS P, 1975); for a modern historical account, see Vincent Harding, *There Is a River: The Black Struggle for Freedom in America* (New York: Random-Vintage, 1981) 94–100.

22. "The Insurrection" in Nelson, *Documents of Upheaval* 30; Garrison had already spelled out his position on slave revolt in a comment of 8 January 1831 on David Walker's *Appeal,* reprinted in Nelson 5–6: "Believing, as we do that men should never do evil that good may come; that a good end does not justify wicked means . . . and that we ought to suffer, as did our Lord and his apostles, unresistingly—knowing that vengeance belongs to God . . . *[w]e* do not preach rebellion—no, but submission and peace. . . . We say, that the possibility of a bloody insurrection at the South fills us with dismay; and we avow, too, as plainly, that if any people were ever justified in

throwing off the yoke of their tyrants, the slaves are that people." For a brief account of David's participation in Spain's 1823 war against France, see Karcher, *First Woman* chap. 2.

23. See the *Liberator* 21 May 1831, p. 84; 21 Jan. 1832, p. 12; 28 Jan. 1832, p. 16. The aphorism titled "Marriage," excerpted from *The Mother's Book,* appears on 10 December 1831 (p. 200); Child included "Stand from Under!" in *The Coronal. A Collection of Miscellaneous Pieces, Written at Various Times* (Boston: Carter and Hendee, 1832) 184–89. The quotation is from *Coronal* 184.

24. Garrison's fellow abolitionist and first biographer, Oliver Johnson, vividly recreates the setting and recalls the antislavery pioneers who gathered there, *W. L. Garrison and His Times* (1881; Miami: Mnemosyne, 1969) 51–53. He does not mention any visits by Maria Child, though he speaks of her elsewhere.

25. LMC to Anne Whitney, 25 May 1879, *SL* 558.

26. *Life* 1:213n; Nina Moore Tiffany, *Samuel E. Sewall: A Memoir* (Boston: Houghton, Mifflin, 1898) 12–13, 36–42.

27. LMC to Louisa May Alcott, 19 June 1878, *CC* 90/2398. Child specifies that her acquaintance with Abba (and probably with Abba's brother Samuel) "began at her father's house, before either of us was married."

28. See the *DAB* articles on David Lee Child and Ellis Gray Loring. David Child taught at the Boston Latin School from 1817 to 1820, the year of Loring's graduation. On Child's prior relationship with Louisa Gilman, see LMC to Louisa Gilman, 4 June [1827?], *CC* 1/24.

29. "Gone," *National Anti-Slavery Standard* 6 June 1868, in *CC* 69/1837. For examples of letters confessing to a similar distaste for "the rough work of reform," see LMC to Ellis Gray Loring, Augusta G. King, and Mary Ann Brown, 6 Mar. and 19 and 26 Sept. 1843 and 2 Dec. 1860, *SL* 192–97, 202–204 and *CC* 47/1271.

30. Johnson, *Garrison and His Times* 83–84, takes issue with the statement by Samuel J. May, in *Some Recollections of Our Antislavery Conflict* (Boston: Fields, Osgood, 1869) 31, that the naysayers disagreed with the principle of immediate emancipation.

31. Johnson, *Garrison and His Times* 83–85; *Life* 1:279. The earliest notices in the *Liberator* of the society's regular monthly meetings read: "All persons interested in the subject of slavery are invited to attend." On 23 June 1832 "Ladies are particularly invited to be present" at a debate over the merits of colonization. Beginning in July 1832, notices of meetings read: "Ladies and gentlemen are respectfully invited to attend." See the *Liberator* 28 Jan., p. 15; 23 June, p. 99; 28 July, p. 119; 25 Aug., p. 135; 22 Sept., p. 151; 27 Oct. 1832, p. 171. In her preface to *The Oasis,* ed. Lydia Maria Child (Boston: Allen and Ticknor, 1834) xv–xvi, Child affirms: "I have, for the last two years, attended almost every Anti-Slavery meeting in this neighborhood. . . ."

32. Oliver Johnson's explanation of why blacks were "not conspicuous among the formers of the new society" underscores how paternalistically abolitionists conceived of the two races' roles in the movement: "It was because they instinctively knew that their presence and co-operation would serve only to increase and intensify the prejudices which the society must encounter. Their very anxiety for its success kept them aloof at first. They were careful not to embarrass in its infancy a movement on which were staked their dearest hopes" (*Garrison and His Times* 99). See also "New-England Anti-Slavery Society," *Liberator* 10 Mar. 1832, p. 39, which invites "friends of the people of color, *and the people of color themselves,*" in other New England towns to "form auxiliaries to this Society." For accounts of black antislavery activity during this period, see Harding, *There Is a River,* especially chaps. 4 and 6; Benjamin

Quarles, *Black Abolitionists* (New York: Oxford UP, 1969); Blackett, *Building an Antislavery Wall,* especially chaps. 1 and 2; and Sterling Stuckey, *Slave Culture: Nationalist Theory and the Foundations of Black America* (New York: Oxford UP, 1987), especially chaps. 2 and 3.

33. Quoted in Child's *Appeal,* p. 130; also in *Life* 1:281.

34. *Life* 1:279–80; "Annual Meeting of the New-England Anti-Slavery Society," *Liberator* 2 Feb. 1833, p. 17; "Proceedings of the New-England Anti-Slavery Society, at its First Annual Meeting," in *First Annual Report of the Board of Managers of the New-England Anti-Slavery Society* (Boston: Garrison and Knapp, 1833) 8.

35. May, *Some Recollections* 97–98. The quotation at the beginning of the next paragraph is from the same page.

36. "Works of Mrs. Child," *North American Review* 38 (July 1833): 138–64. The quotations are from 138–39.

37. [Harriet Winslow Sewall, ed.], *Letters of Lydia Maria Child with a Biographical Introduction by John G. Whittier and an Appendix by Wendell Phillips* (1883; New York: Negro Universities P, 1969) 264.

38. See, for example, Amos A. Phelps, *Lectures on Slavery and Its Remedy* (1834; St. Clair Shores, Mich.: Scholarly P, 1970), which concentrates on showing that slavery is sinful and on answering objections to "immediate emancipation" (frequently quoting Child on the latter topic); William Jay, *Inquiry into the Character and Tendency of the American Colonization, and American Anti-Slavery Societies* (1835; rpt. in *Miscellaneous Writings on Slavery* [Freeport, N.Y.: Books for Libraries P, 1970]), which borrows heavily, without acknowledgment, from Child's discussion of slave law; [Theodore Dwight Weld, Angelina Grimké Weld, and Sarah Grimké], *American Slavery As It Is: Testimony of a Thousand Witnesses* (1839; New York: Arno, 1968), which concentrates on demonstrating the brutality of slavery; and [Richard Hildreth], *Despotism in America; or an Inquiry into the Nature and Results of the Slave-holding System in the United States* (Boston: Whipple and Damrell, 1840), which amplifies the economic analysis offered in chapter 3 of the *Appeal,* as well as aspects of Child's first two chapters.

39. May, *Some Recollections* 98.

40. See, for example, Frank Tannenbaum, *Slave and Citizen: The Negro in the Americas* (1946; New York: Random-Vintage, n.d.); David Brion Davis, *The Problem of Slavery in Western Culture* (Ithaca: Cornell UP, 1966); Carl N. Degler, *Neither Black Nor White: Slavery and Race Relations in Brazil and the United States* (New York: Macmillan, 1971); and Donald Noel, "Slavery and the Rise of Racism," in Noel, ed., *The Origins of American Slavery and Racism* (Columbus: Charles E. Merrill, 1972) 153–74. Child's main source on slave law, George Stroud's *A Sketch of the Laws Relating to Slavery in the Several States of the United States of America* (Philadelphia, 1827), also compares American slave law with biblical, classical, and European colonial slave law, but Stroud's analysis is more narrowly focused. The theoretical insights Child derives from these comparisons seem to be original.

41. For studies of women's antislavery discourse, see Blanche Glassman Hersh, *The Slavery of Sex: Feminist-Abolitionists in America* (Urbana: U of Illinois P, 1978); Nancy A. Hewitt, *Women's Activism and Social Change: Rochester, New York, 1822–1872* (Ithaca: Cornell UP, 1984); and Yellin, *Women and Sisters.* For examples of women's antislavery discourse in the *Liberator,* see [Elizabeth Margaret Chandler], "Our Own Sex," 7 Jan. 1832, p. 2; L.H., "Duty of Females," 5 May 1832, p. 70; "A Dialogue on Slavery" ("Altered from a British Anti-Slavery Tract"), 2 June 1832, p. 86; "The Abuse of Liberty," 26 Mar. 1831, p. 50 (signed "Magawisca" after the Indian

heroine of Catharine Maria Sedgwick's *Hope Leslie*; the author, Sarah Louise Forten, was identified by Dorothy Sterling, *We Are Your Sisters: Black Women in the Nineteenth Century* [New York: Norton, 1984] 121); Sarah Douglass is identified on 21 July 1832, p. 114, as an "accomplished young colored lady" and the author of "several original and truly beautiful articles which have appeared in the Ladies' Department of the Liberator"; a number of speeches by Maria Steward [*sic*] were reprinted in the *Liberator* and later published in books, which, in turn, were advertised in the *Liberator*. Stewart's speeches have been reprinted in Stewart, *Maria W. Stewart: America's First Black Woman Political Writer*, ed. Marilyn Richardson (Bloomington: Indiana UP, 1987).

42. Thomas Clarkson, *The History of the Rise, Progress, and Accomplishment of the Abolition of the African Slave-Trade by the British Parliament*, 2 vols. (1808). Child derived most of her information on the Santo Domingo uprising and some of her economic arguments from Clarkson's pamphlet, *Thoughts on the Necessity of Improving the Condition of the Slaves in the British Colonies, with a View to Their Ultimate Emancipation; and on the Practicability, the Safety, and the Advantages of the Latter Measure* (New York, 1823). See note 40, above, for a full citation of Stroud. Henri Grégoire, *An Enquiry Concerning the Intellectual and Moral Faculties and Literature of Negroes Followed with an Account of the Life and Works of Fifteen Negroes and Mulattoes Distinguished in Science, Literature and the Arts* (1808), trans. D. B. Warden (1810; College Park, Md.: McGrath, 1967). Alexander Everett, *America, or a General Survey of the Political Situation of the Several Powers of the Western Continent*, ed. Michael Hudson (1827; New York: Garland, 1974) 212–25. Child also drew on American antislavery tracts, but these provided her mostly with instances of cruelty and descriptions of the domestic slave trade, rather than with analysis of the workings of the slave system. See, for example, John Rankin, *Letters on American Slavery, Addressed to Mr. Thomas Rankin* (1826; New York: Arno, 1969), which had recently been reprinted in the *Liberator* beginning in August 1832; and Jesse Torrey, *A Portraiture of Domestic Slavery, in the United States: with Reflections on the Practicability of Restoring the Moral Rights of the Slave, without Impairing the Legal Privileges of the Possessor; and a Project of a Colonial Asylum for Free Persons of Colour: Including Memoirs of Facts on the Interior Traffic in Slaves, and on Kidnapping* (1817; St. Clair Shores, Mich.: Scholarly P, 1970).

43. "Annual Meeting of the New-England Anti-Slavery Society," *Liberator* 26 Jan. 1833, p. 14; John Greenleaf Whittier and William Lloyd Garrison to LMC, 23 Sept. and 25 Oct. 1874, *CC* 83/2180, 2191.

44. See note 17 above for a full reference to *The Despotism of Freedom*. Verbal parallels between *Despotism* and the *Appeal* include the following: (1) both works refer to the "quarantine" provision of the Colored Seamen Laws and comment: "as if freedom were as bad as the cholera!" (*Appeal* 64), "as if they had the *cholera*" (*Despotism* 58); (2) both works sum up their analysis of American slave laws by saying: "Our republic is a perfect Pandora's box to the negro, only there is no *hope* at the bottom" (*Appeal* 70), "Our Republic is a complete Pandora's box to the slave, except that *there is no hope at the bottom*" (*Despotism* 21); (3) both works, pointing out that the slaves are ruled by laws they cannot read, comment: "This is worthy of Nero, who caused his edicts to be placed so high that they could not be read, and then beheaded his subjects for disobeying them" (*Appeal* 59), "The standing illustration of Nero's tyranny was, that he issued and executed edicts which he caused to be fixed so high that the subjects could not read them" (*Despotism* 48).

45. Eric Foner, *Free Soil, Free Labor, Free Men: The Ideology of the Republican Party*

before the Civil War (New York: Oxford UP, 1970). See especially the introduction and chap. 1.

46. Edward P. Crapol, "Lydia Maria Child: Abolitionist Critic of American Foreign Policy," in Crapol, ed., *Women and American Foreign Policy: Lobbyists, Critics, and Insiders* (Westport, Conn.: Greenwood, 1987) 1–18.

47. It is perhaps significant that a French Enlightenment philosophe, the Abbé Grégoire, was Child's only precursor and that later abolitionists do not follow Child's lead in devoting comparable space to refuting racist ideology.

48. "Report on the Domestic Slave Trade," *Proceedings of the New-England Anti-Slavery Convention, Held in Boston on the 27th, 28th and 29th of May, 1834* (Boston: Garrison and Knapp, 1834) 25–36.

49. See, for example, Basil Davidson, *Africa in History: Themes and Outlines*, rev. ed. (New York: Collier-Macmillan, 1968) 192–94; Walter Rodney, *How Europe Underdeveloped Africa* (Washington, D.C.: Howard UP, 1982), especially chap. 4.

50. Mungo Park, *Travels in the Interior Districts of Africa* (1799; New York: Arno, 1971); Major Denham, Captain Clapperton, and the late Doctor Oudney, *Narrative of Travels and Discoveries in Northern and Central Africa, in the Years 1822, 1823, and 1824. . . .* 2 vols., 3rd ed. (London: John Murray, 1828); Olaudah Equiano, *The Interesting Narrative of Olaudah Equiano, or Gustavus Vassa, the African* (1789), rpt. in Arna Bontemps, ed., *Great Slave Narratives* (Boston: Beacon, 1969) 1–192; Michaud, *Biographie Universelle, Ancienne et Moderne. . . .* (Paris, 1828). I have not been able to locate the *English Family Library*. The two sources Child quotes and paraphrases most extensively are Park and the Abbé Grégoire (see note 42 for a full citation), but she drew her account of Zhinga from the *Biographie Universelle* 52:314–22.

51. See *The First Settlers of New-England* 131–74, especially 168–69.

52. See Karen Sánchez-Eppler, "Bodily Bonds: The Intersecting Rhetorics of Feminism and Abolition," *Representations* 24 (Fall 1988), rpt. in Shirley Samuels, ed., *The Culture of Sentiment: Race, Gender, and Sentimentality in Nineteenth-Century America* (New York: Oxford UP, 1992) 106–107.

53. May, *Some Recollections* 40–72 offers an eyewitness account.

54. "Comment Is Needless!" *Norwich Republican*, rpt. *Liberator* 6 Apr. 1833, p. 54. (The title is the *Liberator's*.)

55. "Mrs. Child's Appeal in Favor of the Africans," *Quarterly Christian Spectator* 6 (Sept. 1834): 445–56. The quotation is from 448.

56. Convers's attitude can be inferred from Child's replies to his (no longer extant) letters. See LMC to Convers Francis, 22 Nov. 1833 and 25 Sept. and 19 Dec. 1835, *SL* 27, 38–39, 41–42. James Francis is described by a Wayland neighbor as "quite unlike his sister in politics, being an 'old line Democrat' of the Jefferson-Jacksonian stripe, and perhaps more pro- than anti-slavery in sentiment. It is said, he used to declare that 'his sister's attitude on the slavery question had caused him much grief' "; see Alfred Sereno Hudson, "The Home of Lydia Maria Child," *New England Magazine* n.s. 2 (June 1890): 407. Gravestones in the cemetery at Wayland bear the names of James's daughters Lydia Maria and Mary Conant Francis. Child mentions her namesake in LMC to Mary Francis Preston, 26 May 1822, *CC* 1/10. Convers Senior's attitude can be inferred from letters of the 1840s, cited in Karcher, *First Woman* 263–64, and from Convers Junior's reminiscences of his father, quoted in John Weiss, *Discourse Occasioned by the Death of Convers Francis, D.D. . . .* (Cambridge, Mass.: Privately printed, 1863) 62. On the names of Lucretia Child Haskins's children, see Meltzer and Holland, *SL* 67n.

57. George Ticknor Curtis, "Reminiscences of N. P. Willis and Lydia Maria

Child," *Harper's New Monthly Magazine* 81 (Oct. 1890): 720; presumably what Curtis says of himself applies to his mother: "I very seldom met her after the first year or two of her married life. . . . [M]y associations, sympathies, and opinions were with those conservative forces of society which were . . . antagonistic to those in which Mrs. Child's life became absorbed." Lucy Osgood to LMC, 8 May 1843, *CC* 17/493; renewing acquaintance with the "Apostle of Freedom" who "might have lost sight, in her passage down the stream of time, of the scenes & associates of other days," Osgood's letter hints at a long estrangement, probably due to disagreement over abolition. Also LMC to Marian Marshall, 28 Aug. 1836, *CC* 4/105.

58. See Catharine Maria Sedgwick to LMC, 27 May 1834, Sedgwick Collection, Historical Room, Stockbridge (Mass.) Library (courtesy of Patricia G. Holland and Laurie Robertson-Lorant); and LMC to Sarah Shaw, 20 May 1872, *SL* 506.

59. On Ticknor's tactics of enforcing ostracism against abolitionists and other "heretics," see David B. Tyack, *George Ticknor and the Boston Brahmins* (Cambridge, Mass.: Harvard UP, 1967) 185–86. For accounts by Child's friends of the reaction to the *Appeal,* see May, *Some Recollections* 100 and the Introduction and Appendix by Whittier and Phillips respectively in the 1883 edition of Child's *Letters* ix, 264. See also LMC to Samuel J. May, 29 Sept. 1867, *SL* 473–75, written in response to his reminiscences about her ordeal. It was Phillips who supplied the anecdote about Austin, which acquires added significance when we remember that Austin's diatribe at the public meeting called to protest the murder of the abolitionist editor Elijah Lovejoy brought Phillips to his feet with a fiery speech that launched his career as an abolitionist orator. See James Brewer Stewart, *Wendell Phillips: Liberty's Hero* (Baton Rouge: Louisiana State UP, 1986) 59–63. Austin also prosecuted a libel case against David. See "Suffolk, ss. Supreme Judicial Court," *Massachusetts Weekly Journal* 28 Jan. 1829, pp. 2–3. For further details on Child's domestic manuals and the collapse of the *Miscellany,* see Karcher, *First Woman* chaps. 6 and 7.

60. "Mrs. Child's Appeal,' " reprinted in the *Liberator* 14 Dec. 1833, p. 200.

61. "New publication," *Liberator* 10 Aug. 1833, p. 127 (this was by Oliver Johnson, who was editing the *Liberator* in Garrison's absence); "Mrs. Child's New Work" (rpt. from *Christian Watchman*), *Liberator* 7 Sept. 1833, p. 141; "Mrs. Child's Appeal," *Liberator* 7 Sept. 1833, pp. 142–43; "An Appeal in favor of the Africans" (rpt. from *Newburyport Advocate*), *Liberator* 2 Nov. 1833, p. 175.

62. "Facts," *Liberator* 15 Feb. 1834, p. 25; "A Noble Young Lady," *Liberator* 26 July 1834, p. 117.

63. "Mrs. Child's New Work" (rpt. from *Christian Watchman*) and "Mrs. Child's Appeal," *Liberator* 7 Sept. 1833, pp. 141, 142–43.

64. See LMC to Charles Sumner, 7 July 1856, *SL* 286, in which she thanks him for telling her "your public course had been influenced by the effect my anti-slavery writings had on your mind, when you were a younger man"; in this letter Child also mentions similar acknowledgments she has received from Wilson, Channing, and Palfrey. For her influence on Wendell Phillips, see "Gone," *CC* 69/1837. See Higginson, "Lydia Maria Child" 123–24 on the "formative influence" the *Appeal* exerted on him.

Suggestions for Further Reading

Other Antislavery Works by Lydia Maria Child

Many of the short selections and extracts from some of the longer works will be reprinted in *A Lydia Maria Child Reader*, ed. Carolyn L. Karcher, forthcoming from Duke University Press.

"The Little Master and His Little Slave." *Evenings in New England. Intended for Juvenile Amusement and Instruction*. By an American Lady [Lydia Maria Francis]. Boston: Cummings, Hilliard, 1824. 138–47.

Child's earliest published statement on slavery, it expresses her pre-abolitionist views while pointing toward her future involvement in the cause.

"Jumbo and Zairee." *Juvenile Miscellany* n.s. 5 (Jan. 1831): 285–99.

A story about a family kidnapped from Africa, it reflects Child's evolution toward the antislavery ideology articulated in the *Appeal* and shows how she used children's literature as a medium for arousing young readers' sympathies.

"Mary French and Susan Easton." *Juvenile Miscellany* 3rd ser. 6 (May 1834): 186–202.

A story about two girls, one white and the other black, kidnapped into slavery from a free state, it is the most effective and radical of Child's antislavery tales for juveniles and translates the message of the *Appeal* into fictional terms.

The Oasis. Boston: Allen and Ticknor, 1834.

An antislavery gift book edited by Child, the first of its kind, it contains many selections by her and David, including her first antislavery story for adults, "Malem-Boo. The Brazilian Slave."

Anti-Slavery Catechism. Newburyport, Mass.: Charles Whipple, 1836.

Answering questions about slavery and the abolitionist program commonly raised by skeptics and potential converts to the movement, this little tract offers an excellent introduction to early Garrisonian ideology.

"The Black Saxons." *The Liberty Bell*. Boston: Massachusetts Anti-Slavery Fair, 1841. 19–44; reprinted in Child's *Fact and Fiction: A Collection of Stories*. New York: C. S. Francis, 1846. 190–204.

A story about a slave revolt conspiracy, it points up the contradictions between Revolutionary ideology and slavery and draws parallels between Saxon serfs under Norman rule and African American slaves in the South.

"The Quadroons." *The Liberty Bell*. Boston: Massachusetts Anti-Slavery Fair, 1842. 115–41; reprinted in *Fact and Fiction* 61–76.

This tale of a slave mother and daughter, the first of whom dies of grief after being abandoned by her white lover, and the second of whom goes mad after being sold to a profligate, introduced the "tragic mulatto" archetype into American literature.

"Slavery's Pleasant Homes: A Faithful Sketch." *The Liberty Bell*. Boston: Massachusetts Anti-Slavery Fair, 1843. 147–60.

Child apparently judged this story about a slave woman raped and murdered by her master and avenged by her slave husband, too radical to be included in her commercially published collection *Fact and Fiction*. It remained uncollected until its republication in the *Heath Anthology of American Literature,* ed. Paul Lauter et al. (Lexington, Mass.: D.C. Heath, 1990, 1994).

"The Kansas Emigrants." *Autumnal Leaves: Tales and Sketches in Prose and Rhyme.* New York: C. S. Francis, 1857. 302–63.

Exemplifying the style of journalistic realism Child developed in the 1850s, this story about the armed struggle between pro- and antislavery settlers for control of Kansas in the half decade leading up to the Civil War offers readers a fine introduction to the politics of that tense era.

Correspondence between Lydia Maria Child and Gov. Wise and Mrs. Mason, of Virginia. Boston: American Anti-Slavery Society, 1860.

One of Child's most trenchant antislavery tracts, her famous exchange of letters with John Brown and his proslavery detractors sold 300,000 copies and helped mobilize the northern public to wage war against slavery.

The Right Way the Safe Way, Proved by Emancipation in the British West Indies, and Elsewhere. New York: 5 Beekman Street, 1860.

Aimed at southern readers on the eve of the Civil War, this tract presents economic data in favor of emancipation and carefully eschews polemics.

The Patriarchal Institution, As Described by Members of Its Own Family. New York: American Anti-Slavery Society, 1860.

Aimed at northern workers, whom it seeks to influence in favor of the Republican party in the 1860 election, this tract uses tellingly juxtaposed quotations from southern apologists to show that slavery is as much against the interests of white workers as of their black counterparts.

The Duty of Disobedience to the Fugitive Slave Act: An Appeal to the Legislators of Massachusetts. Boston: American Anti-Slavery Society, 1860.

Intended to persuade the Massachusetts legislature to nullify the Fugitive Slave Law, this tract asks politicians to imagine themselves in the situation of fugitive slaves; among the many moving anecdotes Child cites is the story of Margaret Garner, on which Toni Morrison would base her novel *Beloved.*

The Freedmen's Book. Boston: Ticknor and Fields, 1865.

This pioneering school reader, compiled by Child for the emancipated slaves and based on the principle that students learn best when the curriculum fosters pride in their own identity, consists entirely of selections by or about people of African descent.

A Romance of the Republic. Boston: Ticknor and Fields, 1867.

This ambitious novel, which Child considered the capstone of her career, restages the history of slavery and the Civil War and presents interracial marriage as the solution to America's race problem.

Lydia Maria Child: Selected Letters, 1817–1880. Ed. Milton Meltzer, Patricia G. Holland, and Francine Krasno. Amherst: University of Massachusetts Press, 1982.

This beautifully annotated selection of letters is indispensable for understanding the abolitionist movement, as well as Child's personal views on slavery and race. Child's letters contain some of her best writing.

WORKS ABOUT LYDIA MARIA CHILD

Baer, Helene G. *The Heart Is Like Heaven: The Life of Lydia Maria Child.* Philadelphia: University of Pennsylvania Press, 1964.

Though marred by factual errors and superseded by recent studies, this biography reintroduced Child to twentieth-century readers.

Clifford, Deborah Pickman. *Crusader for Freedom: A Life of Lydia Maria Child.* Boston: Beacon Press, 1992.
    The first scholarly biography of Child, it offers a well-researched, readable, and concise overview of her life and achievements.
Holland, Patricia G., Milton Meltzer, and Francine Krasno. *The Collected Correspondence of Lydia Maria Child, 1817–1880. Guide and Index to the Microfiche Edition.* Millwood, N.Y.: Kraus Microform, 1980.
    Indispensable for serious study of Child, this guide and index features a chronology, a brief biography, and an extensive bibliography of works by and about Child, including reviews and "significant references" in general histories.
Karcher, Carolyn L. *The First Woman in the Republic: A Cultural Biography of Lydia Maria Child.* Durham: Duke University Press, 1994.
    Intended as a definitive study and enhanced by the most complete bibliography of Child's writings to date, including periodical publications, this work sets Child's life and writings in the context of nineteenth-century American literary, social, and political history.
Meltzer, Milton. *Tongue of Flame: The Life of Lydia Maria Child.* New York: Thomas Y. Crowell, 1965.
    Intended for young adults, this biography restored to the public Child's legacy as a radical reformer.
Mills, Bruce. *Cultural Reformations: Lydia Maria Child and the Literature of Reform.* Athens: University of Georgia Press, 1994.
    An in-depth critical study of Child's key literary and reformist works, it includes a chapter on the *Appeal,* as well as discussions of her antislavery fiction.
Osborne, William S. *Lydia Maria Child.* Boston: Twayne, 1980.
    The first literary study of Child's writings, it offers a good, brief introduction to her oeuvre.

WORKS BY OTHER ABOLITIONISTS

Bayliss, John F., ed. *Black Slave Narratives.* New York: Collier-Macmillan, 1970.
    Featuring extracts from some twenty slave narratives, this collection provides a varied inside view of slave life.
Douglass, Frederick. *Narrative of the Life of Frederick Douglass, an American Slave. Written by Himself.* Boston: Anti-Slavery Office, 1845.
    The most famous and best written of the slave narratives, it is available in many reprint editions.
Garrison, William Lloyd. *William Lloyd Garrison and the Fight against Slavery: Selections from* THE LIBERATOR. Ed. William E. Cain. Boston: Bedford Books of St. Martin's Press, 1995.
    Garrison and his newspaper represented a major strand of white abolitionist ideology and the one with which Child was most closely associated. This anthology offers an excellent introduction to both.
Grimké, Angelina. *Appeal to the Christian Women of the South.* 1836. Reprint, New York: Arno Press and *New York Times,* 1969.
    A dissenting southern white woman's inside view of slavery, this tract invites comparison with Child's *Appeal* as another example of female antislavery rhetoric.

Jacobs, Harriet A. *Incidents in the Life of a Slave Girl: Written by Herself.* Ed. Lydia
   Maria Child. 1861. Reprint, ed. Jean Fagan Yellin. Cambridge: Harvard University Press, 1987.
      This classic female slave narrative, edited by Child, offers a rare and eloquent
   inside view of the slave woman's experience.
Ripley, C. Peter et al., eds. *Witness for Freedom: African American Voices on Race,
   Slavery, and Emancipation.* Chapel Hill: University of North Carolina Press,
   1993.
      This wide-ranging collection presents a variety of African American views on
   the struggle for freedom as it evolved over a half century.
Ruchames, Louis, ed. *The Abolitionists: A Collection of Their Writings.* New York:
   Putnam, 1963.
      This useful anthology covers the range of white abolitionist thought.
Walker, David. *Appeal to the Coloured Citizens of the World, but in particular, and very
   expressly, to those of the United States of America.* 1829. Reprint, ed. Charles M.
   Wiltse. New York: Hill and Wang, 1965.
      A key expression of African American militant nationalism, this tract's de-
   nunciation of the Colonizationist movement exerted an important influence on
   Garrison and Child and helped prompt a reorientation of the white antislavery
   movement away from Colonization and toward "immediate abolition."
[Weld, Theodore Dwight, Angelina Grimké Weld, and Sarah Grimké]. *American
   Slavery As It Is. Testimony of a Thousand Witnesses.* 1839. Reprint, Arno Press and
   New York Times, 1969.
      One of the most powerful tracts in antislavery archives, its rhetoric and
   presentation of the subject invite comparison with Child's in the *Appeal.*

HISTORIES OF SLAVERY AND ABOLITIONISM

Aptheker, Herbert. *Abolitionism: A Revolutionary Movement.* Boston: Twayne, 1989.
      This study, whose thesis is summed up in its title, presents an incisive
   Marxist analysis of the antislavery movement.
Blassingame, John W. *The Slave Community: Plantation Life in the Antebellum South.*
   New York: Oxford University Press, 1972.
      Relying extensively on slave narratives, as well as on plantation records, this
   study offers a concise introduction to slavery as experienced by field hands and
   goes beyond earlier works in devoting significant attention to the slaves' African
   heritage, culture, and family lives.
Davis, David Brion. *The Problem of Slavery in the Age of Revolution, 1770–1823.*
   Ithaca: Cornell University Press, 1975.
      Exploring the relationships among bourgeois ideology, antislavery senti-
   ment, and the development of capitalism, both in England and in the United
   States, this sophisticated study has generated a stimulating debate among historians.
Dillon, Merton L. *The Abolitionists: The Growth of a Dissenting Minority.* De Kalb:
   Northern Illinois University Press, 1974.
      This is one of several studies providing a readable overview of the antislavery
   movement.
Filler, Louis. *The Crusade against Slavery, 1830–1860.* New York: Harper and Brothers, 1960.
      This early study is useful for its detailed political history of the struggle
   against slavery.

Friedman, Lawrence J. *Gregarious Saints: Self and Community in American Abolitionism, 1830–1870*. New York: Cambridge University Press, 1982.
    The originality of this study lies in its focus on the inner lives and friendships of abolitionists within three different social circles.
Genovese, Eugene D. *Roll, Jordan, Roll: The World the Slaves Made*. New York: Pantheon, 1974.
    This controversial study argues that slave culture developed within a framework of slaveholding "paternalism" resulting in mutual influence and exacting certain compromises from both parties.
Kraditor, Aileen S. *Means and Ends in American Abolitionism: Garrison and His Critics on Strategy and Tactics, 1834–1850*. New York: Pantheon, 1969.
    Despite a strong pro-Garrisonian bias that minimizes the factionalism within the Garrisonian camp, this is still the best analysis of the schisms in the antislavery movement.
Nye, Russel B. *Fettered Freedom: Civil Liberties and the Slavery Controversy, 1830–1860*. 1963. Reprint, Urbana: University of Illinois Press, 1972.
    This study is important for its history of the campaign to suppress the abolitionist movement and debate over slavery.
Pease, Jane H., and William H. Pease. *Bound with Them in Chains: A Biographical History of the Antislavery Movement*. Westport, Conn.: Greenwood Press, 1972.
    The originality of this study lies in presenting the movement through biographical sketches of lesser known figures representing many different political tendencies and cultural backgrounds.
Perry, Lewis. *Radical Abolitionism: Anarchy and the Government of God in Antislavery Thought*. Ithaca: Cornell University Press, 1973.
    This study analyzes the "non-resistance" or radical pacifist ideology embraced by a large segment of the Garrisonian camp and shared to some extent by Child.
Perry, Lewis, and Michael Fellman, eds. *Antislavery Reconsidered: New Perspectives on the Abolitionists*. Baton Rouge: Louisiana State University Press, 1979.
    Most useful to those already familiar with the history of the movement, this is a stimulating collection of essays covering a broad range of topics and issues.
Quarles, Benjamin. *Black Abolitionists*. New York: Oxford University Press, 1969.
    This study is important for redressing the neglect of African Americans in previous histories of the abolitionist movement and for illuminating black abolitionists' distinctive political aims and views.
Rawick, George P. *From Sundown to Sunup: The Making of the Black Community*. Westport, Conn.: Greenwood Press, 1972.
    Paralleling Blassingame's *Slave Community* in its focus on the African heritage, culture, and family lives of field hands, this study draws its data primarily from WPA interviews rather than from slave narratives.
Richards, Leonard L. *"Gentlemen of Property and Standing": Anti-Abolition Mobs in Jacksonian America*. New York: Oxford University Press, 1970.
    Complementing Nye's *Fettered Freedom*, though narrower in focus, this study provides a more detailed account of antiabolitionist mob violence, together with a useful class analysis of the perpetrators.
Stampp, Kenneth M. *The Peculiar Institution: Slavery in the Ante-Bellum South*. New York: Knopf, 1956.
    Though its focus on oppression and resistance has been somewhat superseded by recent works, which grant slaves more agency and place more emphasis on the development of an autonomous culture, this early study is useful

to read in conjunction with abolitionist tracts like Child's *Appeal* and the Welds and Grimké's *American Slavery As It Is,* whose charges it corroborates.

Stewart, James Brewer. *Holy Warriors: The Abolitionists and American Slavery.* New York: Hill and Wang, 1976.

This is one of several studies providing a concise, readable overview of the antislavery movement.

Stuckey, Sterling. *Slave Culture: Nationalist Theory and the Foundations of Black America.* New York: Oxford University Press, 1987.

This stimulating Afrocentric analysis of slave culture includes chapters on key nationalist leaders David Walker and Henry Highland Garnet, as well as on the struggle between integrationists and nationalists in the African American abolitionist movement.

Walters, Ronald G. *The Antislavery Appeal: American Abolitionism after 1830.* Baltimore: Johns Hopkins University Press, 1976.

The originality of this study lies in exploring the culture of the antislavery movement and the commonalities that united abolitionists despite their political and ideological disagreements.

White, Deborah Gray. *Ar'n't I a Woman? Female Slaves in the Plantation South.* New York: Norton, 1985.

This concise study redresses the neglect of female slaves in previous histories of the institution.

Yellin, Jean Fagan. *Women and Sisters: The Antislavery Feminists in American Culture.* New Haven: Yale University Press, 1989.

Exploring interracial alliances among antislavery women, this interdisciplinary study includes chapters on Child, Jacobs, Grimké, and Sojourner Truth.

AN APPEAL

IN FAVOR OF

THAT CLASS OF AMERICANS

Called Africans

We have offended, Oh! my countrymen!
We have offended very grievously,
And been most tyrannous. From east to west
A groan of accusation pierces Heaven!
The wretched plead against us; multitudes,
Countless and vehement, the sons of God,
Our brethren!   —COLERIDGE

When the grim lion urged his cruel chase,
When the stern panther sought his midnight prey
What fate reserved me for this Christian race?
O race more polished, more severe than they!

SHENSTONE.

TO
THE REV. S. J. MAY,
OF BROOKLYN, CONNECTICUT,

THIS VOLUME

IS

MOST RESPECTFULLY INSCRIBED,

AS A MARK OF GRATITUDE,

FOR HIS EARNEST AND DISINTERESTED EFFORTS

IN

AN UNPOPULAR BUT MOST RIGHTEOUS CAUSE.

PREFACE.

READER, I beseech you not to throw down this volume as soon as you have glanced at the title. Read it, if your prejudices will allow, for the very truth's sake:—If I have the most trifling claims upon your good will, for an hour's amusement to yourself, or benefit to your children, read it for *my* sake:—Read it, if it be merely to find fresh occasion to sneer at the vulgarity of the cause:—Read it, from sheer curiosity to see what a woman (who had much better attend to her household concerns) will say upon such a subject:—Read it, on *any* terms, and my purpose will be gained.

The subject I have chosen admits of no encomiums on my country; but as I generally make it an object to supply what is most needed, this circumstance is unimportant; the market is so glutted with flattery, that a little truth may be acceptable, were it only for its rarity.

I am fully aware of the unpopularity of the task I have undertaken; but though I *expect* ridicule and censure, I cannot *fear* them.

A few years hence, the opinion of the world will be a matter in which I have not even the most transient interest; but this book will be abroad on its mission of humanity, long after the hand that wrote it is mingling with the dust.

Should it be the means of advancing, even one single hour, the inevitable progress of truth and justice, I would not exchange the consciousness for all Rothchild's wealth, or Sir Walter's fame.

AN APPEAL, &c.

CHAPTER I.

Brief History of Negro Slavery. —Its Inevitable Effect upon All Concerned in It.

The lot is wretched, the condition sad,
Whether a pining discontent survive,
And thirst for change; or habit hath subdued
The soul depressed; dejected—even to love
Of her dull tasks and close captivity.
—Wordsworth.

My ear is pained,
My soul is sick with every day's report
Of wrong and outrage, with which this earth is filled.
There is no flesh in man's obdurate heart,
It does not feel for man.
—Cowper.

While the Portuguese were exploring Africa, in 1442, Prince Henry ordered Anthony Gonsalez to carry back certain Moorish prisoners, whom he had seized two years before near Cape Bajador: this order was obeyed, and Gonsalez received from the Moors, in exchange for the captives, ten negroes, and a quantity of gold dust. Unluckily, this wicked speculation proved profitable, and other Portuguese were induced to embark in it.

In 1492, the West India islands were discovered by Columbus. The Spaniards, dazzled with the acquisition of a new world and eager to come into possession of their wealth, compelled the natives of Hispaniola to dig in the mines. The native Indians died rapidly, in consequence of hard work and cruel treatment; and thus a new market was opened for the negro slaves captured by the Portuguese. They were accordingly introduced as early as 1503. Those who bought and those who sold were alike prepared to trample on the rights of their fellow beings, by that most demoralizing of all influences, the accursed love of gold.

Cardinal Ximenes, while he administered the government, before the accession of Charles the Fifth, was petitioned to allow a regular commerce in African negroes. But he rejected the proposal with promptitude and firmness, alike honorable to his head and heart. This earliest friend of the Africans, living in a comparatively unenlightened age, has peculiar claims upon our gratitude and reverence. In 1517, Charles the Fifth granted a patent for an annual supply of four thousand negroes to the Spanish islands. He probably soon became aware of the horrible, and ever-increasing evils, attendant upon this traffic; for twenty-five years after he emancipated every negro in his dominions. But when he resigned his crown and retired to a monastery, the colonists resumed their shameless tyranny.

Captain Hawkins, afterward Sir John Hawkins, was the first Englishman, who disgraced himself and his country by this abominable trade. Assisted by some rich people in London, he fitted out three ships, and sailed to the African coast, where he burned and plundered the towns, and carried off three hundred of the defenceless inhabitants to Hispaniola.

Elizabeth afterwards authorized a similar adventure with one of her own vessels. "She expressed her concern lest any of the Africans should be carried off without their free consent; declaring that such a thing would be detestable, and call down the vengeance of Heaven upon the undertakers." For this reason, it has been supposed that the Queen was deceived—that she imagined the negroes were transported to the Spanish colonies as voluntary laborers. But history gives us slight reasons to judge Elizabeth so favorably. It was her system always to preserve an *appearance* of justice and virtue. She was a shrewd, far-sighted politician; and had in perfection the clear head and cold heart calculated to form that character. Whatever she might believe of the trade at its beginning, she was too deeply read in human nature, not to foresee the inevitable consequence of placing power in the hands of avarice.

A Roman priest persuaded Louis the Thirteenth to sanction slavery for the sake of converting the negroes to Christianity; and thus this bloody iniquity, disguised with gown, hood, and rosary, entered the fair dominions of France. To be violently wrested from his home, and condemned to toil without hope, by Christians, to whom he had done no wrong, was, methinks, a very odd beginning to the poor negro's course of religious instruction!

When this evil had once begun, it, of course, gathered strength rapidly; for all the bad passions of human nature were eagerly enlisted in its cause. The British formed settlements in North America, and in the West Indies; and these were stocked with slaves. From 1680 to 1786 *two million, one hundred and thirty thousand* negroes were imported into the British colonies!

In almost all great evils there is some redeeming feature—*some* good results, even where it is not intended: pride and vanity, utterly selfish and wrong in themselves, often throw money into the hands of the poor, and thus tend to excite industry and ingenuity, while they produce comfort. But slavery is *all* evil—within and without—root and branch,—bud, blossom and fruit!

In order to show how dark it is in every aspect—how invariably injurious both to nations and individuals,—I will select a few facts from the mass of evidence now before me.

In the first place, its effects upon *Africa* have been most disastrous. All along the coast, intercourse with Europeans has deprived the inhabitants of their primitive simplicity, without substituting in its place the order, refinement, and correctness of principle, attendant upon true civilization. The soil of Africa is rich in native productions, and honorable commerce might have been a blessing to her, to Europe, and to America; but instead of that, a trade has been substituted, which operates like a withering curse, upon all concerned in it.

There are green and sheltered valleys in Africa,—broad and beautiful rivers,—and vegetation in its loveliest and most magnificent forms.—But no comfortable houses, no thriving farms, no cultivated gardens;—for it is not safe to possess permanent property, where each little state is surrounded by warlike neighbors, continually sending out their armed bands in search of slaves. The white man offers his most tempting articles of merchandize to the negro, as a price for the flesh and blood of his enemy; and if we, with all our boasted knowledge and religion, are seduced by money to do such grievous wrong to those who have never offended us, what can we expect of men just emerging from the limited wants of savage life, too uncivilized to have formed any habits of steady industry, yet earnestly coveting the productions they know not how to earn? The inevitable consequence is, that war is made throughout that unhappy continent, not only upon the slightest pretences, but often without any pretext at all. Villages are set on fire, and those who fly from the flames rush upon the spears of the enemy. Private kidnapping is likewise carried on to a great extent; for he who can catch a neighbor's child is sure to find a ready purchaser; and it sometimes happens that the captor and his living merchandize are both seized by the white slave-trader. Houses are broken open in the night, and defenceless women and children carried away into captivity. If boys, in the unsuspecting innocence of youth, come near the white man's ships, to sell vegetables or fruit, they are ruthlessly seized and carried to slavery in a distant land. Even the laws are perverted to this shameful purpose. If a chief wants European commodities, he accuses a parent of witchcraft; the victim is tried by the ordeal of poisoned water;* and if he sicken at the draught, the king claims a right to punish him by selling his whole family. In African legislation, almost all crimes are punished with slavery; and, thanks to the white man's rapacity, there is always a very powerful motive for finding the culprit guilty. He must be a very good king indeed, that judges his subjects impartially, when he is sure of making money by doing otherwise!

The king of Dahomy, and other despotic princes, do not scruple to seize their own people and sell them, without provocation, whenever they happen to want anything, which slave-ships can furnish. If a chief has conscience enough to object to such proceedings, he is excited by presents of gun-powder and brandy. One of these men, who could not resist the persuasions of the slave traders while he was intoxicated, was conscience-stricken when he recovered his senses, and bitterly reproached his *Christian* seducers. One negro king, debarred by his religion from the use of spirituous liquors, and therefore less dangerously tempted than others, abolished the slave trade throughout his dominions, and exerted himself to encourage honest industry; but his people must have been as sheep among wolves.

Relentless bigotry brings its aid to darken the horrors of the scene. The Mohammedans deem it right to subject the heathen tribes to

---

*Judicial trials by the ordeal of personal combat, in which the vanquished were always pronounced guilty, occurred as late as the sixteenth century both in France and England.

perpetual bondage. The Moors and Arabs think Alla and the Prophet have given them an undisputed right to the poor Caffre, his wife, his children, and his goods. But mark how the slave-trade deepens even the fearful gloom of bigotry! These Mohammedans are by no means zealous to enlighten their Pagan neighbors—they do not wish them to come to a knowledge of what they consider the true religion—lest they should forfeit the only ground, on which they can even pretend to the right of driving them by thousands to the markets of Kano and Tripoli.

This is precisely like our own conduct. We say the negroes are so ignorant that they must be slaves; and we insist upon keeping them ignorant, lest we spoil them for slaves. The same spirit that dictates this logic to the Arab, teaches it to the European and the American:— Call it what you please—it is certainly neither of heaven nor of earth.

When the slave ships are lying on the coast of Africa, canoes well armed are sent into the inland country, and after a few weeks they return with hundreds of negroes, tied fast with ropes. Sometimes the white men lurk among the bushes, and seize the wretched beings who incautiously venture from their homes; sometimes they paint their skins as black as their hearts, and by this deception suddenly surprise the unsuspecting natives; at other times the victims are decoyed on board the vessel, under some kind pretence or other, and then lashed to the mast, or chained in the hold. Is it not very natural for the Africans to say "devilish white"?

All along the shores of this devoted country, terror and distrust prevail. The natives never venture out without arms, when a vessel is in sight, and skulk through their own fields, as if watched by a panther. All their worst passions are called into full exercise, and all their kindlier feelings smothered. Treachery, fraud and violence desolate the country, rend asunder the dearest relations, and pollute the very fountains of justice. The history of the negro, whether national or domestic, is written in blood. Had half the skill and strength employed in the slave-trade been engaged in honorable commerce, the native princes would long ago have directed their energies toward clearing the country, destroying wild beasts, and introducing the arts and refinements of civilized life. Under such influences, Africa might become an earthly paradise;—the white man's avarice has made it a den of wolves.

Having thus glanced at the miserable effects of this system on the condition of Africa, we will now follow the poor *slave* through his wretched wanderings, in order to give some idea of his physical suffering, his mental, and moral degradation.

Husbands are torn from their wives, children from their parents, while the air is filled with the shrieks and lamentations of the bereaved. Sometimes they are brought from a remote country; obliged to wander over mountains and through deserts; chained together in herds; driven by the whip; scorched by a tropical sun; compelled to carry heavy bales of merchandize; suffering with hunger and thirst; worn down with fatigue; and often leaving their bones to whiten in the desert. A large troop of slaves, taken by the Sultan of Fezzan, died in the desert for want of food. In some places, travellers meet with fifty or sixty skeletons in a day, of which the largest proportion were no doubt slaves, on their way to European markets. Sometimes the poor creatures refuse to go a step further, and even the lacerating whip cannot goad them on; in such cases, they become the prey of wild beasts, more merciful than white men.

Those who arrive at the sea-coast, are in a state of desperation and despair. Their purchasers are so well aware of this, and so fearful of the consequences, that they set sail in the night, lest the negroes should know when they depart from their native shores.

And here the scene becomes almost too harrowing to dwell upon. But we must not allow our nerves to be more tender than our consciences. The poor wretches are stowed by hundreds, like bales of goods, between the low decks, where filth and putrid air produce disease, madness, and suicide. Unless they die in *great* numbers, the slave captain does not even concern himself enough to fret; his live stock cost nothing, and he is sure of such a high price for what remains at the end of the voyage, that he can afford to lose a good many.

The following account is given by Dr Walsh, who accompanied Viscount Strangford, as chaplain, on his embassy to Brazil. The vessel in which he sailed chased a slave ship; for to the honor of England be it said, she has asked and obtained permission from other governments to treat as pirates such of their subjects as are discovered carrying on this guilty trade north of the equator. Doctor Walsh was an eye witness of the scene he describes; and the evidence given, at various times, before the British House of Commons, proves that the frightful picture is by no means exaggerated.

"The vessel had taken in, on the coast of Africa, three hundred and thirtysix males, and two hundred and twentysix females, making in all five hundred and sixtytwo; she had been out seventeen days, during which she had thrown overboard fiftyfive. They were all inclosed under grated hatchways, between decks. The space was so low, and they were stowed so close together, that there was no possibility of lying down, or changing their position, night or day. The greater part of them were shut out from light and air; and this when the thermometer, exposed to the open sky, was standing, in the shade on our deck, at eightynine degrees.

"The space between decks was divided into two compartments, three feet three inches high. Two hundred and twentysix women and girls were thrust into one space two hundred and eightyeight feet square; and three hundred and thirtysix men and boys were crammed into another space eight hundred feet square; giving the whole an average of twentythree inches; and to each of the women not more than thirteen inches; though several of them were in a state of health, which peculiarly demanded pity.—As they were shipped on account of different individuals, they were branded like sheep, with the owner's marks of different forms; which, as the mate informed me with perfect indifference, had been burnt in with red-hot iron. Over the hatch-way stood a ferocious looking fellow, the slave-driver of the ship, with a scourge of many-twisted thongs in his hand; whenever he heard the slightest noise from below, he shook it over them, and seemed eager to exercise it.

"As soon as the poor creatures saw us looking down at them, their melancholy visages brightened up. They perceived something of sympathy and kindness in our looks, to which they had not been accustomed; and feeling instinctively that we were friends, they immediately began to shout and clap their hands. The women were particularly excited. They all held up their arms, and when we bent down and shook hands with them, they could not contain their delight; they endeavored to scramble upon their knees, stretching up to kiss our hands, and we understood they knew we had come to liberate them. Some, however, hung down their heads in apparently hopeless dejection; some were greatly emaciated; and some, particularly children, seemed dying. The heat of these horrid places was so great, and the odor so offensive, that it was quite impossible to enter them, even had there been room.

"The officers insisted that the poor, suffering creatures should be admitted on deck to get air and water. This was opposed by the mate of the slaver, who (from a feeling that they deserved it,) declared they should be all murdered. The officers, however, persisted, and the poor beings were all turned out together. It is impossible to conceive the effect of this eruption—five hundred and seventeen fellow-creatures, of all ages and sexes; some children, some adults, some old men and women, all entirely destitute of clothing, scrambling out together to taste the luxury of a little fresh air and water. They came swarming up, like bees from a hive, till the whole deck was crowded to suffocation from stem to stern; so that it was impossible to imagine where they could all have come from, or how they could have been stowed away. On looking into the places where they had been crammed, there were found some children next the sides of the ship, in the places most remote from light and air; they were lying nearly in a torpid state, after the rest had turned out. The little creatures seemed indifferent as to life or death; and when they were carried on deck, many of them could not stand. After enjoying for a short time the unusual luxury of air, some water was brought; it was then that the extent of their sufferings was exposed in a fearful manner. They all rushed like maniacs towards it. No entreaties, or threats, or blows, could restrain them; they shrieked, and struggled, and fought with one another, for a drop of this precious liquid, as if they grew rabid at the sight of it. There is nothing from which slaves in the mid-passage suffer so much as want of water. It is sometimes usual to take out casks filled with sea-water as ballast, and when the slaves are received on board, to start the casks, and re-fill them with fresh. On one occasion, a ship from Bahia neglected to change the contents of their casks, and on the mid-passage found, to their horror, that they were filled with nothing but salt water. All the slaves on board perished! We could judge of the extent of their sufferings from the afflicting sight we now saw. When the poor creatures were ordered down again, several of them came, and pressed their heads against our knees, with looks of the greatest anguish, with the prospect of returning to the horrid place of suffering below."

Alas! the slave-captain proved by his papers that he confined his traffic strictly to the south of the Line, where it was yet lawful; perhaps his papers were forged; but the English officers were afraid to violate an article of the treaty, which their government had made with Brazil. Thus does cunning wickedness defeat benevolence and justice in this world! Dr Walsh continues: "With infinite regret, therefore, we were obliged to restore his papers to the captain, and permit him to proceed, after nine hours' detention and close investigation. It was dark when we separated, and the last parting sounds we heard from the unhallowed ship, were the cries and shrieks of the slaves, suffering under some bodily infliction."

I suppose the English officers acted politically right; but not for the world's wealth, would I have acted politically right, under such circumstances!*

Arrived at the place of destination, the condition of the slave is scarcely less deplorable. They are advertised with cattle; chained in droves, and driven to market with a whip; and sold at auction, with the beasts of the field. They are treated like brutes, and all the influences around them conspire to make them brutes.

"Some are employed as domestic slaves, when and how the owner pleases; by day or by night, on Sunday or other days, in any measure or degree, with any remuneration or with none, with what kind or quantity of food the owner of the human beast may choose. Male or female, young or old, weak or strong, may be punished with or without reason, as caprice or passion may prompt. When the drudge does not suit, he may be sold for some inferior purpose, like a horse that has seen his best days, till like a worn-out beast he dies, unpitied and forgotten! Kept in ignorance of the holy precepts and divine consolations of Christianity, he remains a Pagan in a Christian land, without even an object of idolatrous worship—'having no hope, and without God in the world.' "

From the moment the slave is kidnapped, to the last hour he draws his miserable breath, the white man's influence directly cherishes ignorance, fraud, treachery, theft, licentiousness, revenge, hatred and murder. It cannot be denied that human nature thus operated upon, *must* necessarily yield, more or less, to all these evils.—And thus do we dare to treat beings, who, like ourselves, are heirs of immortality!

And now let us briefly inquire into the influence of slavery on the *white man's* character; for in this evil there is a mighty re-action. "Such is the constitution of things, that we cannot inflict an injury without suffering from it ourselves: he, who blesses another, benefits himself; but he, who sins against his fellow creature, does his own

---

*Dr Walsh's book on Brazil was published in 1831. He says: "Notwithstanding the benevolent and persevering exertions of England, this horrid traffic in human flesh is nearly as extensively carried on as ever, and under circumstances perhaps of a more revolting character. The very shifts at evasion, the necessity for concealment, and the desperate hazard, cause inconvenience and sufferings to the poor creatures in a very aggravated degree."

soul a grievous wrong." The effect produced upon *slave captains* is absolutely frightful. Those who wish to realize it in all its awful extent, may find abundant information in Clarkson's History of Slavery: the authenticity of the facts there given cannot be doubted; for setting aside the perfect honesty of Clarkson's character, these facts were principally accepted as evidence before the British Parliament, where there was a very strong party of slave owners desirous to prove them false.

Indeed when we reflect upon the subject, it cannot excite surprise that slave-captains become as hard hearted and fierce as tigers. The very first step in their business is a deliberate invasion of the rights of others; its pursuit combines every form of violence, bloodshed, tyranny and anguish; they are accustomed to consider their victims as cattle, or blocks of wood;* and they are invested with perfectly despotic powers.

There is a great waste of life among white seamen employed in this traffic, in consequence of the severe punishment they receive, and diseases originating in the unwholesome atmosphere on board. Clarkson, after a long and patient investigation, came to the conclusion that two slave voyages to Africa, would destroy more seamen than eightythree to Newfoundland; and there is this difference to be observed, that the loss in one trade is generally occasioned by weather or accident, in the other by cruelty or disease. The instances are exceedingly numerous of sailors on board slave-ships, that have died under the lash or in consequence of it. Some of the particulars are so painful that it has made me sicken to read them; and I therefore forbear to repeat them. Of the Alexander's crew, in 1785, no less than eleven deserted at Bonny, on the African coast, because life had become insupportable. They chose all that could be endured from a most inhospitable climate, and the violence of the natives, rather than remain in their own ship. Nine others died on the voyage, and the rest were exceedingly abused. This state of things was so universal that seamen were notoriously averse to enter the hateful business. In order

*I have read letters from slave-captains to their employers, in which they declare that they shipped such a number of *billets of wood,* or *pieces of ebony,* on the coast of Africa.

Near the office of the Richmond Enquirer in Virginia, an auction flag was hoisted one day this last winter, with the following curious advertisement: "On Monday the 11th inst., will be sold in front of the High Constable's office, one bright mulatto woman, about twentysix years of age; also, *some empty barrels, and sundry old candle boxes.*"

to obtain them it became necessary to resort to force or deception. (Behold how many branches there are to the tree of crime!) Decoyed to houses where night after night was spent in dancing, rioting and drunkenness, the thoughtless fellows gave themselves up to the merriment of the scene, and in a moment of intoxication the fatal bargain was sealed. Encouraged to spend more than they owned, a jail or the slave-ship became the only alternatives. The superiority of wages was likewise a strong inducement; but this was a cheat. The wages of the sailors were half paid in the currency of the country where the vessel carried her slaves; and thus they were actually lower than in other trades, while they were nominally higher.

In such an employment the morals of the seamen of course became corrupt, like their masters; and every species of fraud was thought allowable to deceive the ignorant Africans, by means of false weights, false measures, adulterated commodities, and the like.

Of the cruelties on board slave-ships, I will mention but a few instances; though a large volume might be filled with such detestable anecdotes perfectly well authenticated.

"A child on board a slave-ship, of about ten months old, took sulk and would not eat; the captain flogged it with a cat-o'-nine tails; swearing that he would make it eat, or kill it. From this, and other ill-treatment, the limbs swelled. He then ordered some water to be made hot to abate the swelling. But even his tender mercies were cruel. The cook, on putting his hand into the water, said it was too hot. Upon this the captain swore at him, and ordered the feet to be put in. This was done. The nails and skin came off. Oiled cloths were then put around them. The child was at length tied to a heavy log. Two or three days afterwards, the captain caught it up again, and repeated that he would make it eat, or kill it. He immediately flogged it again, and in a quarter of an hour it died. And after the babe was dead, whom should the barbarian select to throw it overboard, but the wretched mother! In vain she tried to avoid the office. He beat her, till he made her take up the child and carry it to the side of the vessel. She then dropped it into the sea, turning her head the other way, that she might not see it."*

"In 1780, a slave-trader, detained by contrary winds on the American coast, and in distress, selected one hundred and thirtytwo of his sick slaves, and threw them into the sea, tied together in pairs, that

*Clarkson's History of the Abolition of the Slave Trade.

they might not escape by swimming. He hoped the Insurance Company would indemnify him for his loss; and in the lawsuit, to which this gave birth, he observed that 'negroes cannot be considered in any other light than as beasts of burden; and to lighten a vessel it is permitted to throw overboard its least valuable effects.'

"Some of the unhappy slaves escaped from those who attempted to tie them, and jumped into the sea. One of them was saved by means of a cord thrown by the sailors of another vessel; and the monster who murdered his innocent companions had the audacity to claim him as his property. The judges, either from shame, or a sense of justice, refused his demand."*

Some people speculate in what are called refuse slaves; i.e. the poor diseased ones. Many of them die in the piazzas of the auctioneers; and sometimes, in the agonies of death, they are sold as low as a dollar.

Even this is better than to be unprotected on the wide ocean in the power of such wild beasts as I have described. It may seem incredible to some that human nature is capable of so much depravity. But the confessions of pirates show how habitual scenes of blood and violence harden the heart of man; and history abundantly proves that despotic power produces a fearful species of moral insanity. The wanton cruelties of Nero, Caligula, Domitian, and many of the officers of the Inquisition, seem like the frantic acts of madmen.

The public has, however, a sense of justice, which can never be entirely perverted. Since the time when Clarkson, Wilberforce and Fox made the horrors of the slave trade understood, the slave captain, or slave jockey is spontaneously and almost universally regarded with dislike and horror. Even in the slave-holding States it is deemed disreputable to associate with a professed slave-trader, though few perhaps would think it any harm to bargain with him. This public feeling makes itself felt so strongly, that men engaged in what is called the African traffic, kept it a secret, if they could, even before the laws made it hazardous.

No man of the least principle could for a moment think of engaging in such enterprises; and if he have any feeling, it is soon destroyed by familiarity with scenes of guilt and anguish. The result is, that the slave-trade is a monopoly in the hands of the very wicked; and this is one reason why it has always been profitable.

*The Abbé Grégoire's Inquiry into the Intellect and Morals of Negroes.

Yet even the slave *trade* has had its champions—of course among those who had money invested in it. Politicians have boldly said that it was a profitable branch of commerce, and ought not to be discontinued on account of the idle dreams of benevolent enthusiasts. They have argued before the House of Commons, that others would enslave the negroes, if the English gave it up—as if it were allowable for one man to commit a crime because another was likely to do it! They tell how merciful it is to bring the Africans away from the despotism and wars, which desolate their own continent; but they do not add that the white man is himself the cause of these wars, nor do they prove our right to judge for another man where he will be the happiest. If the Turks, or the Algerines saw fit to exercise this right, they might carry away captive all the occupants of our prisons and penitentiaries.

Some of the advocates of this traffic maintained that the voyage from Africa to the slave-market, called the Middle Passage, was an exceedingly comfortable portion of existence. One went so far as to declare it "the happiest part of a negro's life." They aver that the Africans, on their way to slavery, are so merry, that they dance and sing. But upon a careful examination of witnesses, it was found that their singing consisted of dirge-like lamentations for their native land. One of the captains threatened to flog a woman, because the mournfulness of her song was too painful to him. After meals they jumped up in their irons for exercise. This was considered so necessary for their health, that they were whipped, if they refused to do it. And this was their dancing! "I," said one of the witnesses, "was employed to dance the men, while another person danced the women."

These pretences, ridiculous as they appear, are worth about as much as any of the arguments that can be brought forward in defence of any part of the slave system.

The engraving on the next page will help to give a vivid idea of the Elysium enjoyed by negroes, during the Middle Passage. Fig. A represents the iron hand-cuffs, which fasten the slaves together by means of a little bolt with a padlock.

B represents the iron shackles by which the ancle of one is made fast to the ancle of his next companion. Yet even thus secured, they do often jump into the sea, and wave their hands in triumph at the approach of death. E is a thumb-screw. The thumbs are put into two round holes at the top; by turning a key a bar rises from C to D by means of a screw; and the pressure becomes very painful. By turning

it further, the blood is made to start; and by taking away the key as at
E, the tortured person is left in agony, without the means of helping himself, or being helped by others. This is applied in case of
obstinacy, at the discretion of the captain. I, F, is a speculum oris. The
dotted lines represent it when shut; the black lines when open. It
opens at G, H, by a screw below with a knob at the end of it. This
instrument was used by surgeons to wrench open the mouth in case
of lock-jaw. It is used in slave-ships to compel the negroes to take
food; because a loss to the owners would follow their persevering
attempts to die. K represents the manner of stowing in a slave-ship.

According to Clarkson's estimate, about two and a half out of a
hundred of human beings die annually, in the ordinary course of nature, including infants and the aged: but in an African voyage, where
few babes and no old people are admitted, so that those shipped are
at the firmest period of life, the annual mortality is fortythree in a
hundred. In vessels that sail from Bonny, Benin, and the Calabars,
whence a large proportion of slaves are brought, this mortality is so
much increased by various causes, that eightysix in a hundred die
yearly. He adds, "It is a destruction, which if general but for ten years,
would depopulate the world, and extinguish the human race."

We next come to the influence of this diabolical system on the *slave-
owner;* and here I shall be cautioned that I am treading on delicate
ground, because our own countrymen are slave holders. But I am yet
to learn that wickedness is any the better for being our own.—Let the
truth be spoken—and let those abide its presence who can.

The following is the testimony of Jefferson, who had good opportunities for observation, and who certainly had no New England
prejudices: "There must, doubtless, be an unhappy influence on the
manners of the people, produced by the existence of slavery among
us. The whole commerce between master and slave is a perpetual
exercise of the most boisterous passions; the most unremitting despotism on the one part, and degrading submission on the other. Our
children see this, and learn to imitate it; for man is an imitative
animal. The parent storms; the child looks on, catches the lineaments
of wrath, puts on the same airs in a circle of smaller slaves, gives loose
to the worst of passions; and thus nursed, educated, and daily exercised in tyranny, cannot but be stamped by it with odious peculiarities. The man must be a prodigy, who can retain his morals and
manners undepraved in such circumstances."

In a community where all the labor is done by one class, there must of course be another class, who live in indolence; and we all know how much people that have nothing to do are tempted by what the world calls pleasures; the result is, that slave-holding states and colonies are proverbial for dissipation. Hence too the contempt for industry, which prevails in such a state of society. Where none work but slaves, usefulness becomes degradation. The wife of a respectable mechanic, who accompanied her husband from Massachusetts to the South, gave great offence to her new neighbors by performing her usual household avocations; they begged her to desist from it, (offering the services of their own blacks,) because the sight of a white person engaged in any labor was extremely injurious to the slaves; they deemed it very important that the negroes should be taught, both by precept and example, that they alone were made to work!

Whether the undue importance attached to merely external gentility, and the increasing tendency to indolence and extravagance throughout this country, ought to be attributed, in any degree, to the same source, I am unable to say; if *any* influence comes to us from the example and ridicule of the slave-holding States, it certainly must be of this nature.

There is another view of this system, which I cannot unveil so completely as it ought to be. I shall be called bold for saying so much; but the facts are so important, that it is a matter of conscience not to be fastidious.

The negro woman is unprotected either by law or public opinion. She is the property of her master, and her daughters are his property. They are allowed to have no conscientious scruples, no sense of shame, no regard for the feelings of husband, or parent; they must be entirely subservient to the will of their owner, on pain of being whipped as near unto death as will comport with his interest, or quite to death, if it suit his pleasure.

Those who know human nature would be able to conjecture the unavoidable result, even if it were not betrayed by the amount of mixed population. Think for a moment, what a degrading effect must be produced on the morals of both blacks and whites by customs like these!

Considering we live in the nineteenth century, it is indeed a strange state of society where the father sells his child, and the brother puts his sister up at auction! Yet these things are often practised in our republic.

Doctor Walsh, in his account of Brazil, tells an anecdote of one of these fathers, who love their offspring at market price. "For many years," says he, "this man kept his son in slavery, and maintained the right to dispose of him, as he would of his mule. Being ill, however, and near to die, he made his will, left his child his freedom, and apprised him of it. Some time after, he recovered, and having a dispute with the young man, he threatened to sell him with the rest of his stock. The son, determined to prevent this, assassinated his father in a wood, got possession of the will, demanded his freedom, and obtained it. This circumstance was perfectly well known in the neighborhood, but no process was instituted against him. He was not chargeable, as I could hear, with any other delinquency than the horrible one of murdering his father to obtain his freedom." This forms a fine picture of the effects of slavery upon human relations!*

I have more than once heard people, who had just returned from the South, speak of seeing a number of mulattoes in attendance where they visited, whose resemblance to the head of the family was too striking not to be immediately observed. What sort of feeling must be excited in the minds of those slaves by being constantly exposed to the tyranny or caprice of their own brothers and sisters, and by the knowledge that these near relations will, on a division of the estate, have power to sell them off with the cattle?

But the vices of white men eventually provide a scourge for themselves. They increase the negro race, but the negro can never increase theirs; and this is one great reason why the proportion of colored population is always so large in slave-holding countries. As the ratio increases more and more every year, the colored people must eventually be the stronger party; and when this result happens, slavery must either be abolished, or government must furnish troops, of whose wages the free States must pay their proportion.

As a proof of the effects of slavery on the temper, I will relate but very few anecdotes.

The first happened in the Bahamas. It is extracted from a despatch of Mr Huskisson to the Governor of those islands: "Henry and Helen Moss have been found guilty of a *misdemeanor*, for their cruelty to their slave Kate; and those facts of the case, which seem beyond dispute, appear to be as follows:

*A short time ago a reverend and very benevolent gentleman suggested as the subject of a book, *The Beauty of Human Relations*. What a bitter jest it would be, to send him this volume, with the information that I had complied with his request!

"Kate was a domestic slave, and is stated to have been guilty of theft: she is also accused of disobedience, in refusing to mend her clothes and do her work; and this was the more immediate cause of her punishment. On the twentysecond of July, eighteen hundred and twentysix, she was confined in the stocks, and she was not released till the eighth of August following, being a period of seventeen days. The stocks were so constructed that she could not sit up or lie down at pleasure, and she remained in them night and day. During this period she was flogged repeatedly, one of the overseers thinks about six times; and red pepper was rubbed upon her eyes, to prevent her sleeping. Tasks were given her, which, in the opinion of the same overseer, she was incapable of performing; sometimes because they were beyond her powers, at other times because she could not see to do them, on account of the pepper having been rubbed on her eyes; and she was flogged for failing to accomplish these tasks. A violent distemper had prevailed on the plantation during the summer. It is in evidence, that one of the days of Kate's confinement she complained of fever; and that one of the floggings she received was the day after she made the complaint. When she was taken out of the stocks, she appeared to be cramped, and was then again flogged. The very day of her release, she was sent to field labor (though heretofore a house-servant); and on the evening of the third day ensuing was brought before her owners, as being ill, and refusing to work; and she then again complained of having fever. They were of opinion that she had none then, but gave directions to the driver, if she should be ill, to bring her to them for medicines in the morning. The driver took her to the negro-house, and again flogged her; though at this time apparently without orders from her owners to do so. In the morning at seven o'clock she was taken to work in the field, where she died at noon.

"The facts of the case are thus far incontrovertibly established; and I deeply lament, that, heinous as the offences are which this narrative exhibits, I can discover no material palliation of them amongst the other circumstances detailed in the evidence."

A bill of indictment for murder was preferred against Mr and Mrs Moss: the grand jury threw it out. Upon two other bills, for misdemeanors, a verdict of guilty was returned. Five months' imprisonment, and a fine of three hundred pounds was the only punishment for this deliberate and shocking cruelty!

In the next chapter, it will be seen that similar *misdemeanors* are committed with equal impunity in this country.

I do not know how much odium Mr and Mrs Moss generally incurred in consequence of this transaction; but many of "the most respectable people in the island petitioned for a mitigation of their punishment, visited them in prison, did everything to identify themselves with them, and on their liberation from jail, gave them a public dinner as a matter of triumph!" The witnesses in their favor even went so far as to insist that their character stood high for humanity among the neighboring planters. I believe there never was a class of people on earth so determined to uphold each other, at all events, as slave-owners.

The following account was originally written by the Rev. William Dickey of Bloomingsburgh, to the Rev. John Rankin, of Ripley, Ohio. It was published in 1826, in a little volume of letters, on the subject of slavery, by the Rev. Mr Rankin, who assures us that Mr Dickey was well acquainted with the circumstances he describes.

"In the county of Livingston, Kentucky, near the mouth of Cumberland river, lived Lilburn Lewis, the son of Jefferson's sister. He was the wealthy owner of a considerable number of slaves, whom he drove constantly, fed sparingly, and lashed severely. The consequence was, they would run away. Among the rest was an ill-grown boy, about seventeen, who, having just returned from a skulking spell, was sent to the spring for water, and, in returning, let fall an elegant pitcher, which dashed to shivers on the rocks. It was night, and the slaves were all at home. The master had them collected into the most roomy negro-house, and a rousing fire made." (Reader, what follows is very shocking; but I have already said we must not allow our nerves to be more sensitive than our consciences. If such things are done in our country, it is important that we should know of them, and seriously reflect upon them.) "The door was fastened, that none of the negroes, either through fear or sympathy, should attempt to escape; he then told them that the design of this meeting was to teach them to remain at home and obey his orders. All things being now in train, George was called up, and by the assistance of his younger brother, laid on a broad bench or block. The master then cut off his ancles with a broad axe. In vain the unhappy victim screamed. Not a hand among so many dared to interfere. Having cast the feet into the fire he lectured the negroes at some length. He then proceeded to cut off his limbs below the knees. The sufferer besought him to begin with his head. It was in vain—the master went on thus, until trunk, arms, and head, were all in the fire. Still protracting the intervals with lectures, and threatenings of like punishment, in case any of them were disobedient, or ran away, or disclosed the tragedy they were compelled to witness. In order to consume the bones, the fire was briskly stirred until midnight: when, as if heaven and earth combined to show their detestation of the deed, a sudden shock of earthquake threw down the heavy wall, composed of rock and clay, extinguished the fire, and covered the remains of George. The negroes were allowed to disperse, with charges to keep the secret, under the penalty of like punishment. When his wife asked the cause of the dreadful screams she had heard, he said that he had never enjoyed himself so well at a ball as he had enjoyed himself that evening. Next morning, he ordered the wall to be rebuilt, and he himself superintended, picking up the remains of the boy, and placing them within the new wall, thus hoping to conceal the matter. But some of the negroes whispered the horrid deed; the neighbors tore down the wall, and finding the remains, they testified against him. He was bound over to await the sitting of the court; but before that period arrived, he committed suicide."

"N. B. This happened in 1811; if I be correct, it was on the 16th of December. It was on the Sabbath."

Mr Rankin adds, there was little probability that Mr Lewis would have fallen under the sentence of the law. Notwithstanding the peculiar enormity of his offence, there were individuals who combined to let him out of prison, in order to screen him from justice.

Another instance of summary punishment inflicted on a runaway slave, is told by a respectable gentleman from South Carolina, with whom I am acquainted. He was young, when the circumstance occurred, in the neighborhood of his home; and it filled him with horror. A slave being missing, several planters united in a negro hunt, as it is called. They set out with dogs, guns, and horses, as they would to chase a tiger. The poor fellow, being discovered, took refuge in a tree; where he was deliberately shot by his pursuers.

In some of the West Indies, blood-hounds are employed to hunt negroes; and this fact is the foundation of one of the most painfully interesting scenes in Miss Martineau's Demerara. A writer by the name of Dallas has the hardihood to assert that it is mere sophistry to censure the practice of training dogs to devour men. He asks, "Did not the Asiatics employ elephants in war? If a man were bitten by a mad dog, would he hesitate to cut off the wounded part, in order to save his life?"

It is said that when the first pack of blood-hounds arrived in St Domingo, the white planters delivered to them the first negro they found, merely by way of experiment; and when they saw him immediately torn in pieces, they were highly delighted to find the dogs so well trained to their business.

Some authentic records of female cruelty would seem perfectly incredible, were it not an established law of our nature that tyranny becomes a habit, and scenes of suffering, often repeated, render the heart callous.

A young friend of mine, remarkable for the kindness of his disposition and the courtesy of his manners, told me that he was really alarmed at the change produced in his character by a few months' residence in the West Indies. The family who owned the plantation were absent, and he saw nothing around him but slaves; the consequence was that he insensibly acquired a dictatorial manner, and habitual disregard to the convenience of his inferiors. The candid admonition of a friend made him aware of this, and his natural amiability was restored.

The ladies who remove from the free States into the slave-holding ones almost invariably write that the sight of slavery was at first exceedingly painful; but that they soon become habituated to it; and after a while, they are very apt to vindicate the system, upon the ground that it is extremely convenient to have such submissive servants. This reason was actually given by a lady of my acquaintance, who is considered an unusually fervent Christian. Yet Christianity expressly teaches us to love our neighbor as ourselves. This shows how dangerous it is, for even the best of us, to become *accustomed* to what is wrong.

A judicious and benevolent friend lately told me the story of one of her relatives, who married a slave owner, and removed to his plantation. The lady in question was considered very amiable, and had a serene, affectionate expression of countenance. After several years' residence among her slaves, she visited New England. "Her history was written in her face," said my friend; "its expression had changed into that of a fiend. She brought but few slaves with her; and those few were of course compelled to perform additional labor. One faithful negro woman nursed the twins of her mistress, and did all the washing, ironing, and scouring. If, after a sleepless night with the restless babes (driven from the bosom of their own mother,) she performed her toilsome avocations with diminished activity, her mistress, with her own lady-like hands, applied the cow-skin, and the neighborhood resounded with the cries of her victim. The instrument of punishment was actually kept hanging in the entry, to the no small disgust of her New England visiters. For my part," continued my friend, "I did not try to be polite to her; for I was not hypocrite enough to conceal my indignation."

The following occurred near Natchez, and was told to me by a highly intelligent man, who, being a diplomatist and a courtier, was very likely to make the best of national evils: A planter had occasion to send a female slave some distance on an errand. She did not return so soon as he expected, and he grew angry. At last he gave orders that she should be severely whipped when she came back. When the poor creature arrived, she pleaded for mercy, saying she had been so very ill, that she was obliged to rest in the fields; but she was ordered to receive another dozen of lashes, for having had the impudence to speak. She died at the whipping post; nor did she perish alone—a new born baby died with her. The gentleman who told me this fact, witnessed the poor creature's funeral. It is true, the master was universally blamed and shunned for the cruel deed; but the laws were powerless.

I shall be told that such examples as these are of rare occurrence; and I have no doubt that instances of excessive severity are far from being common. I believe that a large proportion of masters are as kind to their slaves as they can be, consistently with keeping them in bondage; but it must be allowed that this, to make the best of it, is very stinted kindness. And let it never be forgotten that the negro's fate depends entirely on the character of his master; and it is a mere matter of chance whether he fall into merciful or unmerciful hands; his happiness, nay, his very life, depends on chance.

The slave owners are always telling us, that the accounts of slave misery are abominably exaggerated; and their plea is supported by many individuals, who seem to think that charity was made to *cover* sins, not to *cure* them. But without listening to the zealous opposers of slavery, we shall find in the judicial reports of the Southern States, and in the ordinary details of their newspapers, more than enough to startle us; besides, we must not forget that where one instance of cruelty comes to our knowledge, hundreds are kept secret; and the more public attention is awakened to the subject, the more caution will be used in this respect.

Why should we be deceived by the sophistry of those whose interest it is to gloss over iniquity, and who from long habit have learned to believe that it is no iniquity? It is a very simple process to judge rightly in this matter. Just ask yourself the question where you could find a set of men, in whose power you would be willing to place yourself, if the laws allowed them to sin against you with impunity?

But it is urged that it is the interest of planters to treat their slaves well. This argument no doubt has some force; and it is the poor negro's only security. But it is likewise the interest of men to treat their cattle kindly; yet we see that passion and short-sighted avarice do overcome the strongest motives of interest. Cattle are beat unmercifully, sometimes unto death; they are ruined by being over-worked; weakened by want of sufficient food; and so forth. Besides, it is sometimes directly *for* the interest of the planter to work his slaves beyond their strength. When there is a sudden rise in the prices of sugar, a certain amount of labor in a given time is of more consequence to the owner of a plantation, than the price of several slaves; he can well *afford* to waste a few lives. This is no idle hypothesis—such calculations are gravely and openly made by planters. Hence, it is the slave's prayer that sugars may be cheap. When the negro is old, or feeble from incurable disease, is it his master's *interest* to feed him well, and clothe him comfortably? Certainly not: it then becomes desirable to get rid of the human brute as soon as convenient. It is a common remark, that it is not quite safe, in most cases, for even parents to be entirely dependent on the generosity of their children; and if human nature be such, what has the slave to expect, when he becomes a mere bill of expense?

It is a common retort to say that New Englanders, who go to the South, soon learn to patronize the system they have considered so abominable, and often become proverbial for their severity. I have not the least doubt of the fact; for slavery contaminates all that comes within its influence. It would be very absurd to imagine that the inhabitants of one State are worse than the inhabitants of another, unless some peculiar circumstances, of universal influence, tend to make them so. Human nature is everywhere the same; but developed differently, by different incitements and temptations. It is the business of wise legislation to discover what influences are most productive of good, and the least conducive to evil. If we were educated at the South, we should no doubt vindicate slavery, and inherit as a birthright all the evils it engrafts upon the character. If they lived on our rocky soil, and under our inclement skies, their shrewdness would sometimes border upon knavery, and their frugality sometimes degenerate into parsimony. We both have our virtues, and our faults, induced by the influences under which we live, and, of course, totally different in their character. *Our* defects are bad enough; but they cannot, like slavery, affect the destiny and rights of millions.

All this mutual recrimination about horse-jockeys, gamblers, tin-pedlers, and venders of wooden nutmegs, is quite unworthy of a great nation. Instead of calmly examining this important subject on the plain grounds of justice and humanity, we allow it to degenerate into a mere question of *sectional* pride and vanity. [Pardon the Americanism, would we had less *use* for the word!] It is the *system,* not the *men,* on which we ought to bestow the full measure of abhorrence. If we were willing to forget ourselves, and could, like true republicans, prefer the common good to all other considerations, there would not be a slave in the United States, at the end of half a century.

The arguments in support of slavery are all hollow and deceptive, though frequently very specious. No one thinks of finding a foundation for the system in the principles of truth and justice; and the unavoidable result is, that even in *policy* it is unsound. The monstrous fabric rests on the mere *appearance* of present expediency; while, in fact, all its tendencies, individual and national; present and remote, are highly injurious to the true interests of the country. The slave owner will not believe this. The stronger the evidence against his favorite theories, the more strenuously he defends them. It has been wisely said, "Honesty *is* the best policy; but policy without honesty never finds that out."

I hope none will be so literal as to suppose I intend to say that no planter can be honest, in the common acceptation of that term. I simply mean that all who ground their arguments in policy, and not in duty and plain truth, are really blind to the highest and best interests of man.

Among other apologies for slavery, it has been asserted that the Bible does not forbid it. Neither does it forbid the counterfeiting of a bank-bill. It is the *spirit* of the Holy Word, not its particular *expressions,* which must be a rule for our conduct. How can slavery be reconciled with the maxim, "Do unto others, as ye would that others should do unto you"? Does not the command, "Thou shalt not *steal,*" prohibit *kidnapping?* And how does whipping men to death agree with the injunction, "Thou shalt do no *murder"?* Are we not told "to loose the bands of wickedness, to undo the heavy burdens, to let the oppressed go free, and to break every yoke"? It was a Jewish law that he who stole a man, or sold him, or he in whose hands the stolen man was found, should suffer death; and he in whose house a fugitive slave sought an asylum was forbidden to give him up to his master. Modern slavery is so unlike Hebrew servitude, and its regulations are so diametrically opposed to the rules of the Gospel, which came to bring deliverance to the captive, that it is idle to dwell upon this point. The advocates of this system seek for arguments in the history of every age and nation; but the fact is, negro slavery is totally different from any other form of bondage that ever existed; and if it were not so, are we to copy the evils of bad governments and benighted ages?

The difficulty of subduing slavery, on account of the great number of interests which become united in it, and the prodigious strength of the selfish passions enlisted in its support, is by no means its least alarming feature. This Hydra has ten thousand heads, every one of which will bite or growl, when the broad daylight of truth lays open the secrets of its hideous den.

I shall perhaps be asked why I have said so much about the slave *trade,* since it was long ago abolished in this country? There are several good reasons for it. In the first place, it is a part of the system; for if there were no slaves, there could be no slave trade; and while there are slaves, the slave trade *will* continue. In the next place, the trade is still briskly carried on in Africa, and slaves are smuggled into these States through the Spanish colonies. In the third place, a very extensive internal slave trade is carried on in this country. The breeding of negro cattle for the foreign markets, (of Louisiana, Georgia, Alabama, Arkansas, and Missouri,) is a very lucrative branch of business. Whole coffles of them, chained and manacled, are driven through our Capital on their way to auction. Foreigners, particularly those who come here with enthusiastic ideas of American freedom, are amazed and disgusted at the sight.* A troop of slaves once passed through Washington on the fourth of July, while drums were beating, and standards flying. One of the captive negroes raised his hand, loaded with irons, and waving it toward the starry flag, sung with a smile of bitter irony, "Hail Columbia! *happy* land!"

*See the second volume of Stuart's "Three Years in North America." Instead of being angry at such truths, it would be wise to profit by them.

In the summer of 1822, a coffle of slaves, driven through Kentucky, was met by the Rev. James H. Dickey, just before it entered Paris. He describes it thus: "About forty black men were chained together; each of them was handcuffed, and they were arranged rank and file. A chain, perhaps forty feet long, was stretched between the two ranks, to which short chains were joined, connected with the hand-cuffs. Behind them were about thirty women, tied hand to hand. Every countenance wore a solemn sadness; and the dismal silence of despair was only broken by the sound of two violins. Yes—as if to add insult to injury, the foremost couple were furnished with a violin apiece; the second couple were ornamented with cockades; while near the centre our national standard was carried by hands literally in chains. I may have mistaken some of the punctilios of the arrangement, for my very soul was sick. My landlady was sister to the man who owned the drove; and from her I learned that he had, a few days previous, bought a negro woman, who refused to go with him. A blow on the side of her head with the butt of his whip, soon brought her to the ground; he then tied her, and carried her off. Besides those I saw, about thirty negroes, destined for the New Orleans market, were shut up in the Paris jail, for safe keeping."

But Washington is the great emporium of the internal slave trade! The United States jail is a perfect storehouse for slave merchants; and some of the taverns may be seen so crowded with negro captives that they have scarcely room to stretch themselves on the floor to sleep. Judge Morrel, in his charge to the Grand Jury at Washington, in 1816, earnestly called their attention to this subject. He said, "the frequency with which the streets of the city had been crowded with manacled captives, sometimes even on the Sabbath, could not fail to shock the feelings of all humane persons; that it was repugnant to the spirit of our political institutions, and the rights of man; and he believed it was calculated to impair the public morals, by familiarizing scenes of cruelty to the minds of youth."

A free man of color is in constant danger of being seized and carried off by these slave dealers. Mr Cooper, a Representative in Congress from Delaware, told Dr Torrey of Philadelphia, that he was often afraid to send his servants out in the evening, lest they should be encountered by kidnappers. Wherever these notorious slave jockeys appear in our Southern States, the free people of color hide themselves, as they are obliged to do on the coast of Africa.

The following is the testimony of Doctor Torrey, of Philadelphia, published in 1817:

"To enumerate all the horrid and aggravating instances of man-stealing, which are known to have occurred in the state of Delaware, within the recollection of many of the citizens of that State, would require a volume. In many cases, whole families of free colored people have been attacked in the night, beaten *nearly* to death with clubs, gagged and bound, and dragged into distant and hopeless captivity, leaving no traces behind, except the blood from their wounds.

"During the last winter, the house of a free black family was broken open, and its defenceless inhabitants treated in the manner just mentioned, except, that the mother escaped from their merciless grasp, while on their way to the state of Maryland. The plunderers, of whom there were nearly half a dozen, conveyed their prey upon horses; and the woman being placed on one of the horses, behind, improved an opportunity, as they were passing a house, and sprang off. Not daring to pursue her, they proceeded on, leaving her youngest child a little farther along, by the side of the road, in expectation, it is supposed, that its cries would attract the mother; but she prudently waited until morning, and recovered it again in safety.

"I consider myself more fully warranted in particularizing this fact, from the circumstances of having been at Newcastle, at the time that the woman was brought with her child, before the grand jury, for examination; and of having seen several of the persons against whom bills of indictment were found, on the charge of being engaged in the perpetration of the outrage; and also that one or two of them were the same who were accused of assisting in seizing and carrying off another woman and child whom I discovered at Washington. A monster in human shape, was detected in the city of Philadelphia, pursuing the occupation of courting and marrying mulatto women, and selling them as slaves. In his last attempt of this kind, the fact having come to the knowledge of the African population of this city, a mob was immediately collected, and he was only saved from being torn in atoms, by being deposited in the city prison. They have lately invented a method of attaining their object, through the instrumentality of the laws:—Having selected a suitable free colored person, to make a *pitch* upon, the kidnapper employs a confederate, to ascertain the distinguishing marks of his body; he then claims and obtains him as a slave, before a magistrate, by describing those marks, and proving the truth of his assertions, by his well-instructed accomplice.

"From the best information that I have had opportunities to collect, in travelling by various routes through the states of Delaware and Maryland, I am fully convinced that there are, at this time, within the jurisdiction of the United States, several thousands of legally free people of color, toiling under the yoke of involuntary servitude, and transmitting the same fate to their posterity! If the probability of this fact could be authenticated to the recognition of the Congress of the United States, it is presumed that its members, as agents of the constitution, and guardians of the public liberty, would, without hesitation, devise means for the restoration of those unhappy victims of violence and avarice, to their freedom and constitutional personal rights. The work, both from its nature and magnitude, is impracticable to individuals, or benevolent societies; besides, it is perfectly a national business, and claims national interference, equally with the captivity of our sailors in Algiers."

It may indeed be said, in palliation of the internal slave trade, that the horrors of the *middle passage* are avoided. But still the amount of misery is very great. Husbands and wives, parents and children, are rudely torn from each other;—there can be no doubt of this fact: advertisements are very common, in which a mother and her children are offered either in a lot, or separately, as may suit the purchaser. In one of these advertisements, I observed it stated that the youngest child was about a year old.*

The captives are driven by the whip, through toilsome journeys, under a burning sun; their limbs fettered; with nothing before them but the prospect of toil more severe than that to which they have been accustomed.†

The disgrace of such scenes in the capital of our republic cannot be otherwise than painful to every patriotic mind; while they furnish materials for the most pungent satire to other nations. A United States senator declared that the sight of a drove of slaves was so insupportable that he always avoided it when he could; and an intelligent Scotchman said, when he first entered Chesapeake Bay, and cast his eye along our coast, the sight of the slaves brought his heart into his throat. How can we help feeling a sense of shame, when we read Moore's contemptuous couplet,

---

*In Niles's Register, vol. xxxv, page 4, I find the following: "Dealing in slaves has become a large business. Establishments are made at several places in Maryland and Virginia, at which they are sold like cattle. These places are strongly built, and well supplied with thumbscrews, gags, cow-skins, and other whips, oftentimes bloody. But the laws permit the traffic, and it is suffered."

†In the sugar-growing States the condition of the negro is much more pitiable than where cotton is the staple commodity.

"The fustian flag that proudly waves,
    In splendid mockery, o'er a land of slaves"?

The lines would be harmless enough, if they were false; the sting lies in their truth.

Finally, I have described some of the horrors of the slave trade, because when our constitution was formed, the government pledged itself not to abolish this traffic until 1808. We began our career of freedom by granting a twenty years' lease of iniquity—twenty years of allowed invasion of other men's rights—twenty years of bloodshed, violence, and fraud! And this will be told in our annals—this will be heard of to the end of time!*

[While the slave-trade was allowed, the South could use it to advance their views in various ways. In their representation to Congress, five slaves counted the same as three freemen; of course, every fresh cargo was not only an increase of property, but an increase of *political power*. Ample time was allowed to lay in a stock of slaves to supply the new slave states and territories that might grow up; and when this was effected, the prohibition of foreign commerce in human flesh, operated as a complete *tariff*, to protect the domestic supply.]†

Every man who buys a slave promotes this traffic, by raising the value of the article; every man who owns a slave, indirectly countenances it; every man who allows that slavery is a lamentable *necessity*, contributes his share to support it; and he who, votes for admitting a slave-holding State into the Union, fearfully augments the amount of this crime.

*It ought to be remembered to the honor of Denmark that she abolished the slave trade as early as 1803. [Note omitted from 1836 edition.—Ed.]
   †Bracketed passage added to 1836 edition.—Ed.

CHAPTER II.

COMPARATIVE VIEW OF SLAVERY, IN DIFFERENT AGES AND NATIONS.

E'en from my tongue some heart-felt truths may fall;
And outraged Nature claims the care of all.
These wrongs in *any* place would force a tear;
But call for stronger, deeper feeling *here*.

O, sons of freedom ! equalize your laws—
Be all consistent—plead the negro's cause—
Then all the nations in your code may see,
That, black or white, Americans are free.

BETWEEN ancient and modern slavery there is this remarkable distinction—the former originated in motives of humanity; the latter is dictated solely by avarice. The ancients made slaves of captives taken in war, as an amelioration of the original custom of indiscriminate slaughter; the moderns attack defenceless people, without any provocation, and steal them, for the express purpose of making them slaves.

Modern slavery, indeed, in all its particulars, is more odious than the ancient; and it is worthy of remark that the condition of slaves has always been worse just in proportion to the freedom enjoyed by their masters. In Greece, none were so proud of liberty as the Spartans; and they were a proverb among the neighboring States for their severity to slaves. The slave code of the Roman republic was rigid and tyrannical in the extreme; and cruelties became so common and excessive, that the emperors, in the latter days of Roman power, were obliged to enact laws to restrain them. In the modern world, England and America are the most conspicuous for enlightened views of freedom, and bold vindication of the equal rights of man; yet in these two countries slave laws have been framed as bad as they were in Pagan, iron-hearted Rome; and the customs are in some respects more op-pressive;—*modern* slavery unquestionably wears its very worst aspect in the Colonies of England and the United States of North America. I hardly know how to decide their respective claims. My countrymen are fond of preëminence, and I am afraid they deserve it here—especially if we throw into the scale their loud boasts of superiority over all the rest of the world in civil and religious freedom. The slave codes of the United States and of the British West Indies were orig-inally almost precisely the same; but *their* laws have been growing milder and milder, while *ours* have increased in severity. The British have the advantage of us in this respect—they long ago dared to describe the monster as it is; and they are now grappling with it, with the overwhelming strength of a great nation's concentrated ener-gies.—The Dutch, those sturdy old friends of liberty, and the French, who have been stark mad for freedom, rank next for the severity of their slave laws and customs. The Spanish and Portuguese are milder than either.

I will give a brief view of some of our own laws on this subject; for the correctness of which, I refer the reader to Stroud's Sketch of the Slave Laws of the United States of America. In the first place, we will inquire upon what ground the negro slaves in this country are claimed as property. Most of them are the descendants of persons kidnapped on the coast of Africa, and brought here while we were British Colonies; and as the slave trade was openly sanctioned more than twenty years after our acknowledged independence, in 1783, and as the traffic is still carried on by smugglers, there are, no doubt, thousands of slaves, now living in the United States, who were actu-ally stolen from Africa.*

A provincial law of Maryland enacted that any white woman who married a negro slave should serve his master during her husband's lifetime, and that all their children should be slaves. This law was not repealed until the end of eighteen years, and it then continued in full force with regard to those who had contracted such marriages in the intermediate time; therefore the descendants of white women so situated may be slaves unto the present day. The doctrine of the common law is that the offspring shall follow the condition of the *father;* but slave law (with the above temporary exception) reverses the common law, and provides that children shall follow the condi-

---

*In the new slave States, there are a great many negroes, who can speak no other language than some of the numerous African dialects.

tion of the *mother*. Hence mulattoes and their descendants are held in perpetual bondage, though the *father* is a free white man. "Any person whose *maternal* ancestor, even in the *remotest* degree of distance, can be shown to have been a negro, Indian, mulatto, or a mestizo, *not* free at the time this law was introduced, although the *paternal* ancestor at each successive generation may have been a *white free* man, is declared to be the subject of perpetual slavery." Even the code of Jamaica, is on this head, more liberal than ours; by an express law, slavery ceases at the *fourth* degree of distance from a negro ancestor: and in the other British West Indies, the established custom is such, that quadroons or mestizoes (as they call the second and third degrees) are rarely seen in a state of slavery. Here, neither law nor public opinion favors the mulatto descendants of free white men. This furnishes a convenient game to the slave-holder—it enables him to fill his purse by means of his own vices;—the right to sell one half of his children provides a fortune for the remainder. Had the maxim of the common law been allowed,—i. e. that the offspring follows the condition of the *father*,—the mulattoes, almost without exception, would have been free, and thus the prodigious and alarming increase of our slave population might have been prevented. The great augmentation of the servile class in the Southern States compared with the West India colonies, has been thought to indicate a much milder form of slavery; but there are other causes, which tend to produce the result. There are much fewer white men in the British West Indies than in our slave States; hence the increase of the *mulatto* population is less rapid. Here, the descendants of a colored mother *never* become free; in the West Indies, they cease to be slaves in the *fourth generation*, at farthest; and their posterity increase the *free* colored class, instead of adding countless links to the chain of bondage.

The manufacture of sugar is extremely toilsome, and when driven hard, occasions a great waste of negro life; this circumstance, together with the tropical climate of the West Indies, furnish additional reasons for the disproportionate increase of slaves between those islands and our own country, where a comparatively small quantity of sugar is cultivated.

It may excite surprise, that *Indians* and their offspring are comprised in the doom of perpetual slavery; yet not only is *incidental* mention of them as slaves to be met with in the laws of most of the States of our confederacy, but in one, at least, *direct legislation* may be cited to sanction their enslavement. In Virginia, an act was passed, in

1679, declaring that "for *the better encouragement of soldiers,* whatever Indian prisoners were taken in a war, in which the colony was then engaged, should be *free purchase* to the soldiers taking them": and in 1682, it was decreed that "all servants brought into Virginia, by sea or land, not being *Christians,* whether negroes, Moors, mulattoes, or Indians, (except Turks and Moors in amity with Great Britain) and all Indians, which should thereafter be *sold by neighboring* Indians, or any other trafficking with us, as slaves, *should be slaves to all intents and purposes."* These laws ceased in 1691; but the descendants of all Indians sold in the intermediate time are now among slaves.

In order to show the true aspect of slavery among us, I will state distinct propositions, each supported by the evidence of actually existing laws.

1. Slavery is hereditary and perpetual, to the last moment of the slave's earthly existence, and to all his descendants, to the latest posterity.

2. The labor of the slave is compulsory and uncompensated; while the kind of labor, the amount of toil, and the time allowed for rest, are dictated solely by the master. No bargain is made, no wages given. A pure despotism governs the human brute; and even his covering and provender, both as to quantity and quality, depend entirely on the master's discretion.

3. The slave being considered a personal chattel, may be sold, or pledged, or leased, at the will of his master. He may be exchanged for marketable commodities, or taken in execution for the debts, or taxes, either of a living, or a deceased master. Sold at auction, "either individually, or in lots, to suit the purchaser," he may remain with his family, or be separated from them forever.

4. Slaves can make no contracts, and have no legal right to any property, real or personal. Their own honest earnings, and the legacies of friends belong, in point of law, to their masters.

5. Neither a slave, or free colored person can be a witness against any white or free man, in a court of justice, however atrocious may have been the crimes they have seen him commit: but they may give testimony against a fellow-slave, or free colored man, even in cases affecting life.

6. The slave may be punished at his master's discretion—without trial—without any means of legal redress,—whether his offence be real, or imaginary; and the master can transfer the same despotic power to any person, or persons, he may choose to appoint.

7. The slave is not allowed to resist any free man under any circumstances: his only safety consists in the fact that his owner may bring suit, and recover, the price of his body, in case his life is taken, or his limbs rendered unfit for labor.

8. Slaves cannot redeem themselves, or obtain a change of masters, though cruel treatment may have rendered such a change necessary for their personal safety.

9. The slave is entirely unprotected in his domestic relations.

10. The laws greatly obstruct the manumission of slaves, even where the master is willing to enfranchise them.

11. The operation of the laws tends to deprive slaves of religious instruction and consolation.

12. The whole power of the laws is exerted to keep slaves in a state of the lowest ignorance.

13. There is in this country a monstrous inequality of law and right. What is a trifling fault in the white man, is considered highly criminal in the slave; the same offences which cost a white man a few dollars only, are punished in the negro with death.

14. The laws operate most oppressively upon free people of color.

PROPOSITION 1.—*Slavery hereditary and perpetual.*

In Maryland the following act was passed in 1715, and is still in force: "All negroes and other slaves, already imported, or hereafter to be imported into this province, and all children now born, or hereafter to be born, of such negroes and slaves, shall be slaves during their natural lives." The law of South Carolina is, "All negroes, *Indians,* (free Indians in amity with this government, and negroes, mulattoes, and mestizoes, who are *now* free, excepted,) mulattoes or mestizoes, who now are, or shall hereafter be in this province, and all their issue born, or to be born, shall be and remain forever hereafter absolute slaves, and shall follow the condition of *the mother."* Laws similar exist in Virginia, Georgia, Mississippi, and Louisiana. In consequence of these laws, people so nearly white as not to be distinguished from Europeans, may be, and have been, legally claimed as slaves.

PROP. 2.—*Labor compulsory and uncompensated, &c.*

In most of the slave States the law is silent on this subject; but that it is the established custom is proved by laws restraining the excessive abuse of this power, in some of the States. Thus in one State there is a fine of ten shillings, in another of two dollars, for making slaves labor on Sunday, unless it be in works of absolute necessity, or the necessary occasions of the family. There is likewise a law which provides that "any master, who withholds proper sustenance, or clothing, from his slaves, or overworks them, so as to injure their health, shall upon *sufficient information* [here lies the rub] being laid before the grand jury, be by said jury presented; whereupon it shall be the duty of the attorney, or solicitor general, to prosecute said owners, who, on conviction shall be sentenced to pay a fine, or be imprisoned, or both, at the discretion of the court."

The negro act of South Carolina contains the following language: "Whereas many owners of slaves, and *others,* who have the care, management, and overseeing of slaves, *do confine them so closely to hard labor, that they have not sufficient time for natural rest;* be it therefore enacted, that if any owner of slaves, or others having the care, &c., shall put such slaves to labor more than *fifteen* hours in twentyfour, from the twentyfifth of March to the twentyfifth of September; or more than *fourteen* hours in twentyfour hours from the twentyfifth of September to the twentyfifth of March, any such person shall forfeit a sum of money not exceeding twenty pounds, nor under five pounds, current money, for every time, he, she, or they, shall offend therein, at the discretion of the justice before whom complaint shall be made."

In Louisiana it is enacted, that "the slaves shall be allowed half an hour for breakfast, during the whole year; from the first of May to the first of November, they shall be allowed two hours for dinner; and from the first of November to the first of May, one hour and a half for dinner: provided, however, that the owners, who will themselves take the trouble of having the meals of their slaves prepared, be, and they are hereby authorized to abridge, by half an hour a day, the time fixed for their rest."

All these laws, *apparently* for the protection of the slave, are rendered perfectly null and void, by the fact, that the testimony of a negro or mulatto is *never* taken against a white man. If a slave be found toiling in the field on the Sabbath, who can *prove* that his master commanded him to do it?

The law of Louisiana stipulates that a slave shall have *one* linen shirt,* and a pair of pantaloons for the summer, and *one* linen shirt and a woollen great coat and pantaloons for the winter; and for food, one pint of salt, and a barrel of Indian corn, rice, or beans, every month. In North Carolina, the law decides that a quart of corn per

---

*This shirt is usually made of a coarse kind of bagging.

day is sufficient. But, if the slave does not receive this poor allowance, who can *prove* the fact. The withholding of proper sustenance is absolutely incapable of proof, unless the evidence of the sufferer himself be allowed; and the law, as if determined to obstruct the administration of justice, permits the master to exculpate himself by an oath that the charges against him are false. Clothing may, indeed, be ascertained by *inspection;* but who is likely to involve himself in quarrels with a white master because a poor negro receives a few rags less than the law provides? I apprehend that a person notorious for such gratuitous acts of kindness, would have little peace or safety, in any slave-holding country.

If a negro be compelled to toil night and day, (as it is said they sometimes are,* at the season of sugar-making) who is to *prove* that he works more than his fourteen or fifteen hours? No slave can be a witness for himself, or for his fellow-slaves; and should a white man happen to know the fact, there are ninetynine chances out of a hundred, that he will deem it prudent to be silent. And here I would remark that even in the island of Jamaica, where the laws have given a most shocking license to cruelty,—even in Jamaica, the slave is compelled to work but *ten* hours in the day, beside having many holidays allowed him. In Maryland, Virginia, Georgia, Pennsylvania, and New Jersey, the *convicts* condemned to hard labor in the penitentiaries, are required by law to toil only from *eight* to *ten* hours a day, according to the season of the year; yet the law providing that the innocent slave should labor but *fourteen* or *fifteen* hours a day, professes to have been made as a merciful amelioration of his lot!—In Rome, the slaves had a yearly festival called the Saturnalia, during which they were released from toil, changed places with their masters, and indulged in unbounded merriment; at first it lasted but one day; but its duration afterwards extended to two, three, four, and five days in succession. We have no Saturnalia here—unless we choose thus to designate a coffle of slaves, on the fourth of July, rattling their chains to the sound of a violin, and carrying the banner of freedom in hands loaded with irons.

In Georgia, "The inferior courts of the several counties on *receiving information on oath* of any *infirm* slave or slaves, being in a suffering condition, from the neglect of the owner or owners, can make *particular inquiries* into the situation of such slaves, and render

*See Western Review, No. 2, on the Agriculture of Louisiana.

such relief as they think proper. And the said courts may sue for and recover from the owner of such slaves the amount appropriated for their relief." The information must, in the first place, be given by a *white man* upon oath; and of whom must the "particular inquiries" be made? Not of the slave, nor of his companions,—for their evidence goes for nothing; and would a master, capable of starving an aged slave, be likely to confess the whole truth about it? The judges of the inferior courts, if, from defect of evidence, or any other cause, they are unable to *prove* that relief was absolutely needed, must pay all the expenses from their own private purses. Are there many, think you, so desperately enamored of justice, as to take all this trouble, and incur all this risk, for a starving slave?

PROP. 3.—*Slaves considered personal chattels, liable to be sold, pledged, &c.*

The advertisements in the Southern papers furnish a continued proof of this; it is, therefore, unnecessary to go into the details of evidence.* The power to separate mothers and children, husbands and wives, is exercised only in the British West Indies, and the *republic* of the United States!

In Louisiana there is indeed a humane provision in this respect: "If at a public sale of slaves, there happen to be some who are disabled through old age or otherwise, and who have children, such slaves shall not be sold but with such of his or of her children, whom he or she may think proper to go with." But though parents cannot be sold apart from their children, without their consent, yet the master may keep the parents and sell the *children,* if he chooses; in which case the separation is of course equally painful.—"By the *Code Noir,* of Louis the Fourteenth, husbands and wives, parents and children are not allowed to be sold separately. If sales contrary to this regulation are made by process of law, under *seizure for debts,* such sales are declared void; but if such sales are made *voluntarily* on the part of the owner, a wiser remedy is given—the wife, or husband, children, or parent retained by the seller may be claimed by the purchaser, without any additional price; and thus the separated family may be re-united again. The most solemn agreement between the parties contrary to

---

*A white man engaged in a disturbance was accompanied by three or four slaves; his counsel contended that there were not *persons* enough in the affair to constitute a riot, because the slaves were mere *chattels* in the eye of the law. It was however decided that when liable to the *punishment* of the law, they were persons.

this rule has been adjudged void." In the Spanish, Portuguese and French colonies, plantation slaves are considered *real estate,* attached to the soil they cultivate, and of course not liable to be torn from their homes whenever the master chooses to sell them; neither can they be seized or sold by their master's creditors.

The following quotation shows how the citizens of this country bear comparison with men *called* savages. A recent traveller in East Florida says: "Another trait in the character of the Seminole Indians, is their great indulgence to their slaves. The greatest pressure of hunger or thirst never occasions them to impose onerous labors on the negroes, or to dispose of them, though tempted by high offers, if the latter are unwilling to be sold."

PROP. 4.—*Slaves can have no legal claim to any property.*

The civil code of Louisiana declares: "*All that a slave possesses belongs to his master*—he possesses nothing of his own, except his peculium, that is to say, the sum of money or movable estate, which *his master chooses he should possess.*"—"Slaves are incapable of inheriting or transmitting property."—"Slaves cannot dispose of, or receive, by donation, unless they have been enfranchised conformably to law, or are expressly enfranchised by the act, by which the donation is made to them."

In South Carolina "it is not lawful for any slave to buy, sell, trade, &c. without a license from his owner; nor shall any slave be allowed to keep any boat or canoe, for his own benefit, or raise any horses, cattle, sheep or hogs, under pain of forfeiting all the goods, boats, canoes, horses, &c. &c., and it shall be lawful for *any person* to seize and take away from any slave all such goods, boats, &c. and to deliver the same into the hands of the nearest justice of the peace; and if the said justice be satisfied that such seizure has been made according to law, he shall order the goods to be sold at public outcry; one half of the moneys arising from the sale to go to the State, and the other half to him or them that sue for the same." In North Carolina there is a similar law; but half the proceeds of the sale goes to the county poor, and half to the informer.

In Georgia, a fine of thirty dollars a week is imposed upon any master who allows his slave to hire himself out for his own benefit. In Virginia, if a master permit his slave to hire himself out, he is subject to a fine, from ten to twenty dollars; and it is lawful for any person, and the *duty* of the Sheriff, to apprehend the slave. In Maryland, the master, by a similar offence, except during twenty days at harvest time, incurs a penalty of twenty dollars per month.

In Mississippi, if a master allow his slave to cultivate cotton for his own use, he incurs a fine of fifty dollars; and if he license his slave to trade on his own account, he forfeits fifty dollars for each and every offence. Any person trading with a slave forfeits four times the value of the article purchased; and if unable to pay, he receives thirtynine lashes, and pays the cost.

Among the Romans, the Grecians, and the ancient Germans, slaves were permitted to acquire and enjoy property of considerable value, as their own. This property was called the slave's *peculium;* and "the many anxious provisions of the Imperial Code on the subject plainly show the general extent and importance of such acquisitions."—"The Roman slave was also empowered by law to enter into commercial and other contracts, by which the master was bound, to the extent of the value of the slave's *peculium.*"—"The Grecian slaves had also their *peculium;* and were rich enough to make periodical presents to their masters, as well as often to purchase their freedom."

"The Helots of Sparta were so far from being destitute of property, or of legal powers necessary to its acquisition, that they were farmers of the lands of their masters, at low fixed rents, which the proprietor could not raise without dishonor."

"In our own day, the Polish slaves, prior to any recent alleviations of their lot, were not only allowed to hold property, but endowed with it by their lords."—"In the Spanish and Portuguese colonies, the money and effects, which a slave acquires, by his labor at times set apart for his own use, or by any other honest means, are legally his own, and cannot be seized by the master."—"In Africa, slaves may acquire extensive property, which their sable masters cannot take away. In New Calabar, there is a man named Amachree, who has more influence and wealth than all the rest of the community, though he himself is a purchased slave, brought from the Braspan country; he has offered the price of a hundred slaves for his freedom; but according to the laws of the country he cannot obtain it, though his master, who is a poor and obscure individual, would gladly let him have it."

Among the Jews, a servant, or slave, often filled the highest offices of honor and profit, connected with the family. Indeed slavery among this ancient people was in its mildest, patriarchal form; and the same character is now stamped upon the *domestic* slavery of Africa. St Paul says, "The heir, as long as he is a child, differeth nothing from a servant, [the Hebrew word translated *servant* means *slave*] though he be lord of all." Gal. iv. 1. Again: "A wise servant shall have rule over a son that causeth shame, and shall have part of the inheritance among the brethren." Proverbs, xvii. 2. The wealthy patriarch-Abraham, before the birth of Isaac, designed to make his head servant, Eleazer of Damascus, his heir.

PROP. 5.—*No colored man can be evidence against a white man, &c.*

This is an almost universal rule of slave law. The advocates of slavery seem to regard it as a necessary consequence of the system, which neither admits of concealment, nor needs it. "In one or two of our states this rule is founded upon *usage;* in others it is sanctioned by *express legislation.*"

So long as this rule is acted upon, it is very plain, that all regulations made for the protection of the slave are perfectly useless;— however grievous his wrongs, they *cannot be proved.* The master is merely obliged to take the precaution not to starve, or mangle, or murder his negroes, *in the presence of a white man.* No matter if five hundred colored people be present, they cannot testify to the fact. Blackstone remarks, that "rights would be declared vain, and in vain directed to be observed, if there were no method of recovering and asserting those rights, when wrongfully withheld, or invaded."

Stephens says: "It seems to result from the brief and general accounts which we have of the law of the Spanish and Portuguese settlements, though I find it nowhere expressly noticed, that slaves there are not, in all cases at least, incompetent witnesses. But even in the French Windward Islands, the evidence of negro slaves was admitted against all free persons, the master only excepted; and that in criminal as well as in civil cases, where the testimony of white people could not be found to establish the facts in dispute. The *Code Noir* merely allowed a slave's testimony to be heard by the judge, as a suggestion which might throw light on other evidence, without amounting of itself to any degree of legal proof. But the Sovereign Council of Martinique, humbly represented to his majesty that great inconveniences might result from the execution of this law, by the *impunity* of many crimes, which *could not be proved otherwise than by the testimony of slaves;* and they prayed that such evidence might be received in all cases in which there should not be sufficient proof by free witnesses. In consequence of this, the article in question was varied so far as to admit the testimony of slaves, when white witnesses were wanting, except against their masters."

PROP. 6.— *The master has absolute power to punish a slave, &c.*

Stroud says, "There was a time in many, if not in all the slave hold-ing districts of our country, when the murder of a slave was followed by a pecuniary fine only. In one State, the change of the law in this re-spect has been very recent. At the present date (1827) I am happy to say the wilful, malicious, deliberate murder of a slave, by whomsoever perpetrated, is *declared* to be punishable with death in every State. The evil is not that the laws *sanction* crime, but that they do not *punish* it. And this arises chiefly, if not solely, from the exclusion of the testi-mony, on the trial of a white person, of all those who are *not* white."

"The conflicting influences of humanity and prejudice are strangely contrasted in the law of North Carolina on this subject. An act passed in 1798, runs thus: 'Whereas by another act of assembly, passed in the year 1774, the killing of a slave, however wanton, cruel, and deliberate, is only punishable in the first instance by imprison-ment, and paying the value thereof to the owner, which distinction of criminality between the murder of a white person and one *who is equally a human creature, but merely of a different complexion,* is dis-graceful to humanity, and degrading in the highest degree to the laws and principles of a free Christian, and enlightened country, be it enacted, &c. that if any person shall hereafter be guilty of wilfully and maliciously killing a slave, such offenders shall, upon the first conviction thereof, be adjudged guilty of murder, and shall suffer the same punishment as if he had killed a free man; *Provided always, this act shall not extend to the person killing a slave outlawed by virtue of any act of assembly of this state, or to any slave in the act of resistance** to his lawful owner or master, or to any slave* DYING *under* MODERATE CORRECTION.' "

In the laws of Tennessee and Georgia, there is a similar proviso. Where could such a monstrous anomaly be found, save in a code of slave laws? *Die* of *moderate* punishment!! Truly, this *is* an unveiling of consciences!

"To set the matter in its proper light, it may be added that a proclamation of *outlawry*† against a slave is authorized, whenever he

---

*"It has been judicially determined that it is *justifiable* to kill a slave, resisting, or *offering to resist* his master, by force."—*Stroud.*

†"The outlawry of a slave is not, I believe, an unusual occurrence. Very recently, a particular account was given of the killing of a black man, *not charged with any offence* by a person in pursuit of an *outlawed* slave; owing as it was stated, to the person killed not *answering* a call made by his pursuers. Whether the call was *heard* or not, of course could not be ascertained, nor did it appear to have excited any inquiry."—*Stroud.*

runs away from his master, conceals himself in some obscure retreat, and to sustain life, kills a *hog,* or some animal of the cattle kind!

"A pecuniary mulct was the only restraint upon the wilful murder of a slave, from the year 1740 to 1821, a period of more than eighty years. I find in the case of *The State vs. M'Gee, 1 Bay's Reports,* 164. it is said incidentally by Messrs Pinckney and Ford, counsel for the State, that the *frequency* of the offence was owing to the nature of the punishment. This was said in the public court-house by men of great respectability; nevertheless, thirty years elapsed before a change of the law was effected. So far as I have been able to learn, the following section has disgraced the statute-book of South Carolina from the year 1740 to the present hour: 'In case any person shall wilfully cut out the tongue, put out the eye, *cruelly* scald, burn, or deprive any slave of any limb, or member, or shall inflict any other cruel punishment,—[*otherwise than by whipping, or beating, with a horsewhip, cowskin, switch, or small stick, or by putting irons on, or confining, or imprisoning such slave,*]—every such person shall for every such offence, forfeit the sum of one hundred pounds, current money.' Here is direct legislation to *sanction* beating without limit, with horsewhip or cowskin,—the application of irons to the human body,—and perpetual incarceration in a dungeon, according to the will of the master; and the mutilation of limbs is paid by a trifling penalty!

"The revised code of Louisiana declares: 'The slave is entirely subject to the will of the master, who may correct and chastise him, though not with *unusual* rigor, nor so as to maim or mutilate him, or to expose him to the danger of loss of life, or to cause his death.'" Who shall decide what punishment is *unusual?*

In Missouri, if a slave refuses to obey his or her master, mistress, overseer, or employer, in any lawful commands, such slaves may be committed to the county jail, there to remain as long as his owner pleases.

In some of the States there are indeed restraining laws; but they are completely ineffectual from the difficulty of obtaining the evidence of *white men.*

"The same despotic power can be exerted by the attorney, manager, driver, or any other person who is, for the time being, placed over the slave by order of the owner, or his delegates. The following is the language of the Louisiana code; and it represents the established customs of all the slave holding States: 'The condition of a slave being merely a passive one, his subordination to his master, and to all who *represent* him, is not susceptible of any modification, or restriction, [except in what can incite the slave to the commission of crime] in such manner, that he owes to his master, and to all his family a respect without bounds, and an absolute obedience; and he is consequently to execute all the orders, which he receives from his said master, or from them.' "

What chance of mercy the slave has from the generality of overseers, may be conjectured from the following testimony given by a distinguished Virginian: Mr Wirt, in his "Life of Patrick Henry," speaking of the different classes in Virginia, says: "Last and lowest, a *feculum* of beings called overseers—the *most abject, degraded, unprincipled* race—always cap in hand to the Dons who employed them, and furnishing materials for the exercise of their pride, insolence, and spirit of domination."

The Gentoo code, the most ancient in the world, allowed a wife, a son, a pupil, a younger brother, or a slave to be whipped with a lash, or bamboo twig, in such a manner as not to occasion any dangerous hurt; and whoever transgressed the rule, suffered the punishment of a thief. In this case, the slave and other members of the family were *equally* protected.

The Mosaic law was as follows: "If a man smite the eye of his servant, or the eye of his maid, that it perish, *he shall let him go free* for his eye's sake. And if he smite out his man servant's tooth, or his maid servant's tooth, *he shall let him go free* for his tooth's sake." Exodus, xxi. 26, 27.

PROP. 7.— *The slave never allowed to resist a white man.*

It is enacted in Georgia, "If any slave shall presume to strike *any* white man, such slave, upon trial and conviction before the justice, shall for the *first* offence, suffer such punishment as the said justice thinks fit, not extending to life or limb; and for the second offence, *death.*"It is the same in South Carolina, excepting that death is there the punishment of the *third* offence.—However wanton and dangerous the attack upon the slave may be, he must submit; there is only one proviso—he may be excused for striking in defence of his *master, overseer,* &c. and of *their* property. In Maryland, a colored man, even if he be *free,* may have his ears cropped for striking a white man. In Kentucky, it is enacted that "if any negro, mulatto, or Indian, bond or *free,* shall at any time lift his or her hand, in opposition to *any* person not colored, they shall, the offence being proved before a justice of the peace, receive thirty lashes on his or her bare back, well laid on." There is a ridiculous gravity in the following section of a law in Louisiana: "Free people of color ought never to insult or strike white people, nor presume to conceive themselves equal to the whites; but on the contrary, they ought to yield to them *on every occasion,* and never speak or answer them but with respect, under the penalty of imprisonment, according to the nature of the offence."

Such laws are a positive *inducement* to violent and vicious white men to oppress and injure people of color. In this point of view, a negro becomes the slave of every white man in the community. The brutal drunkard, or the ferocious madman, can beat, rob, and mangle him with perfect impunity. Dr Torrey, in his "Portraiture of Domestic Slavery," relates an affecting anecdote, which happened near Washington. A free negro walking along the road, was set upon by two intoxicated ruffians on horseback, who, without any provocation, began to torture him for *amusement.* One of them tied him to the tail of his horse, and thus dragged him along, while the other followed, applying the lash. The poor fellow died by the road-side, in consequence of this treatment.

The *owner* may prosecute when a slave is rendered unfit for labor, by personal violence; and in the Reports of these cases many painful facts come to light which would otherwise have remained forever unknown. See Judicial Reports.

PROP. 8.— *Slaves cannot redeem themselves or change masters.*

Stroud says, "as to the right of *redemption,* this proposition holds good in all the slave-holding States; and is equally true as it respects the right to compel *a change of masters,* except in Louisiana. According to the new civil code of that State, the latter privilege may sometimes, perhaps, be obtained by the slave. But the master must first be *convicted* of cruelty—a task so formidable that it can hardly be ranked among possibilities; and secondly it is *optional* with the judge, whether or not, to make the decree in favor of the slave."

If a slave should *not* obtain a decree in his favor what has he to expect from a master exasperated against him, for making the attempt?

At Athens, so deservedly admired for the mildness of her slave laws, the door of freedom was opened widely. The abused slaves might fly to the Temple of Theseus, whence no one had a right to take them, except for the purpose of publicly investigating their

wrongs. If their complaints were well founded, they were either enfranchised, or delivered to more merciful hands.

In the Roman Empire, from the time of Adrian and the Antonines,
slaves were protected by the laws, and undue severity being proved,
they received freedom or a different master.

By the *Code Noir* of the French islands, a slave cruelly treated is
forfeited to the crown; and the court, which judges the offence, has
power to confer freedom on the sufferer. In the Spanish and Portuguese colonies, a slave on complaint of ill-usage obtains public
protection; he may be manumitted, or change his master.

PROP. 9.—*Slave unprotected in his domestic relations.*

In proof of this it is only necessary to repeat that the slave and his
wife, and his daughters, are considered as the *property* of their owners,
and compelled to yield implicit obedience—that he is allowed to give
no evidence—that he must not resist *any* white man, under *any*
circumstances, which do not interfere with his *master's* interest—and
finally, that public opinion ridicules the slave's claim to any exclusive
right in his own wife and children.

In Athens, the female slave could demand protection from the
magistrates; and if her complaints of insulting treatment were well
founded, she could be sold to another master, who, in his turn,
forfeited his claim by improper conduct.

PROP. 10.—*The laws obstruct emancipation.*

In nearly all slave-holding States, a slave emancipated by his master's will, may be seized and sold to satisfy *any debt.* In Louisiana,
fraud of creditors is by law considered as *proved,* if it can be made to
appear that the master, at the moment of executing the deed of
enfranchisement, had not sufficient property to pay all his debts; and
if after payment of debts, there be not personal estate enough to
satisfy the widow's claim to one third, his slaves, though declared to
be free by his last will, are nevertheless liable to be sold for the
widow's portion.—In South Carolina, Georgia, Alabama, and Mississippi, a valid emancipation can only be gained by authority of the
Legislature, expressly granted. A slave owner *cannot* manumit his
slaves without the formal consent of the Legislature. "In Georgia, any
attempt to free a slave in any other manner than the prescribed form,
is punished by a fine of two hundred dollars for each *offence;* and the
slave or slaves are still, to all intents and purposes, in a state of
slavery." A new act was passed in that State in 1818, by which any

person, who endeavors to enfranchise a slave by will, testament, contract, or stipulation, or who contrives indirectly to confer freedom by allowing his slaves to enjoy the profit of their labor and skill, incurs a penalty not exceeding *one thousand dollars;* and the slaves who have been the object of such benevolence, are ordered to be seized and sold at public outcry.

In North Carolina, "no slave is allowed to be set free, except for *meritorious services,* to be adjudged of and allowed by the county court, and license first had and obtained thereupon;" and any slave manumitted contrary to this regulation may be seized, put in jail, and sold to the highest bidder. In Mississippi *all* the above obstacles to emancipation are combined in one act.

In Kentucky, Missouri, Virginia, and Maryland, greater facilities are afforded to emancipation. An instrument in writing, signed by two witnesses, or acknowledged by the owner of the slave in open court, is sufficient; the court reserving the power to demand security for the maintenance of aged or infirm slaves. By the Virginia laws, an emancipated negro, more than twentyone years old, is liable to be again reduced to slavery, if he remain in the State more than twelve months after his manumission.

In Louisiana, a slave cannot be emancipated, unless he is thirty years old and has behaved well at least four years preceding his freedom; except a slave who has saved the life of his master, his master's wife, or one of his children. It is necessary to make known to the judge the intention of conferring freedom, who may authorize it, after it has been advertised at the door of the court house forty days, without exciting any opposition.

Stephens in his history of West India slavery, supposes that the colonial codes of England are the only ones expressly framed to obstruct emancipation. He is mistaken;—the American *republics* share that distinction with their mother country. There are plenty of better things in England to imitate.

According to the Mosaic law, a Hebrew could not retain his brother, whom he might buy as a servant, more than six years, against his consent, and in the seventh year he went out free for nothing. If he came by himself, he went out by himself; if he were married when he came, his wife went with him. *Exodus,* xxi. *Deut.* xv. *Jeremiah,* xxxiv. Besides this, Hebrew slaves were, without exception, restored to freedom by the *Jubilee.*—"Ye shall hallow the fiftieth year, and proclaim liberty throughout the land, and unto all the inhabitants thereof." *Leviticus,* xxv. 10.

At Athens, if the slave possessed property enough to buy his freedom, the law compelled the master to grant it, whenever the money was offered.

The severe laws of Rome discouraged manumission; but it was a very common thing for slaves to pay for freedom out of their *peculium;* and public opinion made it dishonorable to retain them in bondage under such circumstances. "According to Cicero, sober and industrious slaves, who became such by captivity in war, seldom remained in servitude above six years."

"In Turkey, the right of redemption is expressly regulated by the Koran. The master is commanded to give to all his slaves, that behave themselves faithfully, a writing, fixing beforehand the price at which they may be redeemed; and which he is bound to accept, when tendered by them, or on their behalf."

"In Brazil, a slave who can pay the value of his servitude, (the fair price of which may be settled by the magistrate,) has a right to demand his freedom. And the case frequently happens; for the slaves have one day in the week, and in some places two days, exclusively of Sundays and other festivals, which the industrious employ in providing a fund for their redemption."

"In the Spanish colonies, the law is still more liberal. The civil magistrates are empowered to decide upon the just price of a slave, and when the negro is able to offer this sum, his master is compelled to grant his freedom. He may even redeem himself progressively. For instance, by paying a sixth part of his appreciation, he may redeem for his own use one day in the week; by employing this industriously, he will soon be enabled to buy another day; by pursuing the same laudable course, the remainder of his time may be redeemed with continually accelerated progress, till he becomes entitled to entire manumission."

PROP. II.—*Operation of the laws interferes with religious privileges.*
No places of public worship are prepared for the negro; and churches are so scarce in the slave holding States, compared with the number of *white* inhabitants, that it is not to be supposed great numbers of them follow their masters to such places; and if they did, what could their rude, and merely sensual minds comprehend of a discourse addressed to educated men? In Georgia, there is a law which forbids any congregation or company of negroes to assemble themselves contrary to the act regulating patrols. Every justice of the peace may go in person, or send a constable, to disperse any assembly

or meeting of slaves, which *may* disturb the peace, endanger the safety, &c., and every slave taken at such meetings may, by order of the justice, *without trial,* receive on the bare back twentyfive stripes with whip, switch, or cowskin. In South Carolina, an act forbids the police officers to break into any place of religious meeting before nine o'clock, provided a *majority* of the assembly are *white persons;* but if the quorum of white people should happen to be wanting, every slave would be liable to twentyfive lashes of the cowskin.

These, and various similar regulations, are obviously made to prevent insurrections; but it is plain that they must materially interfere with the slave's opportunities for religious instruction. The fact is, there are *inconveniences* attending a general diffusion of Christianity in a slave holding State—light must follow its path, and that light would reveal the surrounding darkness,—slaves might begin to think whether slavery could be reconciled with religious precepts,—and then the system is quite too republican—it teaches that all men are children of the same Heavenly Father, who careth alike for all.

The West India planters boldly and openly declared, that slavery and Christianity could not exist together; in their minds the immediate inference was, that Christianity must be put down; and very consistently they began to fine and imprison Methodist missionaries, burn chapels,* &c.

In Rome, the introduction of "Christianity abolished slavery; the idea of exclusive property in our fellow men was too obviously at variance with its holy precepts; and its professors, in the sincerity of their hearts, made a formal surrender of such claims. In various ancient instruments of emancipation, the masters begin by declaring, that, 'for the love of God and Jesus Christ, for the easing of their consciences, and the safety of their souls,' they set their bondmen free."

"It is remarkable that the ancient inhabitants of Great Britain used to sell their countrymen, and even their own children, to the Irish. The port of Bristol, afterwards so famous for the African slave trade, was then equally distinguished as a market for the same commodity, though of a different color. But when Ireland, in the year 1172, was

---

*The slaves of any one owner may meet together for religious purposes, if authorized by their master, and private chaplains may be hired to preach to them. The domestic slaves, who are entirely employed in the family, no doubt fare much better in this respect, than the plantation slaves; but this, and all other negro privileges, depend entirely upon the slave's *luck* in the character of his master.

afflicted with public calamities, the clergy and people of that generous nation began to reproach themselves with the unchristian practice of holding their fellow men in slavery. Their English bondmen though fully paid for, were, by an unanimous resolution of the Armagh Assembly, set at liberty. *Their* repentance dictated present restitution to the injured. More than six hundred years afterward, when Mr Wilberforce made his first motion for the abolition of the slave trade, he was supported by every Irish member of the House of Commons." May God bless thee, warm hearted, generous old Ireland!

In the English and Dutch colonies, baptism was generally supposed to confer freedom on the slave; and for this reason, masters were reluctant to have them baptised. They got over this difficulty, however, and married self-interest to conscience, by making a law that "no slave should become free by being a Christian." This is a striking proof how closely Christianity and liberty are associated together.

A French planter of St Domingo, in a book which he published concerning that colony, admits that it is desirable to have negroes know enough of religion to make them friends to humanity, and grateful to their Creator; but he considers it very wrong to load their weak minds with a belief in supernatural dogmas, such as a belief in a future state. He says, "such knowledge is apt to render them intractable, averse to labor, and induces them to commit suicide on themselves and their children, *of which the colony, the state, and commerce have equal need.*"

Our slave holders, in general, seem desirous to have the slave just religious enough to know that insurrections and murder are contrary to the maxims of Christianity; but it is very difficult to have them learn just so much as this, without learning more. In Georgia, I have been told, that a very general prejudice prevails against white missionaries. To avoid this danger, old domestic slaves, who are better informed than the plantation slaves, are employed to hear sermons and repeat them to their brethren; and their repetitions are said to be strange samples of pulpit eloquence. One of these old negroes, as the story goes, told his hearers that the Bible said slaves ought to get their freedom; and if they could not do it in any other way, they must murder their masters. The slaves had never been allowed to learn to read, and of course they could not dispute that such a doctrine was actually in the Scriptures. Thus do unjust and absurd laws "return to plague the inventor."

PROP. 12.— *Whole power of the laws exerted to keep negroes in ignorance.*

South Carolina made the first law upon this subject. While yet a *province,* she laid a penalty of one hundred pounds upon any person who taught a slave to write, or allowed him to be taught to write.* In Virginia, any school for teaching reading and writing, either to slaves, or free people of color, is considered *an unlawful assembly,* and may accordingly be dispersed, and punishment administered upon each pupil not exceeding twenty lashes.

In South Carolina, the law is the same.

The city of Savannah, in Georgia, a few years ago, passed an ordinance, by which "any person that teaches a person of color, slave or free, to read or write, or causes such persons to be so taught, is subjected to a fine of thirty dollars for each offence; and every person of color who shall teach reading or writing, is subject to a fine of thirty dollars, or to be imprisoned ten days and whipped thirtynine lashes."

From these facts it is evident that legislative power prevents a master from giving liberty and instruction to his slave, even when such a course would be willingly pursued by a benevolent individual. The laws allow almost unlimited power to do *mischief;* but the power to do *good* is effectually restrained.

PROP. 13.— *There is a monstrous inequality of law and right.*

In a civilized country, one would expect that if any disproportion existed in the laws, it would be in favor of the ignorant and defenceless; but the reverse is lamentably the case here. *Obedience* to the laws is the price freemen pay for the *protection* of the laws;—but the same legislatures which absolutely sanction the negro's *wrongs,* and, to say the least, make very inadequate provisions for his *safety,* claim the right to *punish* him with inordinate severity.

"In Kentucky, white men are condemned to death for *four* crimes only; slaves meet a similar punishment for *eleven* crimes. In South Carolina, white persons suffer death for *twentyseven* crimes; slaves incur a similar fate for *thirtysix* crimes. In Georgia, whites are punished capitally for *three* crimes only; slaves for at *least nine.*

Stroud says there are *seventyone* crimes in the slave States, for which negroes are punished with *death,* and for each and every one of these

---

*Yet it has been said that these laws are entirely owing to the rash efforts of the abolitionists.

crimes the white man suffers nothing worse than imprisonment in the penitentiary.

"Trial by jury is utterly denied to the slave, *even in criminal accusations which may affect his life;* in South Carolina, Virginia, and Louisiana, instead of a jury, is substituted a tribunal composed of two justices of the peace and from three to five *free*-holders, (i. e. *slave*-holders.) In Virginia it is composed of five justices merely. What chance has an ignorant slave before a tribunal chosen by his accuser, suddenly convoked, and consisting of but five persons?"

If a slave is found out of the limits of the town in which he lives, or beyond the plantation on which he is usually employed, without a written permission from his master, or the company of some white person, *any body* may inflict twenty lashes upon him; and if the slave resist such punishment, he may be lawfully *killed.*

If a slave visit another plantation without leave in writing from his master, the owner of the plantation may give him ten lashes.

More than seven slaves walking or standing together in the road, without a white man, may receive twenty lashes each from any person.

Any slave, or Indian, who takes away, or lets loose a boat, from any place where it is fastened, receives thirty-nine lashes for the first offence; and, according to some laws, one ear is cut off for the second offence.

For carrying gun, powder, shot, a club, or any weapon whatsoever, offensive or defensive, thirtynine lashes by order of a justice; and in some States, twenty lashes from the nearest constable, *without* a conviction by the justice.

For selling any article, without a specific ticket from his master, ten lashes by the captain of the patrollers,* or thirtynine by order of a magistrate. The same punishment for being at any assembly deemed *unlawful.*

For travelling by himself from his master's land to any other place, unless by the most accustomed road, forty lashes; the same for travelling in the night without a pass; the same for being found in another negro's kitchen, or quarters; and every negro found *in company* with such vagrant, receives twenty lashes.

For hunting with dogs, even in the woods of his master, thirty lashes.

*The patrols are very generally low and dissipated characters, and the cruelties which negroes suffer from them, while in a state of intoxication, are sometimes shocking. The law endows these men with very great power.

For running away and lurking in swamps, a negro may be lawfully *killed* by any person. If a slave *happen* to die of *moderate* correction, it is likewise justifiable homicide.

For endeavoring to entice another slave to run away, if provisions are prepared, the slave is punished with DEATH; and any negro aiding or abetting suffers DEATH.

Thirtynine stripes for harboring a runaway slave one hour.

For disobeying orders, imprisonment, as long as the master chooses.

For riding on horseback, without written permission, or for keeping a dog, twentyfive lashes.

For rambling, riding, or going abroad in the night, or riding horses in the day without leave, a slave may be whipped, cropped, or branded on the cheek with the letter R, or otherwise punished, not extending to life, or *so as to unfit him for labor.*

For beating the Patuxent river, to catch fish, ten lashes; for placing a seine across Transquakin, and Chickwiccimo creeks, thirtynine lashes by order of a justice.

For advising the murder of a person, one hundred lashes may be given.

A runaway slave may be put into jail, and the jailer must forthwith send a letter by mail, to the man whom the negro says is his owner. If an answer does not arrive at the proper time, the jailer must inflict twentyfive lashes, well laid on, and interrogate anew. If the slave's second statement be not corroborated by the letter from the owner, twentyfive lashes are again administered.—The act very coolly concludes thus: "and so on, for the space of *six months,* it shall be the duty of the jailer to interrogate and whip as aforesaid."

The letter may miscarry—the owner may reside at a great distance from the Post-Office, and thus long delays may occur—the ignorant slave may not know his master's christian name—the jailer may not spell it aright; but no matter—"it is the jailer's duty to interrogate and whip, as aforesaid."

The last authorized edition of the laws of Maryland, comprises the following: "If any slave be convicted of any petit treason, or murder, or wilfully burning of dwelling houses, it may be lawful for the justices to give judgment against such slave to have the right hand cut off, to be hanged in the usual manner, the head severed from the body, the body divided into four quarters, and the head and quarters set up in the most public places of the county," &c.

The laws of Tennessee and Missouri are comparatively mild; yet in Missouri it is *death* to prepare or administer medicine without the master's consent, unless it can be *proved* that there was no evil intention. The law in Virginia is similar; it requires proof that there was no evil intention, and that the medicine produced no bad consequences.

To estimate fully the cruel injustice of these laws, it must be remembered that the poor slave is without religious instruction, unable to read, too ignorant to comprehend legislation, and holding so little communication with any person better informed than himself, that the chance is, he does not even know the *existence* of half the laws by which he suffers. This is worthy of Nero, who caused his edicts to be placed so high that they could not be read, and then beheaded his subjects for disobeying them.

PROP. 14.— *The laws operate oppressively on free colored people.*

Free people of color, like the slaves, are excluded by law from all means of obtaining the common elements of education.

The free colored man may at any time be taken up on suspicion, and be condemned and imprisoned as a runaway slave, unless he can *prove* the contrary; and be it remembered, none but *white* evidence, or written documents, avail him. The common law supposes a man to be innocent, until he is proved guilty; but slave law turns this upside down. Every colored man is *presumed* to be a slave, till it can be proved otherwise; this rule prevails in all the slave States, except North Carolina, where it is confined to negroes. Stephens supposes this harsh doctrine to be peculiar to the British Colonial Code; but in this he is again mistaken—the American *republics* share the honor with England.

A law passed in December, 1822, in South Carolina, provides that any free colored persons coming into port on board of any vessel shall be seized and imprisoned during the stay of the vessel; and when she is ready to depart, the captain shall take such free negroes and pay the expenses of their arrest and imprisonment; and in case of refusing so to do, he shall be indicted and fined not less than one thousand dollars, and imprisoned not less than two months; and such free negroes shall be sold for slaves. The Circuit Court of the United States, adjudged the law unconstitutional and void. Yet nearly *two years* after this decision, four colored English seamen were taken out of the brig Marmion. England made a formal complaint to our Government. Mr Wirt the Attorney General gave the opinion that the law was unconstitutional. This, as well as the above mentioned decision, excited strong indignation in South Carolina. Notwithstanding the decision, the law still remains in force, and other States have followed the example of South Carolina, though with a more cautious observance of appearances.

In South Carolina, if any free negro harbor, conceal, or entertain, any runaway slave, or a slave charged with *any* criminal matter, he forfeits ten pounds for the first day, and twenty shillings for every succeeding day. In case of inability to pay, the free negro is sold at auction, and if any overplus remain, after the fines and attendant expenses are paid, it is put into the hands of the public treasurer.

The free negro may entertain a slave without *knowing* that he has done anything wrong; but his declaration to that effect is of no avail. Where every effort is made to prevent colored people from obtaining any money, they are of course often unable to pay the penalties imposed.

If any omission is made in the forms of emancipation established by law, *any person whatsoever* may seize the negro so manumitted, and appropriate him to their own use.

If a free colored person remain in Virginia twelve months after his manumission, he can be sold by the overseers of the poor for the benefit of the *literary fund!*

In Georgia, a free colored man, except a regular articled seaman, is fined one hundred dollars for coming into the State; and if he cannot pay it, may be sold at public outcry. This act has been changed to one of increased severity. A free colored person cannot be a witness against a white man. They may therefore be robbed, assaulted, kidnapped and carried off with impunity; and even the legislatures of the old slave States adopt it as a maxim that it is very desirable to get rid of them. It is of no avail to *declare* themselves free; the law *presumes* them to be slaves, unless they can *prove* to the contrary. In many instances written documents of freedom have been wrested from free colored people and destroyed by kidnappers. A lucrative internal slave trade furnishes constant temptation to the commission of such crimes; and the *new* States of Alabama, Mississippi, Missouri, and the territories of Arkansas, and the Floridas, are not likely to be glutted for years to come.

In Philadelphia, though remote from a slave market, it has been ascertained that *more than thirty* free persons of color, were stolen and carried off within *two* years. Stroud says: "Five of these have been restored to their friends, by the interposition of humane gentlemen, though not without great expense and difficulty. The others are still in bondage; and if rescued at all, it must be by sending *white* witnesses a journey of more than a thousand miles."

I know the names of four colored citizens of Massachusetts, who went to Georgia on board a vessel, were seized under the laws of that State, and sold as slaves. They have sent the most earnest exhortations to their families and friends to do something for their relief; but the attendant expenses require more money than the friends of negroes are apt to have, and the poor fellows as yet remain unassisted.

A New York paper, November, 1829, contains the following caution:

"*Beware of kidnappers!*—It is *well understood* that there is at present in this city, a gang of kidnappers, busily engaged in their vocation of stealing colored children for the Southern market! It is believed that three or four have been stolen within as many days. A little negro boy came to this city from the country three or four days ago. Some strange white persons were very friendly to him, and yesterday morning he was mightily pleased that they had given him some new clothes. And the persons pretending thus to befriend him, entirely secured his confidence. This day he cannot be found.—Nor can he be traced since seen with one of his new friends yesterday. There are suspicions of a foul nature, connected with some who serve the police in subordinate capacities. It is hinted that there may be those in some authority, not altogether ignorant of these diabolical practices. Let the public be on their guard! It is still fresh in the memories of all, that a cargo, or rather drove, of negroes was made up from this city and Philadelphia, about the time that the emancipation of all the negroes in this State took place under our present constitution, and were taken through Virginia, the Carolinas, and Tennessee, and disposed of in the state of Mississippi. Some of those who were taken from Philadelphia were persons of intelligence, and after they had been driven through the country in chains, and disposed of by sale on the Mississippi, wrote back to their friends, and were rescued from bondage. The persons who were guilty of this abominable transaction are known, and now reside in North Carolina; they may, very probably, be engaged in similar enterprises at the present time—at least there is reason to believe that the system of kidnapping free persons of color from the Northern cities has been carried on more extensively than the public are generally aware of."

This, and other evils of the system, admit of no radical cure but the utter extinction of slavery. To enact *laws* prohibiting the slave traffic, and at the same time tempt avarice by the allurements of an *insatiable market,* is irreconcilable and absurd.

To my great surprise, I find that the free States of Ohio and Indiana disgrace themselves by admitting the same maxim of law, which prevents any black or mulatto from being witness against a white man!

It is naturally supposed that free negroes will sympathize with their enslaved brethren, and that, notwithstanding all exertions to the contrary, they will become a little more intelligent; this excites a peculiar jealousy and hatred in the white population, of which it is impossible to enumerate all the hardships. Even in the *laws,* slaves are always mentioned before free people of color; so desirous are they to degrade the latter class below the level of the former. To complete the wrong, this unhappy class are despised in consequence of the *very* evils we ourselves have induced—for as slavery inevitably makes its victims servile and vicious, and as none but negroes are allowed to be slaves, we, from our very childhood, associate everything that is de-graded with the *mere color;* though in fact the object of our contempt may be both exemplary and intelligent. In this way the Africans are doubly the victims of our injustice; and thus does prejudice "*make* the meat it feeds on."

I have repeatedly said that our slave laws are continually increasing in severity: as a proof of this I will give a brief view of some of the most *striking,* which have been passed since Stroud published his compendium of slave laws, in 1827. In the first class are contained those enactments *directly* oppressive to people of color; in the second are those which injure them *indirectly,* by the penalties or disabilities imposed upon the whites, who instruct, assist, or employ them, or endeavor, in any way, to influence public opinion in their favor.

Class First.—The Legislature of Virginia passed a law in 1831, by which any free colored person who undertakes to preach, or conduct any religious meeting, by day or night, may be whipped not exceed-ing thirtynine lashes, at the discretion of *any* justice of the peace; and anybody may apprehend any such free colored person without a warrant. The same penalty, adjudged and executed in the same way, falls upon any slave, or free colored person, who attends such preach-ing; and any slave who listens to any *white* preacher, in the night time, receives the same punishment. The same law prevails in Georgia, and Mississippi. A master may permit a slave to preach on *his* plantation, to none but *his* slaves.

There is a *naïveté* in the following preamble to a law passed by North Carolina, in 1831, which would be amusing, if the subject were not too serious for mirth: "*Whereas teaching slaves to read and write has a tendency to excite dissatisfaction in their minds,* and to produce insurrection and rebellion," therefore it is enacted that teaching a slave to read or write, or giving or selling to a slave *any* book, or pamphlet, shall be punished with thirtynine lashes, if the offender be a free black, or with imprisonment at the discretion of the court; if a slave, the *offence* is punishable with thirtynine lashes, on his or her bare back, on conviction before a justice of the peace.

In Georgia, any slave, or free person of color, is for a similar offence, fined or whipped, or fined *and* whipped at the discretion of the court.

In Louisiana, twelve months' imprisonment is the penalty for teaching a slave to read or write.

For publishing, or circulating, in the state of North Carolina, any pamphlet or paper having an *evident tendency* to excite slaves, or free persons of color, to insurrection or resistance, imprisonment not less than one year, *and* standing in the pillory, *and* whipping, at the discretion of the court for the first offence; and death for the second. The same offence punished with death in Georgia, without any reservation. In Mississippi, the same as in Georgia. In Louisiana, the same offence punished either with imprisonment for life, or death, at the discretion of the court. In Virginia, the first offence of this sort is punished with thirtynine lashes, the second with death.

With regard to publications having a *tendency* to promote discontent among slaves, their masters are so very jealous, that it would be difficult to find *any* book, that would not come under their condemnation. The Bible, and the Declaration of Independence are certainly unsafe. The preamble to the North Carolina law declares, that the *Alphabet* has a tendency to excite dissatisfaction; I suppose it is because *freedom* may be spelt out of it. A store keeper in South Carolina was nearly ruined by having unconsciously imported certain printed *handkerchiefs*, which his neighbors deemed seditious. A friend of mine asked, "Did the handkerchiefs contain texts from scripture? or quotations from the Constitution of the United States?"

Emancipated slaves must quit North Carolina in ninety days after their enfranchisement, on pain of being sold for life. Free persons of color who shall *migrate into* that State, may be seized and sold as runaway slaves; and if they *migrate out* of the State for more than ninety days, they can never return under the same penalty.

This extraordinary use of the word *migrate* furnishes a new battering ram against the free colored class, which is everywhere so odious to slave owners. A *visit* to relations in another State may be called *migrating;* being taken up and detained by *kidnappers,* over ninety days, may be called *migrating;*—for where neither the evidence of the sufferer nor any of his own color is allowed, it will evidently amount to this.

In South Carolina, if a free negro cross the line of the State, he can *never* return.

In 1831, Mississippi passed a law to expel all colored persons under sixty and over sixteen years of age from the State, within ninety days, unless they could prove good characters, and obtain from the court a certificate of the same, for which they paid three dollars; these certificates might be revoked at the discretion of the county courts. If such persons do not quit the State within the time specified, or if they return to it, they may be sold for a term not exceeding five years.

In Tennessee, slaves are not allowed to be emancipated unless they leave the State forthwith. Any free colored person emigrating into this State, is fined from ten to fifty dollars, and hard labor in the penitentiary from one to two years.

North Carolina has made a law subjecting any vessel with *free* colored persons on board to thirty days' quarantine; as if freedom were as bad as the cholera! Any person of color coming on shore from such vessels is seized and imprisoned, till the vessel departs; and the captain is fined five hundred dollars; and if he refuse to take the colored seaman away, and pay all the expenses of his imprisonment, he is fined five hundred more. If the sailor do not depart within ten days after his captain's refusal, he must be whipped thirtynine lashes; and all colored persons, bond or free, who *communicate* with him, receive the same.

In Georgia, there is a similar enactment. The prohibition is, in both States, confined to *merchant* vessels, (it would be imprudent to meddle with *vessels of war;*) and any colored person communicating with such seamen is whipped not exceeding *thirty* lashes. If the captain refuse to carry away seamen thus detained, and *pay the expenses of their imprisonment,* he shall be fined five hundred dollars, and also imprisoned, not exceeding three months.

These State laws are a direct violation of the Laws of Nations, and our treaties; and may involve the United States in a foreign war.

Colored seamen are often employed in Spanish, Portuguese, French, and English vessels. These nations are bound to know the United States Laws; but can they be expected to know the enactments of particular States and cities? and if they know them, are they bound to observe them, if they interfere with the established rules of nations? When Mr Wirt pronounced these laws unconstitutional, great excitement was produced in South Carolina. The Governor of that State in his Message to the Legislature implied that separation from the Union was the only remedy, if the laws of the Southern States could not be enforced. They seem to require unconditional submission abroad as well as at home.

The endeavor to prevent insurrections in this way, is as wise as to attempt to extinguish fire with spirits of wine. The short-sighted policy defeats itself. A free colored sailor was lately imprisoned with seven slaves: Here was a fine opportunity to sow the seeds of sedition in their minds!

The upholders of slavery will in vain contend with the liberal spirit of the age; it is too strong for them.—They may as well try to bottle up the sunshine for their own exclusive use, as to attempt to keep knowledge and freedom to themselves. We all know that such an experiment would result in bottling up darkness for themselves, while exactly the same amount of sunshine remained abroad for the use of their neighbors.

In North Carolina, free negroes are whipped, fined, and imprisoned at the discretion of the court, for intermarrying with slaves.

In Georgia, free colored persons when unable to pay *any* fine, may be sold for a space of time not exceeding five years. This limitation does not probably avail much; if sold to another master before the five years expired, they would never be likely to be free again.

Several other laws have been passed in Georgia, prohibiting slaves from living apart from their master, either to labor for other persons, or to sell refreshments, or to carry on any trade or business although with their master's consent. Any person of color, bond or free, is forbidden to occupy any tenement except a *kitchen* or an *outhouse,* under penalty of from twenty to fifty lashes. Some of these laws are applicable only to particular cities, towns, or counties; others to several counties.

Sundry general laws of a penal nature have been made more penal;

and the number of offences, for which a colored person may suffer *death,* is increased.

A law passed in Tennessee, in 1831, provides that negroes for conspiracy to rebel, shall be punished with whipping, imprisonment and pillory, at the discretion of the court; it has this curious proviso—"Householders *may* serve as jurors, if *slave-holders* cannot be had!"* The Southern courts need to have a great deal of *discretion,* since so much is trusted to it.

Class Second.—In Virginia, *white* persons who teach any colored person to read or write, are fined not exceeding fifty dollars; for teaching slaves for pay, from ten to twenty dollars for each offence.

In Georgia, a similar offence is fined not exceeding five hundred dollars, and imprisoned at the discretion of the court. Knowledge seems to be peculiarly *pokerish* in Georgia.

In North Carolina, if a white person teach a slave to read or write, or give or sell him *any* book, &c., he is fined from one to two hundred dollars.

In Louisiana, any white person, who teaches a slave to read or write, is imprisoned one year. And if any person shall use any language from the *bar, bench, stage, pulpit,* or any other place,—or hold any conversation having a *tendency* to promote discontent among free colored people, or insubordination among slaves, he may be imprisoned at hard labor, not less than three, nor more than twentyone years; or he may suffer death—at the discretion of the court.

In Mississippi, a white man, who prints or circulates doctrines, sentiments, advice, or *innuendoes,* likely to produce discontent among the colored class, is fined from one hundred to a thousand dollars, and imprisoned from three to twelve months.

All the States which have pronounced an anathema against books and alphabets, have likewise forbidden that any colored man shall be employed in a printing office, under the penalty of ten dollars for every offence.

In Mississippi, any white who employs, or receives a free colored person, without a certificate of freedom, written on parchment, forfeits *one thousand dollars.*

If any master, in that State, allows his slaves to sell any wares or merchandise out of the incorporated towns, he is liable to a fine of from fifty to five hundred dollars.

*The Common Law assigns for the trial of a foreigner, six jurors of his own nation, and six native Englishmen.

In Virginia, any person who buys of a slave any article belonging to his master, forfeits from ten to fifty dollars; if the purchase be made on Sunday, ten dollars more are added to the fine for each article.

This enactment is evidently made to prevent a slave from obtaining any money, or holding communication with freemen; a particular proviso is made against Sunday, because the slave has usually more leisure on that day. It is to be remembered that all a slave has belongs to his master.

To carry a slave out of North Carolina, or conceal him with intent to carry him out, is punished with death.

If a runaway slave die in prison, before he or she can be sold, *the county pays the sheriff and jailer;* formerly these officers depended on the life and marketableness of their prisoners for security; but even this poor motive for kindness is now taken away. If ninetynine out of a hundred die in prison, they will be heard of only in the *jailer's bill.* I never heard or read of an *inquest* upon the body of a slave found dead. Under the term "runaway slaves" are included many free colored persons taken up unjustly.

Well might Jefferson say, "I tremble for my country, when I reflect that God is just!"

In travelling over this dreary desert, it is pleasant to arrive at one little oasis: Louisiana *has* enacted that slaves brought into that State for sale, shall forthwith be set free; but they must be sent out of the State.

It is worthy of remark that England pursues a totally different course with regard to allowing slaves to communicate with free people. Their recent laws are all calculated to make it easy for the slave to obtain a fair hearing from people who have no interest to suppress his complaints. He may go upon any plantation, and communicate with any person; and whoever tries to prevent his going to a magistrate is guilty of a misdemeanor.

They have abolished all distinction between white and colored witnesses.

The law expressly stipulates the quality and quantity of provisions.

Inquest is held upon the bodies of slaves dying suddenly, or from any suspected violence.

Use of the cart whip prohibited; and no female to be punished except by order of the court.

Only fifteen lashes allowed as a punishment to men for one offence, and in one day; two kinds of punishment never allowed for one offence.

When a slave is punished, two competent witnesses must be present.

The owner is obliged to keep a record of domestic punishments and the causes.

Marriages among slaves are encouraged, and husband and wife are not allowed to be sold separately. Children under sixteen years old cannot be separated from their parents.

Masters illegally punishing their slaves, are subject to fine, imprisonment, and loss of the slave, for the first offence; for the second offence, sequestration of all their slaves.

Free colored representatives are allowed to take their seat in the legislature, and share all the other privileges of British subjects.

Yet these humane laws, so carefully framed in favor of the defenceless, have been found insufficient to protect the slave. Experience proves, what reason clearly points out, that the force of good laws must be weakened by the very nature of this unholy relation. Where there is knowledge and freedom on one side, and ignorance and servitude on the other, evasions and subterfuges will of course be frequent. Hence English philanthropists have universally come to the conclusion that nothing effectual can be done, unless slavery itself be destroyed.

The limits of this work compel me to pass by many enactments in our slave-holding States, which would throw still more light on this dark subject.

I have laid open some of the laws which do actually exist, and are constantly enforced in this free country; and knowing all this, and still more, to be true, I blush and hang my head, whenever I hear any one boast of our "glorious institutions."

The slave-holders insist that their *humanity* is so great, as to render all their ferocious laws perfectly harmless. Are the laws then made on purpose to urge tender-hearted masters to be so much worse than they really desire to be? The democrats of the South appear to be less scrupulous about the liberties of others, than the Autocrat of the Russias;—for, when Madame de Staël told the Emperor Alexander that his *character* answered instead of a *constitution* for his country, he replied, "Then, madam, I am but a lucky *accident.*" How much more emphatically may it be said, that the slave's destiny is a matter of chance! Reader, would you trust the very best man you know, with your time, your interests, your family, and your life, unless the contract were guarded on every side by the strong arm of the law? If a money-loving neighbor could force you to toil, and could gain a certain number of dollars for every hour of your labor, how much rest should you expect to have?

It is utter nonsense to say that generosity of disposition is a protection against tyranny, where all the power is on one side. It may be, and it no doubt is so, in particular instances; but they must be exceptions to the general rule.

We all know that the Southerners have a high sense of what the world calls honor, and that they are brave, hospitable, and generous to people of their own color; but the more we respect their virtues, the more cause is there to lament the demoralizing *system,* which produces such unhappy effects on all who come within its baneful influence. Most of them may be as kind as can be expected of human nature, endowed with almost unlimited power to do wrong; and some of them may be even more benevolent than the warmest friend of the negro would dare to hope; but while we admit all this, we must not forget that there is in every community a class of men, who will not be any better than the laws compel them to be.

Captain Riley, in his Narrative, says: "Strange as it may seem to the philanthropist, my free and proud spirited countrymen still hold a million and a half* of human beings in the most cruel bonds of slavery; who are kept at hard labor, and smarting under the lash of inhuman, mercenary drivers; in many instances enduring the miseries of hunger, thirst, imprisonment, cold, nakedness, and even tortures. This is no picture of the imagination. For the honor of human nature, I wish likenesses were nowhere to be found! I myself have witnessed such scenes in different parts of my own country; and the bare recollection of them now chills my blood with horror."

When the slave owners talk of their gentleness and compassion, they are witnesses in their own favor, and have strong motives for showing the fairest side. But what do the laws themselves imply? Are enactments ever made against exigencies which do not exist? If negroes have never been scalded, burned, mutilated, &c. why are such crimes forbidden by an express law, with the marvellous proviso, except said slave *die* of *"moderate* punishment"? If a law sanctioning whipping to any extent, incarceration at the discretion of the master, and the body loaded with irons, is called a *restraining* law, let me ask what crimes must have been committed, to require *prohibition,*

*There are now over two millions.

where so much is *allowed?* The law, which declares that slaves shall be compelled to labor *only* fourteen or fifteen hours a day, has the following preamble: "Whereas *many* owners of slaves, managers, &c. do confine them so closely to hard labor that they have not sufficient time for natural rest," &c. Mr Pinckney, in a public argument, speaking of slaves murdered by severe treatment, says: "The *frequency* of the crime is no doubt owing to the nature of the punishment." The reader will observe that I carefully refrain from quoting the representations of party spirit, and refer to *facts* only for evidence.

Where the laws are made by the people, a majority of course approve them; else they would soon be changed. It must therefore in candor be admitted, that the *laws* of the State speak the prevailing *sentiments* of the inhabitants.

Judging by this rule, what inference must be drawn from the facts stated above? "At Sparta, the freeman is the freest of all men, and the slave is the greatest of slaves."

Our republic is a perfect Pandora's box to the negro, only there is no *hope* at the bottom. The wretchedness of his fate is not a little increased by being a constant witness of the unbounded freedom enjoyed by others: the slave's labor must necessarily be like the labor of Sisiphus; and here the torments of Tantalus are added.

Slavery is so inconsistent with free institutions, and the spirit of liberty is so contagious under such institutions, that the system must either be given up, or sustained by laws outrageously severe; hence we find that our slave laws have each year been growing more harsh than those of any other nation.

Shall I be told that all these regulations are necessary for the white man's safety? What then, let me indignantly ask, what must the system be that *requires* to be supported by such unnatural, such tyrannical means! The very apology pronounces the condemnation of slavery—for it proves that it cannot exist without producing boundless misery to the oppressed, and perpetual terror to the oppressor.

In our fourth of July orations, we are much in the habit of talking about the tyranny of England! and there is no doubt that broad and deep stains do rest upon her history. But there is a vulgar proverb that "those who live in glass houses should not throw stones." In judging of national, as well as individual wrong, it is fair to consider the amount of temptation. England has had power, more extensive and permanent than any nation since the decline of Rome: the negroes and the Indians are the only people who have been dependent on *our* justice and generosity—and how have we treated *them*?

It is a favorite argument that we are not to blame for slavery, because the British engrafted it upon us, while we were colonies. But did we not take the liberty to *change* English laws and customs, when they did not suit us? Why not put away *this*, as well as other evils of much less consequence? It could have been done easily, at the time of our confederation; it *can* be done now.—Have not other nations been making alterations for the better, on this very subject, since we became independent? Is not England trying with all her might to atone for the wrong she has done? Does not the constitution of the United States, and the constitution of each individual State, make provision for such changes as shall tend to the public good?

The plain truth is, the continuation of this system is a sin; and the sin rests upon us: It has been eloquently said that "by this excuse, we try to throw the blame upon our ancestors, and leave repentance to posterity."

CHAPTER III.

FREE LABOR AND SLAVE LABOR.
—POSSIBILITY OF SAFE
EMANCIPATION.

Wo onto him that useth his neighbor's service
without wages, and giveth him not for his work.
— *Jeremiah*, xxii. 13.

Who can reflect, unmoved, upon the round
Of smooth and solemnized complacencies,
By which, on Christian lands, from age to age,
Profession mocks performance. Earth is sick,
And Heaven is weary, of the hollow words,
Which states and kingdoms utter when they talk
Of truth and justice.
— WORDSWORTH.

POLITICAL economists found their systems on those broad and general principles, the application of which has been proved by reason and experience to produce the greatest possible happiness to the greatest number of people. All writers of this class, I believe without exception, prefer free labor to slave labor.

Indeed a very brief glance will show that slavery is inconsistent with *economy*, whether domestic, or political.

The slave is bought, sometimes at a very high price; in free labor there is no such investment of capital.—When the slave is ill, a physician must be paid by the owner; the free laborer defrays his own expenses. The children of the slave must be supported by his master; the free man maintains his own. The slave is to be taken care of in his old age, which his previous habits render peculiarly helpless; the free laborer is hired when he is wanted, and then returns to his home. The slave does not care how slowly or carelessly he works; it is the free man's interest to do his business well and quickly. The slave is indifferent how many tools he spoils; the free man has a motive to be careful. The slave's clothing is indeed very cheap, but it is of no consequence to him how fast it is destroyed—his master *must* keep him covered, and that is all he is likely to do; the hired laborer pays more for his garments, but makes them last three times as long. The free man will be honest for reputation's sake; but reputation will make the slave none the richer, nor invest him with any of the privileges of a human being—while his poverty and sense of wrong both urge him to steal from his master. A salary must be paid to an overseer to compel the slave to work; the free man is impelled by the desire of increasing the comforts of himself and family. Two hired laborers will perform as much work as three slaves; by some it is supposed to be a more correct estimate that slaves perform only *half* as much labor as the same number of free laborers. Finally, *where* slaves are employed, manual industry is a degradation to white people, and indolence becomes the prevailing characteristic.

Slave owners have indeed frequently shown great adroitness in defending this bad system; but, with few exceptions, they base their arguments upon the necessity of continuing slavery because it is already begun. Many of them have openly acknowledged that it was highly injurious to the prosperity of the State.

The Hon. Henry Clay, in his address before the Colonization Society of Kentucky, has given a view of the causes affecting, and likely to affect, slavery in this country, which is very remarkable, for its completeness, its distinctness, and its brevity. The following sentences are quoted from this address: "As a mere laborer, the slave feels that he toils for his master, and not for himself; that the laws do not recognise his capacity to acquire and hold property, which depends altogether upon the pleasure of his proprietor, and that all the fruits of his exertions are reaped by others. He knows that, whether sick or well, in times of scarcity or abundance, his master is bound to provide for him by the all-powerful influence of self-interest. He is generally, therefore, indifferent to the adverse or prosperous fortunes of his master, being contented if he can escape his displeasure or chastisement, by a careless and slovenly performance of his duties.

"This is the state of the relation between master and slave, prescribed by the law of its nature, and founded in the reason of things. There are undoubtedly many exceptions, in which the slave dedicates himself to his master with a zealous and generous devotion, and the master to the slave with a parental and affectionate attachment. But it is my purpose to speak of the *general* state of this unfortunate relation.

"That labor is best, in which the laborer knows that he will derive the profits of his industry, that his employment depends upon his diligence, and his reward upon this assiduity. He then has every motive to excite him to exertion, and to animate him in perseverance. He knows that if he is treated badly he can exchange his employer, for one who will better estimate his service; and that whatever he earns is *his,* to be distributed by himself as he pleases, among his wife, and children, and friends, or enjoyed by himself. In a word, he feels that he is a free agent, with rights, and privileges, and sensibilities.

"Wherever the option exists to employ, at an equal hire, free or slave labor, the former will be decidedly preferred, for the reasons already assigned. It is more capable, more diligent, more faithful, and in every respect more worthy of confidence.

"It is believed that nowhere in the *farming* portion of the United States would slave labor be generally employed, if the proprietor were not tempted to raise slaves by the high price of the Southern market, which keeps it up in his own."

Speaking of an attempt more than thirtyfive years ago, to adopt gradual emancipation in Kentucky, Mr Clay says: "We were overpowered by numbers, and submitted to the decision of the majority, with the grace which the minority, in a republic, should ever yield to such a decision. I have nevertheless never ceased, and never shall cease, to regret a decision, the effects of which have been, to place us in the rear of our neighbors, who are exempt from slavery, in the state of agriculture, the progress of manufactures, the advance of improvement, and the general prosperity of society."

Mr Appleton, in his reply to Mr McDuffie in the winter of 1832,— a speech distinguished for its good temper and sound practical sense,—says: "I do not think the gentleman from South Carolina has overrated the money price of New England labor at fifty cents; but most of the labor is performed by the *owners of the soil.* It is great industry alone, which makes New England prosperous. The circumstance that with this cheap slave labor, the South is complaining of suffering, while the North is content and prosperous with dear free labor, is a striking fact and deserves a careful and thorough examination. The experience of all ages and nations proves that high wages are the most powerful stimulus to exertion, and the best means of attaching the people to the institutions under which they live. It is apparent that this political effect upon the character of society cannot have any action upon slaves. Having no choice or volition, there is nothing for stimulus to act upon; they are in fact no part of society. So that, in the language of political economy, they are, like machinery, merely capital; and the productions of their labor consist wholly of profits of capital. But it is not perceived how the tariff can lessen the value of the productions of their labor, in comparison with that of the other States. New York and Virginia both produce wheat; New York with dear labor is content, and Virginia with cheap labor is dissatisfied.

"What is the *occupation* of the white population of the planting States? I am at a loss to know how this population is employed. We hear of no products of these States, but those produced by slave labor. It is clear the white population cannot be employed in raising cotton or tobacco, because in doing so they can earn but twelve and a half cents per day, since the same quantity of labor performed by a slave is worth no more. I am told also that the wages of overseers, mechanics, &c. are higher than the white labor of the North; and it is well known that many mechanics go from the North to the South, to get employment during the winter. These facts suggest the inquiry whether this cheap slave labor does not paralyze the industry of the whites? Whether *idleness* is not the greatest of their evils?"

During the famous debate in the Virginia Legislature, in the winter of 1832, Mr Brodnax made the following remark: "That slavery in Virginia is an evil, and a transcendent evil, it would be more than idle for any human being to doubt or deny. It is a mildew which has blighted every region it has touched, from the creation of the world. Illustrations from the history of other countries and other times might be instructive and profitable, had we the time to review them; but we have evidence tending to the same conviction nearer at hand and accessible to daily observation, in the short histories of the different States of this great confederacy, which are impressive in their admonitions and conclusive in their character."

During the same session, Mr Faulkner of Virginia, said: "Sir, I am gratified to perceive that no gentleman has yet risen in this Hall, the avowed *advocate* of slavery. The day has gone by, when such a voice could be listened to with patience, or even forbearance. I even regret, sir, that we should find one amongst us, who enters the lists as its *apologist*, except on the ground of uncontrollable necessity. If there be one, who concurs with the gentleman from Brunswick (Mr Gholson) in the harmless character of this institution, let me request him to compare the condition of the slave holding portion of this Commonwealth—barren, desolate, and seared as it were by the avenging hand of Heaven,—with the descriptions which we have of this same country from those who first broke its virgin soil. To what is this change ascribable? Alone to the withering and blasting effects of slavery. If this does not satisfy him, let me request him to extend his travels to the Northern States of this Union,—and beg him to contrast the happiness and contentment which prevails throughout the country— and busy and cheerful sound of industry—the rapid and swelling growth of their population—their means and institutions of education—their skill and proficiency in the useful arts—their enterprise, and public spirit—the monuments of their commercial and manufacturing industry; and, above all, their devoted attachment to the government from which they derive their protection, with the division, discontent, indolence, and poverty of the Southern country. To what, sir, is all this ascribable? To that vice in the organization of society, by which one half of its inhabitants are arrayed in interest and feeling against the other half—to that unfortunate state of society in which freemen regard labor as disgraceful—and slaves shrink from it as a burden tyrannically imposed upon them—to that condition of things, in which half a million of your population can feel no sympathy with the society in the prosperity of which they are forbidden to participate, and no attachment to a government at whose hands they receive nothing but injustice.

"If this should not be sufficient, and the curious and incredulous inquirer should suggest that the contrast which has been adverted to, and is so manifest, might be traced to a difference of climate, or other causes distinct from slavery itself, permit me to refer him to the two states of Kentucky and Ohio—no difference of soil—no diversity of climate—no diversity in the original settlement of those two States, can account for the remarkable disproportion in their national advancement.—Separated by a river alone, they seem to have been purposely and providentially designed to exhibit in their future histories the difference, which necessarily results from a country free from, and a country afflicted with, the curse of slavery. The same may be said of the two states of Missouri and Illinois.

"Slavery, it is admitted, is an evil—it is an institution which presses heavily against the best interests of the State. It banishes free white labor—it exterminates the mechanic—the artisan—the manufacturer. It deprives them of occupation. It deprives them of bread. It converts the energy of a community into indolence—its power into imbecility—its efficiency into weakness. Sir, being thus injurious, have we not a right to demand its extermination! Shall society suffer, that the slave holder may continue to gather his *vigintial crop* of human flesh? What is his mere pecuniary claim, compared with the great interests of the common weal? Must the country languish and die, that the slave holder may flourish? Shall all interests be subservient to one?—all rights subordinate to those of the slave holder? Has not the mechanic—have not the middle classes their rights?—rights incompatible with the existence of slavery?"

Sutcliff, in his Travels in North America, says: "A person not conversant with these things would naturally think that where families employ a number of slaves, everything about their houses, gardens, and plantations, would be kept in the best order. But the reverse of this is generally the case. I was sometimes tempted to think that the more slaves there were employed, the more disorder appeared. I am persuaded that one or two hired servants, in a well regulated family, would preserve more neatness, order, and comfort, than treble the number of slaves.

"There is a very striking contrast between the appearance of the horses or teams in Pennsylvania, and those in the Southern States, where slaves are kept. In Pennsylvania we met with great numbers of wagons, drawn by four or more fine fat horses, and carriages firm and well made, and covered with stout good linen, bleached almost white: and it is not uncommon to see ten or fifteen together, travelling cheerfully along the road, the driver riding on one of his horses. Many of these come more than three hundred miles to Philadelphia, from the Ohio, Pittsburg, and other places; and I have been told by a respectable friend, a native of Philadelphia, that more than one thousand covered carriages frequently come to Philadelphia market.

"The appearance of things in the slave States is quite the reverse of this. We sometimes meet a ragged black boy or girl driving a team, consisting of a lean cow or a mule, sometimes a lean bull, or an ox and a mule; and I have seen a mule, a bull, and a cow, each miserable in its appearance, composing one team, with a half naked black slave or two, riding or driving, as occasion suited. The carriage or wagon, if it may be called such, appeared in as wretched a condition as the team and its driver. Sometime a couple of horses, mules, or cows, &c.

would be dragging a hogshead of tobacco, with a pivot, or axle, driven into each end of the hogshead, and something like a shaft attached, by which it was drawn, or rolled along the road. I have seen two oxen and two slaves pretty fully employed in getting along a single hogshead; and some of these come from a great distance inland."

The inhabitants of free States are often told that they cannot argue fairly upon the subject of slavery because they know nothing about its actual operation; and any expression of their opinions and feelings with regard to the system, is attributed to ignorant enthusiasm, fanatical benevolence, or a wicked intention to do mischief.

But Mr Clay, Mr Brodnax, and Mr Faulkner, belong to slave holding States; and the two former, if I mistake not, are slave owners. *They* surely are qualified to judge of the system; and I might fill ten pages with other quotations from Southern writers and speakers, who acknowledge that slavery is a great evil. There are zealous partisans indeed, who defend the system strenuously, and some of them very eloquently. Thus, Mr Hayne, in his reply to Mr Webster, denied that the South suffered in consequence of *slavery;* he maintained that the slave holding States were prosperous, and the principal cause of all the prosperity in the Union. He laughed at the idea of any danger, however distant, from an overgrown slave population, and supported the position by the fact that slaves had always been kept in entire subjection in the British West Indies, where the white population is less than ten per cent of the whole. But the distinguished gentleman from South Carolina did not mention that the *peace* establishment of the British West Indies costs England *two million pounds annually!* Yet such is the fact. This system is so closely entwined with the apparent interests and convenience of individuals, that it will never want for able defenders, so long as it exists. But I believe I do not misrepresent the truth, when I say the prevailing opinion at the South is, that it would have been much better for those States, and for the country in general, if slavery had never been introduced.

Miss Martineau, in her most admirable little book on Demerara, says: "Labor is the product of mind as much as of body; and to secure that product, we must sway the mind by the natural means—by motives. Laboring against self-interest is what nobody ought to expect of white men—much less of slaves. Of course every man, woman and child, would rather play for nothing than work for nothing.

"It is the mind, which gives sight to the eye, and hearing to the ear, and strength to the limbs; and the mind cannot be purchased. Where a man is allowed the possession of himself, the purchaser of his labor is benefited by the vigor of his mind through the service of his limbs: where man is made the possession of another, the possessor loses at once and forever all that is most valuable in that for which he has paid the price of crime. He becomes the owner of that which only differs from an idiot in being less easily drilled into habits, and more capable of effectual revenge.

"Cattle are fixed capital, and so are slaves: But slaves differ from cattle on the one hand, in yielding (from internal opposition) a less return for their maintenance; and from free laborers on the other hand, in not being acted upon by the inducements which stimulate production as an effort of mind as well as body. In all three cases the labor is purchased. In free laborers and cattle, all the faculties work together, and to advantage; in the slave they are opposed; and therefore he is, so far as the amount of labor is concerned, the least valuable of the three. The negroes *can* invent and improve—witness their ingenuity in their dwellings, and their skill in certain of their sports; but their masters will never possess their faculties, though they have purchased their limbs. Our true policy would be to divide the work of the slave between the ox and the hired laborer; we should get more out of the sinews of the one and the soul of the other, than the produce of double the number of slaves."

As a matter of humanity, let it be remembered that men having more *reason* than brutes, must be treated with much greater severity, in order to keep them in a state of abject submission.

It seems unnecessary to say that what is unjust and unmerciful, can never be expedient; yet men often write, talk, and act, as if they either forgot this truth, or doubted it. There is genuine wisdom in the following remark, extracted from the petition of Cambridge University to the Parliament of England, on the subject of slavery: "A firm belief in the Providence of a benevolent Creator assures us that no system, founded on the oppression of one part of mankind, *can* be beneficial to another."

But the tolerator of slavery will say, "No doubt the system is an evil; but we are not to blame for it; we received it from our English ancestors. It is a lamentable *necessity;*—we cannot do it away if we would;—insurrections would be the inevitable result of any attempt to remove it"—and having quieted their consciences by the use of the word *lamentable,* they think no more upon the subject.

These assertions have been so often, and so dogmatically repeated, that many truly kind-hearted people have believed there was some truth in them. I myself, (may God forgive me for it!) have often, in thoughtless ignorance, made the same remarks.

An impartial and careful examination has led me to the conviction that slavery causes insurrections, while emancipation prevents them.

The grand argument of the slave holder is that sudden freedom occasioned the horrible massacres of St Domingo.—If a word is said in favor of abolition, he shakes his head, and points a warning finger to St Domingo! But it is a remarkable fact that this same vilified island furnishes a strong argument *against* the lamentable necessity of slavery. In the first place, there was a bloody civil war there before the act of emancipation was passed; in the second place enfranchisement produced the most blessed effects; in the third place, no difficulties whatever arose, until Bonaparte made his atrocious attempt *to restore slavery* in the island.

Colonel Malenfant, a slave proprietor, resident in St Domingo at the time, thus describes the effect of sudden enfranchisement, in his Historical and Political Memoir of the Colonies:

"After this public act of emancipation, the negroes remained quiet both in the south and in the west, and they continued to work upon all the plantations. There were estates which had neither owners nor managers resident upon them, yet upon these estates, though abandoned, the negroes continued their labors where there were any, even inferior agents, to guide them; and on those estates where no white men were left to direct them, they betook themselves to the planting of provisions; but upon all the plantations where the whites resided, the blacks continued to labor as quietly as before." Colonel Malenfant says, that when many of his neighbors, proprietors or managers, were in prison, the negroes of their plantations came to him to beg him to direct them in their work.

He adds, "If you will take care not to talk to them of the restoration of slavery, but to talk to them of freedom, you may with this word chain them down to their labor. How did Toussaint succeed?— How did I succeed before this time in the plain of the Culde-Sac on the plantation Gouraud, during more than eight months after liberty had been granted to the slaves? Let those who knew me at that time, let the blacks themselves, be asked: they will all reply that not a single negro upon that plantation, consisting of more than four hundred and fifty laborers, refused to work: and yet this plantation was thought to be under the worst discipline and the slaves the most idle of any in the plain. I inspired the same activity into three other plantations of which I had the management. If all the negroes had come from Africa within six months, if they had the love of independence that the Indians have, I should own that force must be employed; but ninetynine out of a hundred of the blacks are aware that without labor they cannot procure the things that are necessary for them; that there is no other method of satisfying their wants and their tastes. They know that they must work, they wish to do so, and they will do so."

Such was the conduct of the negroes for the first nine months after their liberation, or up to the middle of 1794. In the latter part of 1796, Malenfant says, "the colony was flourishing under Toussaint, the whites lived happily and in peace upon their estates, and the negroes continued to work for them." General Lecroix who published his "Memoirs for a History of St Domingo" in 1819, says, that in 1797 the most wonderful progress had been made in agriculture. "The Colony," says he, "marched as by enchantment towards its ancient splendor: cultivation prospered; every day produced perceptible proof of its progress." General Vincent,* who was a general of brigade of artillery in St Domingo and a proprietor of estates in the island, was sent by Toussaint to Paris in 1801 to lay before the Directory the new constitution which had been agreed upon in St Domingo. He arrived in France just at the moment of the peace of Amiens, and found that Bonaparte was preparing an armament for the purpose of restoring slavery in St Domingo. He remonstrated against the expedition; he stated that it was totally unnecessary and therefore criminal, for everything was going on well in St Domingo. The proprietors were in peaceable possession of their estates; cultivation was making rapid progress; the blacks were industrious and beyond example happy. He conjured him, therefore, not to reverse this beautiful state of things; but his efforts were ineffectual, and the expedition arrived upon the shores of St Domingo. At length, however, the French were driven from the island. Till that time the planters had retained their property, and then it was, and not till then, that they lost their all. In 1804, Dessalines was proclaimed Emperor; in process of time a great part of the black troops were disbanded, and returned to cultivation again. From that time to this, there has been no want of subordination or industry among them."

*Clarkson's Thoughts, p. 2.

The following account of Hayti at a later period is quoted from Mr Harvey's sketches of that island, during the latter part of the reign of Christophé:

"Those who by their exertions and economy were enabled to procure small spots of land of their own or to hold the smaller plantations at an annual rent, were diligently engaged in cultivating coffee, sugar, and other articles, which they disposed of to the inhabitants of the adjacent towns and villages. It was an interesting sight to behold this class of the Haytians, now in possession of their freedom, coming in groups to the market nearest which they resided, bringing the produce of their industry for sale; and afterwards returning, carrying back the necessary articles of living which the disposal of their commodities had enabled them to purchase; all evidently cheerful and happy. Nor could it fail to occur to the mind that their present condition furnished the most satisfactory answer to that objection to the general emancipation of slaves, founded on their alleged unfitness to value and improve the benefits of liberty.

"Though of the same race and possessing the same general traits of character as the negroes of the other West India islands, they are already distinguished from them by habits of industry and activity, such as slaves are seldom known to exhibit. As they would not suffer, so they do not require, the attendance of one acting in the capacity of a driver with the instrument of punishment in his hand."

"In Guadaloupe, the conduct of the freed negroes was equally satisfactory. The perfect subordination which was established and the industry which prevailed there, are proved by the official Reports of the Governor of Guadaloupe, to the French government. In 1793 liberty was proclaimed universally to the slaves in that island, and during their ten years of freedom, their governors bore testimony to their regular industry and uninterrupted submission to the laws."

"During the first American war, a number of slaves ran away from their North American masters and joined the British army. When peace came, it was determined to give them their liberty, and to settle them in Nova Scotia, upon grants of land, as British subjects and as free men. Their number, comprehending men, women and children, was two thousand and upwards. Some of them worked upon little portions of land as their own; others worked as carpenters; others became fishermen; and others worked for hire in various ways. In time, having embraced Christianity, they raised places of worship of their own, and had ministers of their own from their own body. They led a harmless life, and gained the character of an industrious and honest people from their white neighbors. A few years afterwards, the land in Nova Scotia being found too poor to answer, and the climate too cold for their constitutions, a number of them, to the amount of between thirteen and fourteen hundred, volunteered to form a new colony which was then first thought of at Sierra Leone, to which place they were accordingly conveyed. Many hundreds of the negroes who had formed the West Indian black regiments were removed in 1819 to Sierra Leone, where they were set at liberty at once, and founded the villages of Waterloo, Hastings and others. Several hundred maroons (runaway slaves and their descendants,) being exiled from Jamaica, were removed in 1801 to Sierra Leone, where they were landed with no other property than the clothes which they wore and the muskets which they carried in their hands. A body of revolted slaves were banished from Barbadoes in 1816, and sent also to Sierra Leone. The rest of the population of this colony consists almost entirely of negroes who have been recaptured from slave ships, and brought to Sierra Leone in the lowest state of misery, debility and degradation: naked, diseased, destitute, wholly ignorant of the English language, in this wretched, helpless condition they have been suddenly made free, and put into possession at once of the rights and privileges of British subjects. All these instances of sudden emancipation have taken place in a colony where the disproportion between black and white is more than a hundred to one. Yet this mixed population of suddenly emancipated slaves—runaway slaves—criminal slaves—and degraded recaptured negroes, are in their free condition living in order, tranquillity and comfort, and many of them in affluence."

"During the last American war, 774 slaves escaped from their masters, and were at the termination of the war settled in Trinidad as free laborers, where they are earning their own livelihood with industry and good conduct. The following extract of a letter, received in 1829 from Trinidad by Mr Pownall, will show the usefulness and respectability of these liberated negroes. 'A field negro brings four hundred dollars, but most of the work is done by free blacks and people from the main at a much cheaper rate; and as these are generally employed by foreigners, this accounts for their succeeding better than our own countrymen, who are principally from the old islands, and are unaccustomed to any other management than that of slaves; however, they are coming into it fast. In Trinidad, there are upwards of fifteen thousand free people of color; *there is not a single pauper amongst them;* they live independently and comfortably, and nearly half of the property of the island is said to be in their hands. It is admitted that they are highly respectable in character, and are rapidly advancing in knowledge and refinement.' Mr Mitchell, a sugar planter who had resided twentyseven years in Trinidad, and who is the superintendent of the liberated negroes there, says he knows of no instance of a manumitted slave not maintaining himself. In a paper printed by the House of Commons in 1827, (No. 479,) he says of the liberated blacks under his superintendence, that each of them possessed an allotment of land which he cultivated, and on which he raised provisions and other articles for himself and his family; his wife and children aiding him in the work. A great part, however, of the time of the men (the women attending to the domestic menage) was freely given to laboring on the neighboring plantations, on which they worked not in general by the day, but by the piece. Mr Mitchell says that their work is well executed, and that they can earn as much as four shillings a day. If, then, these men who have land on which they can support themselves are yet willing to work for hire, how is it possible to doubt that in case of general emancipation, the freed negroes who would have no land of their own would gladly work for wages?"

"A few years ago, about 150 negro slaves, at different times, succeeded in making their escape from Kentucky into Canada. Captain Stuart, who lived in Upper Canada from 1817 to 1822, was generally acquainted with them, and employed several of them in various ways.—He found them as good and as trustworthy laborers, in every respect, as any emigrants from the islands, or from the United States, or as the natives of the country. In 1828, he again visited that country, and found that their numbers had increased by new refugees to about three hundred. They had purchased a tract of woodland, a few miles from Amherstburgh, and were settled on it, had formed a little village, had a minister of their own number, color, and choice, a good old man of some talent, with whom Captain Stuart was well acquainted, and though poor, were living soberly, honestly and industriously, and were peacefully and usefully getting their own living.— In consequence of the Revolution in Colombia, all the slaves who joined the Colombian armies, amounting to a considerable number, were declared free.—General Bolivar enfranchised his own slaves to the amount of between seven and eight hundred, and many proprietors followed his example. At that time Colombia was overrun by hostile armies, and the masters were often obliged to abandon their property. The black population (including Indians) amounted to nine hundred thousand persons. Of these, a large number was suddenly emancipated, and what has been the effect?—Where the opportunities of insurrection have been so frequent, and so tempting, what has been the effect? M. Ravenga declares that the effect has been a *degree of docility on the part of the blacks, and a degree of security on the part of the whites,* unknown in any preceding period of the history of Colombia."

"Dr Walsh* states that in Brazil there are six hundred thousand enfranchised persons, either Africans or of African descent, who were either slaves themselves or are the descendants of slaves. He says they are, generally speaking, 'well conducted and industrious persons, who compose indiscriminately different orders of the community. There are among them merchants, farmers, doctors, lawyers, priests and officers of different ranks. Every considerable town in the interior has regiments composed of them.' The benefits arising from them, he adds, have disposed the whites to think of making free the whole negro population."

"Mr Koster, an Englishman living in Brazil, confirms Mr Walsh's statement.† 'There are black regiments,' he observes, 'composed entirely and exclusively of black creole soldiers, commanded by black creole officers from the corporal to the colonel. I have seen the several guard houses of the town occupied by these troops. Far from any apprehension being entertained on this score, it is well known that the quietude of this country, and the feeling of safety which every one possesses, although surrounded by slaves, proceed from the contentedness of the free people.'"

"The actual condition of the hundred thousand emancipated blacks and persons of color in the British West India Colonies, certainly gives no reason to apprehend that if a general emancipation should take place, the newly freed slaves would not be able and willing to support themselves. On this point the Returns from fourteen of the Slave Colonies, laid before the House of Commons, in 1826, give satisfactory information: they include a period of five years from January 1, 1821, to December 31, 1825, and give the following account of the state of pauperism in each of these colonies.

*Walsh's Notes on Brazil, vol. ii, page 365.
†Amelioration of Slavery, published in No. 16 of the Pamphleteer.

"*Bahamas.*—The only establishment in the colony for the relief of the poor, appears to be a hospital or poor house. The number passing through the hospital annually was, on the average, fifteen free black and colored persons and thirteen whites. The number of free black and colored persons is about *double* that of the whites; so that the proportion of white to that of colored paupers in the Bahamas, is nearly two to one.

"*Barbadoes.*—The average annual number of persons supported in the nine parishes, from which returns have been sent, is nine hundred and ninetyeight, all of whom, with a single exception, are white. The probable amount of white persons in the island is fourteen thousand five hundred—of free black and colored persons, four thousand five hundred.

"*Berbice.*—The white population appears to amount to about six hundred, the free black and colored to nine hundred. In 1822, it appears that there were seventeen white and two colored paupers.

"*Demerara.*—The free black and colored population, it is supposed, are twice the number of the whites. The average number of white pensioners on the poor fund appears to be fiftyone, that of colored pensioners twentysix. In occasional relief, the white paupers receive about three times as much as the colored.

"*Dominica.*—The white population is estimated at about nine hundred; the free black and colored population was ascertained, in 1825, to amount to three thousand one hundred and twentytwo. During the five years ending in November, 1825, thirty of the former class had received relief from the poor fund, and only ten of the latter, making the proportion of more than nine white paupers to one colored one in the same number of persons.

"*Jamaica* is supposed to contain twenty thousand whites, and double that number of free black and colored persons. The returns of paupers from the parishes which have sent returns, exhibits the average number of white paupers to be two hundred and ninetyfive, of black and colored paupers, one hundred and fortyeight; the proportion of white paupers to those of the other class, according to the whole population, being as four to one.

"*Nevis.*—The white population is estimated at about eight hundred, the free black and colored at about eighteen hundred. The number of white paupers receiving relief is stated to be twentyfive; that of the other class, two; being in the proportion of twentyeight to one.

"*St Christophers.*—The average number of white paupers appears to be one hundred and fifteen; that of the other class, fourteen; although there is no doubt that the population of the latter class greatly outnumbers that of the former.

"*Tortola.*—In 1825 the free black and colored population amounted to six hundred and seven. The whites are estimated at about three hundred. The number of white paupers relieved appears to be twentynine: of the other class, four: being in proportion of fourteen to one.

"In short, in a population of free black and colored persons amounting to from eighty thousand to ninety thousand, only two hundred and twentynine persons have received any relief whatever as paupers during the years 1821 to 1825; and these chiefly the concubines and children of destitute whites; while of about sixtyfive thousand whites, in the same time, sixteen hundred and seventyfive received relief. The proportion, therefore, of enfranchised persons receiving any kind of aid as paupers in the West Indies, is about one in three hundred and seventy: whereas the proportion among the whites of the West Indies is about one in forty; and in England, generally one in twelve or thirteen—in some counties, one in eight or nine.

"Can any one read these statements, made by the colonists themselves, and still think it necessary to keep the negroes in slavery, lest they should be unable to maintain themselves if free?

"In 1823, the Assembly of Grenada passed a resolution, declaring that the free colored inhabitants of these colonies, were a respectable, well behaved class of the community, were possessed of considerable property, and were entitled to have their claims viewed with favor.

"In 1824, when Jamaica had been disturbed for months by unfounded alarms relating to the slaves, a committee of the legislative assembly declared that 'the conduct of the freed people evinced not only zeal and alacrity, but a warm interest in the welfare of the colony, and every way identified them with those who are the most zealous promoters of its internal security.' The assembly confirmed this favorable report a few months ago, by passing a bill conferring on all free black and colored persons the same privileges, civil and political, with the white inhabitants.

"In the orders issued in 1829, by the British Government, in St Lucia, placing all freemen of African descent upon the footing of equal rights with their white neighbors, the loyalty and good conduct of that class are distinctly acknowledged, and they are declared 'to have shown, hitherto, readiness and zeal in coming forward for the maintenance of order.' As similar orders have been issued for Trinidad, Berbice, and the Cape of Good Hope, it may be presumed that the conduct of the free blacks and colored persons in those colonies has likewise given satisfaction to Government.

"In the South African Commercial Advertiser of 9th of February, 1831, we are happy to find recorded one more of the numerous proofs which experience affords of the safety and expediency of immediate abolition.

"*Three thousand* prize negroes have received their *freedom; four hundred in one day;* but not the least difficulty or disorder occurred;— *servants found masters—masters hired servants; all gained homes, and at night scarcely an idler was to be seen.* In the last month, one hundred and fifty were liberated under precisely similar circumstances, and with the same result. These facts are within our own observation; and to state that sudden and abrupt emancipation would create disorder and distress to those you mean to serve, is not reason; but the plea of all men who are adverse to emancipation.

"As far as it can be ascertained from the various documents which have been cited, and from others, which, from the fear of making this account too long, are not particularly referred to, it appears that in every place and time in which emancipation has been tried, *not one drop of white blood has been shed, or even endangered by it;* that it has everywhere greatly improved the condition of the blacks, and in most places has removed them from a state of degradation and suffering to one of respectability and happiness. Can it, then, be justifiable, on account of any vague fears of we know not what evils, to reject this just, salutary and hitherto uninjurious measure; and to cling to a system which we know, by certain experience, is producing crime, misery and death, during every day of its existence?"

In Mexico, September 15, 1829, the following decree was issued; "Slavery is forever abolished in the republic; and consequently all those individuals, who, until this day, looked upon themselves as slaves, are free." The prices of slaves were settled by the magistrates, and they were required to work with their master, for stipulated wages, until the debt was paid. If the slave wished to change masters he could do so, if another person would take upon himself the liability of payment, in exchange for his labor; and provided the master was secured against loss, he was obliged to consent to the transaction. Similar transfers might take place to accommodate the master, but never without the consent of the servant. The law regulated the allowance of provisions, clothing, &c., and if the negro wished for more, he might have it charged, and deducted from his wages; but lest masters should take advantage of the improvidence of their servants, it was enacted, that all charges exceeding half the earnings of any slave, or family of slaves, should be void in law. The duties of servants were defined as clearly as possible by the laws, and magistrates appointed to enforce them; but the master was entrusted with no power to punish, in any manner whatever. It was expressly required that the masters should furnish every servant with suitable means of religious and intellectual instruction.

A Vermont gentleman, who had been a slave holder in Mississippi, and afterward resident at Matamoras, in Mexico, speaks with enthusiasm of the beneficial effects of these regulations, and thinks the example highly important to the United States. He declares that the value of the plantations was soon increased by the introduction of free labor. "No one was made poor by it. It gave property to the servant, and increased the riches of the master."

The republics of Buenos Ayres, Chili, Bolivia, Peru, Colombia, Guatemala and Monte Video, likewise took steps for the abolition of slavery, soon after they themselves came into possession of freedom. In some of these states, means were taken for the instruction of young slaves, who were all enfranchised by law, on arriving at a certain age; in others, universal emancipation is to take place after a certain date, fixed by the laws. The empire of Brazil, and the United States are the only American nations, that have taken no measures to destroy this most pestilent system; and I have recently been assured by intelligent Brazilians, that public opinion in that country is now so strongly opposed to slavery, that something effectual will be done toward abolition, at the very next meeting of the Cortes. If this *should* take place, the United States will stand alone in most hideous preëminence.

When Necker wrote his famous book on French finances, he suggested a universal compact of nations to suppress the slave trade. The exertions of England alone have since nearly realized his generous plan, though avarice and cunning do still manage to elude her vigilance and power. She has obtained from Spain, Portugal, France, Holland, and Denmark, a mutual right to search all vessels suspected of being engaged in this wicked traffic.* I believe I am correct in

---

*The British government actually paid Spain 400,000 pounds, as an indemnity to those engaged in the slave trade, on condition that the traffic should be abolished by law throughout her dominions.

saying that ours is now the *only* flag, which can protect this iniquity from the just indignation of England. When a mutual right of search was proposed to us, a strong effort was made to blind the people with their own prejudices, by urging the old complaint of the impressment of seamen; and alas, when has an unsuccessful appeal been made to passion and prejudice? It is evident that nothing on earth ought to prevent coöperation in a cause like this. Besides, "It is useless for us to attempt to linger on the skirts of the age that is departing. The action of existing causes and principles is steady and progressive. It cannot be retarded, unless we would 'blow out all the moral lights around us;' and if we refuse to keep up with it, we shall be towed in the wake, whether we are willing or not."*

When I think of the colonies established along the coast of Africa—of Algiers, conquered and civilized—of the increasing wealth and intelligence of Hayti—of the powerful efforts now being made all over the world to sway public opinion in favor of universal freedom—of the certain emancipation of slaves in all British Colonies—and above all, the evident union of purpose existing between the French and English cabinets,—I can most plainly see the hand of God working for the deliverance of the negroes. We may resist the blessed influence, if we will; but we cannot conquer. Every year the plot is thickening around us, and the nations of the earth, either consciously or unconsciously, are hastening the crisis. The defenders of the slave system are situated like the man in the Iron Shroud, the walls of whose prison daily moved nearer and nearer, by means of powerful machinery, until they crushed all that remained within them.

But to return to the subject of emancipation. Nearly every one of the States north of Mason and Dixon's line once held slaves. These slaves were manumitted without bloodshed, and there was no trouble in making free colored laborers obey the laws.

I am aware that this desirable change must be attended with much more difficulty in the Southern States, simply because the evil has been suffered until it is fearfully overgrown; but it must not be forgotten that while they are using their ingenuity and strength to sustain it for the present, the mischief is increasing more and more rapidly. If this be not a good time to apply a remedy, when will be a better? They must annihilate slavery, or slavery will annihilate them.

It seems to be forgotten that emancipation from tyranny is not an

*Speech of Mr Brodnax of Virginia.

emancipation from law; the negro, after he is made free, is restrained from the commission of crimes by the same laws which restrain other citizens: if he steals, he will be imprisoned: if he commits murder, he will be hung.

It will, perhaps, be said that the free people of color in the slave portions of *this* country are peculiarly ignorant, idle, and vicious? It may be so; for our laws and our influence are peculiarly calculated to make them bad members of society. But we trust the civil power to keep in order the great mass of ignorant and vicious foreigners continually pouring into the country; and if the laws are strong enough for this, may they not be trusted to restrain the free blacks?

In those countries where the slave codes are mild, where emancipation is rendered easy, and inducements are offered to industry, insurrections are not feared, and free people of color form a valuable portion of the community. If we persist in acting in opposition to the established laws of nature and reason, how can we expect favorable results? But it is pronounced *unsafe* to change our policy. Every progressive improvement in the world has been resisted by despotism, on the ground that changes were dangerous. The Emperor of Austria thinks there is need of keeping his subjects ignorant, that good order may be preserved. But what he calls good order, is sacrificing the happiness of many to the advancement of a few; and no doubt knowledge *is* unfavorable to the continuation of such a state of things. It is precisely so with the slave holder; he insists that the welfare of millions must be subordinate to his private interest, or else all good order is destroyed.

It is much to be regretted that Washington enfranchised his slaves in the manner he did; because their poverty and indolence have furnished an ever ready argument for those who are opposed to emancipation.* To turn slaves adrift in their old age, unaccustomed to take care of themselves, without employment, and in a community

---

*With all my unbounded reverence for Washington, I have, I confess, sometimes found it hard to forgive him for not manumitting his slaves long before his death. A fact which has lately come to my knowledge, gave me great joy; for it furnishes a reason for what had appeared to me unpardonable. It appears that Washington possessed a gang of negroes in right of his wife, with which his own negroes had intermarried. By the marriage settlement, the former were limited, in default of issue of the marriage, to the representation of Mrs Washington at her death; so that *her* negroes could not be enfranchised. An unwillingness to separate parents and children, husbands and wives, induced Washington to postpone the manumission of his own slaves. This motive is briefly, and as it were accidentally, referred to in his will.

where all the prejudices were strongly arrayed against free negroes, was certainly an unhappy experiment.

But if slaves were allowed to redeem themselves progressively, by purchasing one day of the week after another, as they can in the Spanish colonies, habits of industry would be gradually formed, and enterprise would be stimulated, by their successful efforts to acquire a little property. And if they afterward worked better as free laborers than they now do as slaves, it would surely benefit their masters, as well as themselves.

That strong-hearted republican, La Fayette, when he returned to France in 1785, felt strongly urged by a sense of duty, to effect the emancipation of slaves in the Colony of Cayenne. As most of the property in the colony belonged to the crown, he was enabled to prosecute his plans with less difficulty than he could otherwise have done. Thirty thousand dollars were expended in the purchase of plantations and slaves, for the sole purpose of proving by experiment the safety and good policy of conferring freedom.* Being afraid to trust the agents generally employed in the colony, he engaged a prudent and amiable man at Paris to undertake the business. This gentleman, being fully instructed in La Fayette's plans and wishes, sailed for Cayenne. The first thing he did when he arrived, was to collect all the cartwhips, and other instruments of punishment, and have them burnt amid a general assemblage of the slaves; he then made known to them the laws and rules by which the estates would be governed. The object of all the regulations was to encourage industry by making it the means of freedom. This new kind of stimulus had a most favorable effect on the slaves, and gave promise of complete success. But the judicious agent died in consequence of the climate, and the French Revolution threw everything into a state of convulsion at home and abroad. The new republic of France bestowed unconditional emancipation upon the slaves in her colonies; and had she persevered in her promises with good faith and discretion, the horrors of St Domingo might have been spared. The emancipated negroes in Cayenne came in a body to the agents, and declared that if the plantations still belonged to General La Fayette they were ready and willing to resume their labors for the benefit of one who had treated them like men, and cheered their toil by making it a certain means of freedom.

*It is now reported that the Hon. Mr Wirt has purchased a plantation in Florida, with the same benevolent intent. Such a step is worthy of that noble minded and distinguished man. [Note omitted from 1836 edition.—Ed.]

I cannot forbear paying a tribute of respect to the venerable Moses Brown, of Providence, Rhode Island, now living in virtuous and vigorous old age. He was a slave owner in early life, and, unless I have been misinformed, a slave dealer, likewise. When his attention became roused to religious subjects, these facts troubled his conscience. He easily and promptly decided that a Christian could not consistently keep slaves; but he did not dare to trust his own nature to determine the best manner of doing justice to those he had wronged. He therefore appointed a committee, before whom he laid a statement of the expenses he had incurred for the food and clothing of his slaves, and of the number of years, during which he had had the exclusive benefit of their labors. He conceived that he had no right to charge them for their freedom, because God had given them an inalienable right to that possession, from the very hour of their birth; but he wished the committee to decide what wages he ought to pay them for the work they had done. He cordially accepted the decision of the committee, paid the negroes their dues, and left them to choose such employments as they thought best. Many of the grateful slaves preferred to remain with him as hired laborers. It is hardly necessary to add that Moses Brown is a Quaker.

It is commonly urged against emancipation that white men cannot possibly labor under the sultry climate of our most southerly States. This is a good reason for not sending the slaves out of the country, but it is no argument against making them free. No doubt we do need their labor; but we ought to pay for it. Why should their presence be any more disagreeable as hired laborers, than as slaves? In Boston, we continually meet colored people in the streets, and employ them in various ways, without being endangered, or even incommoded. There is no moral impossibility in a perfectly kind and just relation between the two races.

If white men think otherwise, let *them* remove from climates which nature has made too hot for their constitutions. Wealth or pleasure often induces men to change their abode; an emigration for the sake of humanity would be an agreeable novelty. Algernon Sidney said, "When I cannot live in my own country, but by such means as are worse than dying in it, I think God shows me that I ought to keep myself out of it."

But the slave holders try to stop all the efforts of benevolence, by vociferous complaints about infringing upon their *property;* and justice is so subordinate to self-interest, that the unrighteous claim is silently allowed, and even openly supported, by those who ought to blush for themselves, as Christians and as republicans. Let men *simplify* their arguments—let them confine themselves to one single question, "What right can a man have to compel his neighbor to toil without reward, and leave the same hopeless inheritance to his children, in order that *he* may live in luxury and indolence?" Let the doctrines of *expediency* return to the Father of Lies, who invented them, and gave them power to turn every way for evil. The Christian knows no appeal from the decisions of God, plainly uttered in his conscience.

The laws of Venice allowed *property* in human beings; and upon this ground Shylock demanded his pound of flesh, cut nearest to the heart. Those who advertise mothers to be sold separately from their children, likewise claim a right to human flesh; and they too cut it nearest to the *heart*.

The personal liberty of one man can never be the property of another. All ideas of property are founded upon the mutual agreement of the human race, and are regulated by such laws as are deemed most conducive to the general good. In slavery there is no *mutual* agreement; for in that case it would not be slavery. The negro has no voice in the matter—no alternative is presented to him—no bargain is made. The beginning of his bondage is the triumph of power over weakness; its continuation is the tyranny of knowledge over ignorance. One man may as well claim an exclusive right to the air another man breathes, as to the possession of his limbs and faculties. Personal freedom is the birthright of every human being. God himself made it the first great law of creation; and no human enactment can render it null and void. "If," says Price, "you have a right to make another man a slave, he has a right to make you a slave;" and Ramsay says, "If we have in the beginning no right to sell a man, no person has a right to buy him."

Am I reminded that the *laws* acknowledge these vested rights in human flesh? I answer, the laws themselves were made by individuals, who wished to justify the wrong and profit by it. We ought never to have recognised a claim, which cannot exist according to the laws of God; it is our duty to atone for the error; and the sooner we make a beginning, the better will it be for us all. Must our arguments be based upon justice and mercy to the slave holders *only?* Have the negroes no right to ask compensation for their years and years of unrewarded toil? It is true that they have food and clothing, of such kind, and in such quantities, as their masters think proper. But it is evident that this is not the worth of their labor; for the proprietors can give from one hundred to five and six hundred dollars for a slave, beside the expense of supporting those who are too old or too young to labor. They could not *afford* to do this, if the slave did not earn more than he receives in food and clothing. If the laws allowed the slave to redeem himself progressively, the owner would receive his money back again; and the negro's years of uncompensated toil would be more than lawful interest.

The southerners are much in the habit of saying they really wish for emancipation, if it could be effected in safety; but I search in vain for any proof that these assertions are sincere. (When I say this, I speak collectively; there are, no doubt, individual exceptions.)

Instead of profiting by the experience of other nations, the slave owners, as a body, have resolutely shut their eyes against the light, because they preferred darkness. Every change in the laws has rivetted the chain closer and closer upon their victims; every attempt to make the voice of reason and benevolence heard has been overpowered with threatening and abuse. A cautious vigilance against improvement, a keen-eyed jealousy of all freedom of opinion, has characterized their movements. There *can* be no doubt that the *majority* wish to perpetuate slavery. They support it with loud bravado, or insidious sophistry, or pretended regret; but they never abandon the point. Their great desire is to keep the public mind turned in another direction. They are well aware that the ugly edifice is built of rotten timbers, and stands on slippery sands—if the loud voice of public opinion could be made to reverberate through its dreary chambers, the unsightly frame would fall, never to rise again.

Since so many of their own citizens admit that the policy of this system is unsound, and its effects injurious, it is wonderful that they do not begin to destroy the "costly iniquity" in good earnest. But long continued habit is very powerful; and in the habit of slavery are concentrated the strongest evils of human nature—vanity, pride, love of power, licentiousness, and indolence.

There is a minority, particularly in Virginia and Kentucky, who sincerely wish a change for the better; but they are overpowered, and have not even ventured to speak, except in the great Virginia debate of 1832. In the course of that debate the spirit of slavery showed itself without disguise. The members *talked* of emancipation; but with one or two exceptions, they merely wanted to emancipate or rather to send away, the *surplus* population, which they could neither keep nor sell, and which might prove dangerous. They wished to get rid of the consequences of the evil, but were determined to keep the evil itself. Some members from Western Virginia, who spoke in a better spirit, and founded their arguments on the broad principles of justice, not on the mere convenience of a certain class, were repelled with angry excitement. The eastern districts threatened to separate from the western, if the latter persisted in expressing opinions opposed to the continuance of slavery. From what I have uniformly heard of the comparative prosperity of Eastern and Western Virginia, I should think this was very much like the town's poor threatening to separate from the town.

The mere circumstance of daring to debate on the subject was loudly reprimanded; and there was a good deal of indignation expressed that "reckless editors, and imprudent correspondents, had presumed so far as to allude to it in the columns of a newspaper." Discussion in the Legislature was strongly deprecated until a plan had been formed; yet they must have known that no plan could be formed, in a republican government, without previous discussion. The proposal contained within itself that self-perpetuating power, for which the schemes of slave owners are so remarkable.

Mr Gholson sarcastically rebuked the restless spirit of improvement, by saying "he really had been under the *impression* that he *owned* his slaves. He had lately purchased four women and ten children, in whom he thought he had obtained a great bargain; for he supposed they were his own property, *as were his brood mares.*" To which Mr Roane replied, "I own a considerable number of slaves, and am perfectly sure they are mine; and I am sorry to add that I have occasionally, though not often, been compelled to make *them* feel the *impression* of that ownership. I would not touch a hair on the head of the gentleman's slave, any sooner than I would a hair in the *mane of his horse.*"

Mr R. likewise remarked, "I think slavery as much a correlative of liberty as cold is of heat. History, experience, observation and reason, have taught me that the torch of liberty has ever burned brighter when surrounded by the dark and filthy, yet *nutritious* atmosphere of slavery! I do not believe in the fanfaronade that all men are by nature equal. But these abstract speculations have nothing to do with the question, which I am willing to view as one of cold, sheer state policy, in which the safety, prosperity, and happiness of the *whites alone* are concerned."

Would Mr Roane carry out his logic into all its details? Would he cherish intemperance, that sobriety might shine the brighter? Would he encourage theft, in order to throw additional lustre upon honesty? Yet there seems to be precisely the same relation between these things that there is between slavery and freedom. Such sentiments sound oddly enough in the mouth of a republican of the nineteenth century!

When Mr Wirt, before the Supreme Federal Court, said that slavery was contrary to the laws of nature and of nations, and that the law of South Carolina concerning seizing colored seamen, was unconstitutional, the Governor directed several reproofs at him. In 1825, Mr King laid on the table of the United States Senate a resolution to appropriate the proceeds of the public lands to the emancipation of slaves, and the removal of free negroes, provided the same could be done under and agreeable to, the laws of the respective States. He said he did not wish it to be debated, but considered at some future time. Yet kindly and cautiously as this movement was made, the whole South resented it, and Governor Troup called to the Legislature and people of Georgia, to "stand to their arms." In 1827 the people of Baltimore presented a memorial to Congress, praying that slaves born in the District of Columbia after a given time, specified by law, might become free on arriving at a certain age. A famous member from South Carolina called this an "impertinent interference, and a violation of the principles of *liberty!*" and the petition was not even *committed.* Another Southern gentleman in Congress objected to the Panama mission because Bolivar had proclaimed liberty to the slaves.

Mr Hayne, in his reply to Mr Webster, says: "There is a spirit, which, like the father of evil, is constantly walking to and fro about the earth, seeking whom it may devour; it is the spirit of *false philanthropy.* When this is infused into the bosom of a statesman (if one so possessed can be called a statesman) it converts him at once into a visionary enthusiast. Then he indulges in golden dreams of national greatness and prosperity. He discovers that 'liberty is power,' and not content with vast schemes of improvement at home, which it would bankrupt the treasury of the world to execute, he flies to foreign lands to fulfil 'obligations to the human race, by inculcating the principles of civil and religious liberty,' &c. This spirit has long been busy with the slaves of the South; and it is even now displaying itself in vain efforts to drive the government from its *wise* policy in relation to the Indians."

Governor Miller, of South Carolina, speaking of the tariff and "the remedy," asserted that slave labor was preferable to free, and challenged the free states to competition on fair terms. Governor Hamilton of the same State, in delivering an address on the same subject, uttered a eulogy upon slavery; concluding as usual that nothing but the tariff—nothing but the rapacity of Northerners, could have nullified such great blessings of Providence, as the cheap labor and fertile soil of Carolina. Mr Calhoun, in his late speech in the Senate, alludes in a tone of strong disapprobation, and almost of reprimand, to the remarkable debate in the Virginia Legislature; the occurrence of which offence he charges to the opinions and policy of the north.

If these things evince any real desire to do away the evil, I cannot discover it. There are many who inherit the misfortune of slavery, and would gladly renounce the miserable birthright if they could; for their sakes, I wish the majority were guided by a better spirit and a wiser policy. But this state of things cannot last. The operations of Divine Providence are hastening the crisis, and move which way we will, it must come in some form or other; if we take warning in time, it may come as a blessing. The spirit of philanthropy, which Mr Hayne calls 'false,' *is* walking to and fro in the earth; and it will not pause, or turn back, till it has fastened the golden band of love and peace around a sinful world.—The sun of knowledge and liberty is already high in the heavens—it is peeping into every dark nook and corner of the earth—and the African cannot be always excluded from its beams.

The advocates of slavery remind me of a comparison I once heard differently applied: Even thus does a dog, unwilling to follow his master's carriage, bite the wheels, in a vain effort to stop its progress.

CHAPTER IV.

INFLUENCE OF SLAVERY ON THE POLITICS OF THE UNITED STATES.

Casca. I believe these are portentous things
Unto the climate that they point upon.
Cicero. Indeed it is a strange disposed time:
But men may construe things after their fashion,
Clean from the purpose of the things themselves.
—JULIUS CÆSAR.

WHEN slave representation was admitted into the Constitution of the United States, a wedge was introduced, which has ever since effectually sundered the sympathies and interests of different portions of the country. By this step, the slave States acquired an undue advantage, which they have maintained with anxious jealousy, and in which the free States have never perfectly acquiesced. The latter would probably never have made the concession, so contrary to their principles, and the express provisions of their State constitutions, if powerful motives had not been offered by the South. These consisted, first, in taking upon themselves a proportion of *direct taxes,* increased in the same ratio as their representation was increased by the concession to their slaves.

Second.—In conceding to the small States an entire equality in the Senate. This was not indeed proposed as an item of the adjustment, but it operated as such; for the small States, with the exception of Georgia, (which in fact expected to become one of the largest,) lay in the North, and were either free, or likely soon to become so.

During most of the contest, Massachusetts, then one of the large States, voted with Virginia and Pennsylvania for unequal representation in the Senate; but on the final question she was divided, and gave no vote. There was probably an increasing tendency to view this part of the compromise not merely as a concession of the large to the small States, but also of the largely slave-holding, to the free, or slightly slave-holding States. The two questions of slave representation with a proportional increase of direct taxes, and of perfect equality in the Senate, were always connected together; and a large committee of compromise, consisting of one member from each State, expressly recommended that both provisions should be adopted, but neither of them without the other.

Such were the equivalents, directly or indirectly offered, by which the free States were induced to consent to slave representation. It was not without very considerable struggles that they overcame their repugnance to admitting such a principle in the construction of a republican government. Mr Gerry, of Massachusetts, *at first* exclaimed against it with evident horror, but *at last,* he was chairman of the committee of compromise. Even the slave States themselves, seem to have been a little embarrassed with the discordant element. A curious proof of this is given in the language of the Constitution. The ugly feature is covered as cautiously as the deformed visage of the Veiled Prophet. The words are as follows: "Representatives and direct taxes shall be apportioned among the States according to their respective numbers; which shall be ascertained by adding to the whole number of free persons, *including those bound to servitude for a term of years, and excluding Indians not taxed, three fifths of all other persons.*" In this most elaborate sentence, a foreigner would discern no slavery. None but those who already knew the venomous serpent, would be able to discover its sting.

Governor Wright, of Maryland, a contemporary of all these transactions, and a slave holder, after delivering a eulogy upon the kindness of masters* expressed himself as follows: "The Constitution guaranties to us the services of these persons. It does not say *slaves;* for the feelings of the framers of that glorious instrument would not suffer them to use *that* word, on account of its anti-congeniality—its incongeniality to the idea of a constitution for freemen. It says, '*persons held to service, or labor.*'"—*Gov. Wright's Speech in Congress, March,* 1822.

This high praise bestowed on the *form* of our constitution, reminds me of an anecdote. A clergyman in a neighboring State, being

*It was stated, at the time, that this person frequently steamed his negroes, in order to reduce their size to an equal weight for riding race horses. This practice is understood to be common at the South.

obliged to be absent from his parish, procured a young man to supply his place, who was very worldly in his inclinations, and very gay in his manners. When the minister returned, his people said somewhat reproachfully, "How could you provide such a man to preach for us; *you might at least have left us a hypocrite.*"

While all parties agreed to act in opposition to the *principles* of justice, they all concurred to pay homage to them by hypocrisy of *language!* Men are willing to try all means to *appear* honest, except the simple experiment of *being* so. It is true, there were individuals who distrusted this compromise at the time, if they did not wholly disapprove of it. It is said that Washington, as he was walking thoughtfully near the Schuylkill, was met by a member of the Convention, to whom, in the course of conversation, he acknowledged that he was meditating whether it would not be better to separate, without proposing a constitution to the people; for he was in great doubt whether the frame of government, which was now nearly completed, would be better for them, than to trust to the course of events, and await future emergencies.

This anecdote was derived from an authentic source, and I have no doubt of its truth; neither is there any doubt that Washington had in his mind this great compromise, the pivot on which the system of government was to turn.

If avarice was induced to shake hands with injustice, from the expectation of increased direct taxation upon the South, she gained little by the bargain. With the exception of two brief periods, during the French war, and the last war with England, the revenue of the United States has been raised by *duties on imports.*—The heavy debts and expenditures of the several States, which they had been accustomed to provide for by direct taxes, and which they probably expected to see provided for by the same means in time to come, have been all paid by duties on imports. The greatest proportion of these duties are, of course, paid by the free States; for here, the poorest laborer daily consumes several articles of foreign production, of which from one eighth to one half the price is a tax paid to government. The clothing of the slave population increases the revenue very little, and their food almost none at all.

Wherever free labor and slave labor exist under the same government, there must be a perpetual clashing of interests. The legislation required for one, is, in its spirit and maxims, diametrically opposed to that required for the other. Hence Mr Madison predicted, in the

convention, which formed our Federal Constitution, that the con-
tests would be between the great geographical sections; that such had
been the division, even during the war and the confederacy.

In the same convention, Charles Pinckney, a man of great sagacity,
spoke of the equal representation of large and small States as a matter
of slight consequence; no difficulties would ever arise on that point,
he said; the question would always be between the slave-holding and
non-slave-holding interests.

If the pressure of common danger, and the sense of individual
weakness, during our contest for independence, could not bring the
States to mutual confidence, nothing ever can do it, except a change
of character.—From the adoption of the constitution to the present
time, the breach has been gradually widening. The South has pursued a uniform and sagacious system of policy, which, in all its bear-
ings, direct and indirect, has been framed for the preservation and ex-
tension of slave power. This system, has in the very nature of the two
things, constantly interfered with the interests of the free States; and
hitherto the South have always gained the victory. This has principally been accomplished by yoking all important questions together
in pairs, and strenuously resisting the passage of one, unless accompanied by the other. The South was desirous of removing the seat of
government from Philadelphia to Washington, because the latter is in
a slave territory, where republican representatives and magistrates can
bring their slaves without danger of losing them, or having them
contaminated by the principles of universal liberty: The assumption
of the State debts, likely to bring considerable money back to the
North, was *linked* with this question, and both were carried. The
admission of Maine into the Union as a free State, and of Missouri as
a slave State, were two more of these Siamese twins, not allowed to be
separated from each other. A numerous smaller progeny may be
found in the laying of imposts, and the successive adjustment of
protection to navigation, the fisheries, agriculture, and manufactures.

There would perhaps be no harm in this system of compromises,
or any objection to its continuing in infinite series, if no injustice
were done to a third party, which is never heard or noticed, except for
purposes of oppression.

I reverence the wisdom of our early legislators; but they certainly
did very wrong to admit slavery as an element into a free constitution; and to sacrifice the known and *declared* rights of a third and
weaker party, in order to cement a union between two stronger ones.

Such an arrangement ought not, and could not, come to good. It has given the slave States a controlling power which they will always keep, so long as we remain together.

President John Adams was of opinion, that this ascendency might be attributed to an early mistake, originating in what he called the "Frankford advice." When the first Congress was summoned in Philadelphia, Doctor Rush, and two or three other eminent men of Pennsylvania, met the Massachusetts delegates at Frankford, a few miles from Philadelphia, and conjured them, as they valued the success of the common cause, to let no measure of importance *appear* to originate with the North, to yield precedence in all things to Virginia, and lead her if possible to commit herself to the Revolution. Above all, they begged that not a word might be said about "independence;" for that a strong prejudice already existed against the delegates from New England, on account of a supposed design to throw off their allegiance to the mother country. "The Frankford advice" was followed. The delegates from Virginia took the lead on all occasions.

His son, John Q. Adams, finds a more substantial reason. In his speech on the Tariff, February 4, 1833, he said: "Not three days since, Mr Clayton of Georgia, called that species of population (viz. slaves) the machinery of the South. Now that machinery had twenty odd representatives* in that hall,—not elected by the machinery, but by those who owned it. And if he should go back to the history of this government from its foundation, it would be easy to prove that its decisions had been effected, in general, by less majorities than that. Nay, he might go farther, and insist that that very representation had ever been, in fact, *the ruling power of this government.*"

"The history of the Union has afforded a continual proof that this representation of property, which they enjoy, as well in the election of President and Vice President of the United States, as upon the floor of the House of Representatives, has secured to the slave-holding States the entire control of the national policy, and, almost without exception, the possession of the highest executive office of the Union. Always united in the purpose of regulating the affairs of the whole Union by the standard of the slave-holding interest, their disproportionate numbers in the electoral colleges have enabled them, in ten out of twelve quadrennial elections, to confer the Chief Magistracy

*There are now twentyfive *odd* representatives—that is, representatives of slaves.

upon one of their own citizens.—Their suffrages at every election, without exception, have been almost exclusively confined to a candidate of their own caste. Availing themselves of the divisions which, from the nature of man, always prevail in communities entirely free, they have sought and found auxiliaries in the other quarters of the Union, by associating the passions of parties, and the ambition of individuals, with their own purposes, to establish and maintain throughout the confederated nation the slave-holding policy. The office of Vice President, a station of high dignity, but of little other than contingent power, had been usually, by their indulgence, conceded to a citizen of the other section; but even this political courtesy was superseded at the election before the last, and both the offices of President and Vice President of the United States were, by the preponderancy of slave-holding votes, bestowed upon citizens of two adjoining and both slave-holding States. At this moment the President of the United States, the President of the Senate, the Speaker of the House of Representatives, and the Chief Justice of the United States, are all citizens of that favored portion of the united republic. The last of these offices, being, under the constitution, held by the tenure of good behaviour, has been honored and dignified by the occupation of the present incumbent upwards of thirty years. An overruling sense of the high responsibilities under which it is held, has effectually guarded him from permitting the sectional slave-holding spirit to ascend the tribunal of justice; and it is not difficult to discern, in this inflexible impartiality, the source of the obloquy which that same spirit has not been inactive in attempting to excite against the Supreme Court of the United States itself; and of the insuperable aversion of the votaries of nullification to encounter or abide by the decision of that tribunal, the true and legitimate umpire of constitutional, controverted law."*

It is worthy of observation that this slave representation is always used to protect and extend slave power; and in this way, the slaves themselves are made to vote for slavery: they are compelled to furnish halters to hang their posterity.

Machiavel says that "the whole politics of rival states consist in checking the growth of one another." It is sufficiently obvious, that the slave and free States are, and must be, rivals, owing to the inevitable contradiction of their interests. It needed no Machiavel to predict

*It seems to me that a political pamphlet was never written with more ability, clearness, and moderation, than Mr Adams's Report on the Tariff.

the result. A continual strife has been going on, more or less earnest, according to the nature of the interests it involved, and the South has always had strength and skill to carry her point. Of all our Presidents, Washington alone had power to keep the jealousies of his countrymen in check; and he used his influence nobly.—Some of his successors have cherished those jealousies, and made effective use of them.

The people of the North have to manage a rocky and reluctant soil; hence commerce and the fisheries early attracted their attention. The products of these employments were, as they should be, proportioned to the dexterity and hard labor required in their pursuit. The North grew opulent; and her politicians, who came in contact with those of the South with anything like rival pretensions, represented the commercial class, which was the nucleus of the old Federal party.

The Southerners have a genial climate and a fertile soil; but in consequence of the cumbrous machinery of slave labor, which is slow for everything, (except exhausting the soil,) they have always been less prosperous than the free States. It is said, I know not with how much truth, but it is certainly very credible, that a great proportion of their plantations are deeply mortgaged in New York and Philadelphia. It is likewise said that the expenses of the planters are generally one or two years in advance of their income. Whether these statements be true or not, the most casual observer will decide, that the free States are uniformly the most prosperous, notwithstanding the South possesses a political power, by which she manages to checkmate us at every important move. When we add this to the original jealousy spoken of by Mr Madison, it is not wonderful that Southern politicians take so little pains to conceal their strong dislike of the North.

A striking difference of manners, also caused by slavery, serves to aggravate other differences. Slave holders have the habit of command; and from the superior ease with which it sits upon them, they seem to imagine that they were "born to command," and we to obey. In time of war, they tauntingly told us that we might furnish the *men*, and they would furnish the *officers;* but in time of peace they find our list of pensioners so large, they complain that we did furnish so many men.

At the North, every body is busy in some employment, and politics, with very few exceptions, form but a brief episode in the lives of the citizens. But the Southern politicians are men of leisure. They have nothing to do but to ride round their plantations, hunt, attend the races, study politics for the next legislative or congressional campaign, and decide how to use the prodigious mechanical power, of slave representation, which a political Archimedes may effectually wield for the destruction of commerce, or anything else, involving the prosperity of the free States.*

It has been already said, that most of the wealth in New England was made by commerce; consequently the South became unfriendly to commerce. There was a class in New England, jealous, and not without reason, of their own commercial aristocracy. It was the policy of the South to foment these passions; and increase these prejudices. Thus was the old Democratic party formed; and while that party honestly supposed they were merely resisting the encroachments of a nobility at home, they were actually playing a game for one of the most aristocratic classes in the world—viz. the Southern planters. A famous slave owner and politician openly boasted, that the South could always put down the aristocracy of the North, by means of her own democracy. In this point of view, democracy becomes a machine used by one aristocratic class against another, that has less power, and is therefore less dangerous.

There are features in the organization of society, resulting from slavery, which are conducive to anything but the union of these States. A large class are without employment, are accustomed to command, and have a strong contempt for habits of industry. This class, like the nobility of feudal times, are restless, impetuous, eager for excitement, and prompt to settle all questions with the sword. Like the fierce old barons, at the head of their vassals, they are ever ready to resist and nullify the *central* power of the State, whenever it interferes with their individual interests, or even approaches the strong holds of their prejudices. All history shows, that men possessing hereditary, despotic power, cannot easily be brought to acknowledge a superior, either in the administrators of the laws, or in the law itself. It was precisely such a class of men that covered Europe with camps, for upwards of ten centuries.

A Southern governor has dignified duelling with the name of an

*The Hon. W. B. Seabrook, a southern gentleman, has lately written a pamphlet on the management of slaves in which he says: "An addition of one million dollars to the private fortune of Daniel Webster, would not give to Massachusetts more than she now possesses in the federal councils. On the other hand, every increase of slave property in South Carolina, is a fraction thrown into the scale, by which her representation in *Congress* is determined." [Note added to 1836 edition.—Ed.]

"institution"; and the planters generally, seem to regard it as among those which they have denominated their "peculiar institutions." General Wilkinson, who was the son of a slave owner, expresses in his memoirs, great abhorrence of duelling, and laments the powerful influence which his father's injunction, when a boy, had upon his after life: "James," said the old gentleman, "if you ever take an insult, I will disinherit you."

A young lawyer, who went from Massachusetts to reside at the South, has frequently declared that he could not take any stand there as a lawyer, or a gentleman, until he had fought: he was subject to continual insult and degradation, until he had evinced his readiness to kill, or be killed. It is obvious that such a state of morals elevates mere physical courage into a most undue importance. There are indeed emergencies, when all the virtues, and all the best affections of man, are intertwined with personal bravery; but this is not the kind of courage, which makes duelling in fashion. The patriot nobly sacrifices himself for the good of others; the duellist wantonly sacrifices others to himself.

Brow-beating, which is the pioneer of the pistol, characterizes, particularly of late years, the Southern legislation. By these means, they seek to overawe the Representatives from the free States, whenever any question even remotely connected with slavery is about to be discussed; and this, united with our strong reverence for the Union, has made our legislators shamefully cautious with regard to a subject, which peculiarly demands moral courage, and an abandonment of selfish considerations. If a member of Congress does stand his ground firmly, if he wants no preferment or profit, which the all powerful Southern influence can give, an effort is then made to intimidate him. The instances are numerous in which Northern men have been insulted and challenged by their Southern brethren, in consequence of the adverse influence they exerted over the measures of the *Federal* government. This turbulent evil exists only in our slave States; and the peace of the country is committed to their hands whenever *twentyfive* votes in Congress can turn the scale in favor of war.

The statesmen of the South have generally been planters. Their agricultural products must pay the merchants—foreign and domestic,—the ship owner, the manufacturer,—and all others concerned in the exchange or manipulation of them. It is universally agreed that the production of the raw materials is the least profitable employment of capital. The planters have always entertained a jealous dislike of those engaged in the more profitable business of the manufacture and exchange of products; particularly as the existence of slavery among them destroys ingenuity and enterprise, and compels them to employ the merchants, manufacturers, and sailors of the free States.* Hence there has ever been a tendency to check New England, whenever she appears to shoot up with vigorous rapidity. Whether she tried to live by *hook* or by *crook,* there is always an effort to restrain her within certain limited bounds. The embargo, passed without limitation of time, (a thing unprecedented,) was fastened upon the bosom of her commerce, until life was extinguished. The ostensible object of this measure, was to force Great Britain to terms, by distressing the West Indies for food. But while England commanded the seas, her colonies were not likely to starve; and for the sake of this doubtful experiment, a certain and incalculable injury was inflicted upon the Northern States. Seamen, and the numerous classes of mechanics connected with navigation, were thrown out of employment, as suddenly as if they had been cast on a desert island by some convulsion of nature. Thousands of families were ruined by that ill-judged measure. Has any government a right to inflict so much direct suffering on a very large portion of their own people, for the sake of an indirect and remote evil which may possibly be inflicted on an enemy?

It is true, agriculture suffered as well as commerce; but agricultural products could be converted into food and clothing; they would not decay like ships, nor would the producers be deprived of employment and sustenance, like those connected with navigation.

Whether this step was intended to paralyze the North or not, it most suddenly and decidedly produced that effect. We were told that it was done to save our commerce from falling into the hands of the English and French. But our merchants earnestly entreated not to be thus saved. At the very moment of the embargo, underwriters were ready to *insure* at the *usual* rates.

The non-intercourse was of the same general character as the embargo, but less offensive and injurious. The war crowned this course of policy; and like the other measures, was carried by slave votes. It was emphatically a Southern, not a national war. Individuals gained glory by it, and many of them nobly deserved it; but the amount of

*Virginia has great natural advantages for becoming a manufacturing country; but slavery, that does evil to all and good to none, produces a state of things which renders that impossible.

benefit which the country derived from that war might be told in much fewer words than would enumerate the mischiefs it produced.

The commercial States, particularly New England, have been frequently reproached for not being willing to go to war for the protection of their own interests; and have been charged with pusillanimity and ingratitude for not warmly seconding those who were so zealous to defend their cause. Mr Hayne, during the great debate with Mr Webster, in the Senate, made use of this customary sarcasm. It is revived whenever the sectional spirit of the South, or party spirit in the North, prompts individuals to depreciate the talents and character of any eminent Northern man. The Southern States have even gone so far on this subject, as to assume the designation of "*patriot States,*" in contra-distinction to their northern neighbors—and this too, while Bunker Hill and Faneuil Hall are still standing! It certainly was a pleasant idea to exchange the appellation of *slave* States for that of *patriot* States—it removed a word which in a republic is unseemly and inconsistent.

Whatever may be thought of the justice and expediency of the last war, it was certainly undertaken against the earnest wishes of the commercial States—two thirds of the Representatives from those States voted in opposition to the measure. According to the spirit of the constitution it ought not to have passed unless there were two thirds in favor of it. Why then should the South have insisted upon conferring a boon, which was not wanted; and how happened it, that *Yankees,* with all their acknowledged shrewdness in money matters, could never to this day perceive how they were protected by it? Yet New England is reproached with cowardice and ingratitude to her Southern benefactors! If one man were to knock another down with a broad axe, in the attempt to brush a fly from his face, and then blame him for not being sufficiently thankful, it would exactly illustrate the relation between the North and the South on this subject.

If the protection of commerce had been the real object of the war, would not some preparations have been made for a navy? It was ever the policy of the slave States to destroy the navy. Vast conquests by *land* were contemplated, for the protection of Northern commerce. Whatever was intended, the work of destruction was done. The policy of the South stood for a while like a giant among ruins. New England received a blow, which crushed her energies, but could not annihilate them. Where the system of free labor prevails, and there is work of any kind to be done, there is a safety valve provided for *any* pressure. In such a community there is a vital and active principle, which cannot be long repressed. You may dam up the busy waters, but they will sweep away obstructions, or force a new channel.

Immediately after the peace, when commerce again began to try her broken wings, the South took care to keep her down, by multiplying permanent embarrassments, in the shape of duties. The *direct* tax (which would have borne equally upon them, and which in the original compact was the equivalent for slave representation), was forthwith repealed, and commerce was burdened with the payment of the national debt. The encouragement of *manufactures*, the consumption of domestic products, or *living within ourselves*, was then urged upon us. This was an ancient doctrine of the democratic party. Mr Jefferson was its strongest advocate. Did he think it likely to bear unfavorably upon "the nation of shop keepers and pedlers?"* The Northerners adopted it with sincere views to economy, and more perfect independence. The duties were so adjusted as to embarrass commerce, and to guard the interests of a few in the North, who, from patriotism, party spirit, or private interest, had established manufactures on a considerable scale. This system of protection opposed by the North, was begun in 1816 by Southern politicians, and enlarged and confirmed by them in 1824. It was carried nearly as much by Southern influence, as was the war itself; and if the votes were placed side by side, there could not be a doubt of the identity of the interests and passions, which lay concealed under both. But enterprise, that moral perpetual-motion, overcomes all obstacles. Neat and flourishing villages rose in every valley of New England. The busy hum of machinery made music with her neglected waterfalls. All her streams, like the famous Pactolus, flowed with gold. From her discouraged and embarrassed commerce arose a greater blessing, apparently indestructible. Walls of brick and granite could not easily be overturned by the Southern *lever,* and left to decay, as the ship timber had done. Thus Mordecai was again seated in the king's gate, by means of the very system intended for his ruin. As soon as this state of things became perceptible, the South commenced active hostility with manufactures. Doleful pictures of Southern desolation and decay were given, and all attributed to manufactures. The North was said to be plundering the South, while she, poor dame, was enriching

*Mr Jefferson's description of New England.

her neighbors, and growing poor upon her extensive labors. (If this statement be true, how much gratitude do we owe the *negroes;* for they do all the work that is done at the South. Their masters only serve to keep them in a condition, where they do not accomplish half as much as they otherwise would.)

New England seems to be like the poor lamb that tried to drink at the same stream with the wolf. "You make the water so muddy I can't drink," says the wolf: "I stand below you," replied the lamb, "and therefore it cannot be." "You did me an injury last year," retorted the wolf. "I was not born last year," rejoined the lamb. "Well, well," exclaimed the wolf, "then it was your father or mother. I'll eat you, at all events."

The bitter discussions in Congress have grown out of this strong dislike to the free States; and the crown of the whole policy is nullification. The single state of South Carolina has undertaken to abolish the revenues of the whole nation; and threatened the Federal Government with secession from the Union, in case the laws were enforced by any other means than through the judicial tribunals.

"It is not a little extraordinary that this new pretension of South Carolina, the State which above all others enjoys this unrequited privilege of excessive representation, released from all payment of the direct taxes, of which her proportion would be nearly double that of any non-slave-holding State, should proceed from that very complaint that she bears an unequal proportion of duties of imposts, which, by the constitution of the United States, are required to be uniform throughout the Union. Vermont, with a free population of two hundred and eighty thousand souls, has five representatives in the popular House of Congress, and seven Electors for President and Vice President. South Carolina, with a free population of less than two hundred and sixty thousand souls, sends nine members to the House of Representatives, and honors the Governor of Virginia with eleven votes for the office of President of the United States. If the rule of representation were the same for South Carolina and for Vermont, they would have the same number of Representatives in the House, and the same number of Electors for the choice of President and Vice President. She has nearly double the number of both."

What would the South have? They took the management at the very threshold of our government, and, excepting the rigidly just administration of Washington, they have kept it ever since. They claimed slave representation, and obtained it. For their convenience the revenues were raised by imposts instead of direct taxes, and thus they give little or nothing in exchange for their excessive representation. They have increased the slave States, till they have twentyfive votes in Congress—They have laid the embargo, and declared war—They have controlled the expenditures of the nation—They have acquired Louisiana and Florida for an eternal slave market, and perchance for the manufactory of more slave States—They have given five presidents out of seven to the United States—And in their attack upon manufactures, they have gained Mr Clay's *concession* bill. "But all this availeth not, so long as Mordecai the Jew sitteth in the king's gate." The free States must be kept down. But change their policy as they will, free States *cannot* be kept down. There is but one way to ruin them; and that is to make them slave States. If the South with all her power and skill cannot manage herself into prosperity, it is because the difficulty lies at her own doors, and she will not remove it. At one time her deserted villages were attributed to the undue patronage bestowed upon settlers on the public lands; at another, the tariff is the cause of her desolation. Slavery, the real root of the evil, is carefully kept out of sight, as a "delicate subject," which must not be alluded to. It is a singular fact in the present age of the world, that delicate and indelicate subjects mean precisely the same thing.

If any proof were wanted, that *slavery* is the cause of all this discord, it is furnished by Eastern and Western Virginia. They belong to the same State, and are protected by the same laws; but in the former, the slave-holding interest is very strong—while in the latter, it is scarcely anything. The result is, warfare, and continual complaints, and threats of separation. There are no such contentions between the different sections of *free* States; simply because slavery, the exciting cause of strife, does not exist among them.

The constant threat of the slave-holding States is the dissolution of the Union; and they have repeated it with all the earnestness of sincerity, though there are powerful reasons why it would not be well for them to venture upon that untried state of being. In one respect only, are these threats of any consequence—they have familiarized the public mind with the subject of separation, and diminished the reverence, with which the free States have hitherto regarded the Union. The farewell advice of Washington operated like a spell upon the hearts and consciences of his countrymen. For many, many years after his death, it would almost have been deemed blasphemy to speak of separation as a possible event. I would that it still continued so! But it is now an everyday occurrence, to hear politicians, of all parties, conjecturing what system would be pursued by different sections of the country, in case of a dissolution of the Union. This evil is likewise chargeable upon slavery. The threats of separation have *uniformly* come from the slave-holding States; and on many important measures the free States have been awed into acquiescence by their respect for the Union.

Mr Adams, in the able and manly report before alluded to, says: "It cannot be denied that in a community spreading over a large extent of territory, and politically founded upon the principles proclaimed in the declaration of independence, but differing so widely in the elements of their social condition, that the inhabitants of one half the territory are wholly free, and those of the other half divided into masters and slaves, deep if not irreconcilable collisions of interest must abound. The question whether such a community can exist under one common government, is a subject of profound, philosophical speculation in theory. Whether it can continue long to exist, is a question to be solved only by the experiment now making by the people of this Union, under that national compact, the constitution of the United States."

The admission of Missouri into the Union is another clear illustration of the slave-holding power. That contest was marked by the same violence and the same threats as have characterized nullification. On both occasions the planters were pitted against the commercial and manufacturing sections of the country. On both occasions the democracy of the North was, by one means or another, induced to throw its strength upon the Southern *lever,* to increase its already prodigious power. On both, and on all occasions, some little support has been given to Northern principles in Maryland, Virginia, and North Carolina; because in portions of those States there is a considerable commercial interest, and some encouragement of free labor. So true it is, in the minutest details, that slavery and freedom are always arrayed in opposition to each other.

At the time of the Missouri question, the pestiferous effects of slavery had become too obvious to escape the observation of the most superficial statesman. The new free States admitted into the Union enjoyed tenfold prosperity compared with the new slave States. Give a free laborer a barren rock, and he will soon cover it with vegetation; while the slave and his task-master, would change the garden of Eden to a desert.

But Missouri must be admitted as a slave State, for two strong reasons. First, that the planters might perpetuate their predominant influence by adding to the slave representation,—the power of which is always concentrated against the interests of the free States.— Second, that a new market might be opened for their surplus slaves. It is lamentable to think that two votes in favor of Missouri slavery, were given by Massachusetts men; and that those two votes would have turned the scale. The planters loudly threatened to dissolve the Union, if slavery were not extended beyond the Mississippi. If the Union cannot be preserved without crime, it is an eternal truth that nothing good can be preserved *by* crime. The immense territories of Louisiana, Arkansas, and Florida are very likely to be formed into slave States; and every new vote on this side, places the free States more and more at the mercy of the South, and gives a renewed and apparently interminable lease to the duration of slavery.

The purchase or the conquest of the Texas, is a favorite scheme with Southerners, because it would occasion such an inexhaustible demand for slaves. A gentleman in the Virginia convention thought the acquisition of the Texas so certain, that he made calculations upon the increased value of negroes. We have reason to thank God that the jealousy of the Mexican government places a barrier in that direction.

The existence of slavery among us prevents the recognition of Haytian independence. That republic is fast increasing in wealth, intelligence and refinement.—Her commerce is valuable to us and might become much more so. But our Northern representatives have never even made an effort to have her independence acknowledged, because a colored ambassador would be so disagreeable to our prejudices.

Few are aware of the extent of *sectional* dislike in this country; and I would not speak of it, if I thought it possible to add to it. The late John Taylor, a man of great natural talent, wrote a book on the agriculture of Virginia, in which he acknowledges impoverishment, but attributes it all to the mismanagement of *overseers*. In this work, Mr Taylor has embodied more of the genuine spirit, the ethics and politics, of planters, than any other man; excepting perhaps, John Randolph in his speeches. He treats merchants, capitalists, bankers, and all other people not planters, as so many robbers, who live by plundering the slave owner, apparently forgetting by what plunder they themselves live.

Mr Jefferson and other eminent men from the South, have occasionally betrayed the same strong prejudices; but they were more guarded, lest the democracy of the North should be undeceived, and their votes lost. Mr Taylor's book is in high repute in the Southern States, and its sentiments widely echoed; but it is little known here.

A year or two since, I received a letter from a publisher who largely supplies the Southern market, in which he assured me that no book from the North would sell at the South, unless the source from which it came, were carefully concealed! Yet New England has always yielded to Southern policy in preference to uniting with the Middle States, with which she has in most respects, a congeniality of interests and habits. It has been the constant policy of the slave States to prevent the free States from acting together.

Who does not see that the American people are walking over a subterranean fire, the flames of which are fed by slavery?

The South no doubt gave her influence to General Jackson, from the conviction that a slave owner would support the slave-holding interest. The Proclamation against the nullifiers, which has given the President such sudden popularity at the North, has of course offended them. No person has a right to say that Proclamation is insincere. It will be extraordinary if a slave owner does in *reality* depart from the uniform system of his brethren. In the President's last Message, it is maintained that the wealthy land holders, that is, the planters, are the *best* part of the population;—it admits that the laws for raising of revenue by imposts have been in their operation oppressive to the South;—it recommends a gradual withdrawing of protection from manufactures;—it advises that the public lands shall cease to be a source of revenue, as soon as practicable—that they be sold to settlers—and in a *convenient time* the disposal of the soil be surrendered to *the States respectively in which it lies;*—lastly, the Message tends to discourage future appropriations of public money for purposes of internal improvement.

Every one of these items is a concession to the slave-holding policy. If the public lands are taken from the nation, and given to the States in which the soil lies, who will get the largest share? That *best* part of the population called planters.

The Proclamation and the Message are very unlike each other. Perhaps South Carolina is to obtain her own will by a route more certain, though more circuitous, than open rebellion. Time will show.

CHAPTER V.

COLONIZATION SOCIETY, AND ANTI-SLAVERY SOCIETY.

It is not madness
That I have utter'd:—For love of grace,
Lay not that flattering unction to your soul,
That not your trespass but my madness speaks:
It will but *skin* and *film* the ulcerous place;
While rank corruption, mining all within,
Infects unseen. Confess yourself to Heaven;
Repent what's past; avoid what is to come;
And do not spread the compost on the weeds,
To make them ranker.
—HAMLET, *Act III. Scene 3d.*

When doctrines meet with general approbation,
It is not heresy, but reformation.
—GARRICK.

So much excitement prevails with regard to these two societies at present, that it will be difficult to present a view of them which will be perfectly satisfactory to all. I shall say what appears to me, to be candid and true, without any anxiety as to whom it may please, and whom it may displease. I need not say that I have a decided predilection, because it has been sufficiently betrayed in the preceding pages; and I allude to it for the sake of perfect sincerity, rather than from any idea that my opinion is important.

The American Colonization Society was organized a little more than sixteen years ago at the city of Washington, chosen as the most central place in the Union.—Auxiliary institutions have since been formed in almost every part of the country; and nearly all the distinguished men belong to it. The doing away of slavery in the United

States, by gradually removing all the blacks to Africa, has been generally supposed to be its object.—The project at first excited some jealousy in the Southern States; and the Society in order to allay this, were anxious to make all possible concessions to slave owners, in their Addresses, Reports, &c. In Mr Clay's speech, printed in the first Annual Report of the Society, he said, "It is far from the intention of this Society to affect, in *any manner,* the tenure by which a certain species of property is held. I am myself a slave-holder, and I consider that kind of property as inviolable as any other in the country. I would resist encroachment upon it as soon, and with as much firmness as I would upon any other property that I hold. Nor am I prepared to go as far as the gentleman, who has just spoken (Mr Mercer) in saying that I would emancipate my slaves, if the means were provided of sending them from the country."

At the same meeting Mr Randolph said, "He thought it necessary, being himself a slave-holder, to show that so far from being in the *smallest degree* connected with the abolition of slavery, the proposed Society *would prove one of the greatest securities to enable the master to keep in possession his own property."*

In Mr Clay's speech, in the second Annual Report, he declares: "It is not proposed to deliberate upon, or consider at all, any question of emancipation, or any that is *connected* with the abolition of slavery. On this condition alone gentlemen from the South and West can be expected to coöperate. On this condition only, I have myself attended."

In the seventh Annual Report it is said, "An effort for the benefit of the blacks, in which all parts of the country can unite, of course must not have the abolition of slavery for its immediate object; nor *may it aim directly at the instruction of the blacks."*

Mr Archer of Virginia, fifteenth Annual Report, says, "The object of the Society, if I understand it aright, involves no intrusion on property, *nor even upon prejudice."*

In the speech of James S. Green, Esq. he says: "This Society have ever disavowed, and they do yet disavow that their object is the emancipation of slaves. They have no *wish* if they *could* to interfere in the smallest degree with what they deem the most interesting and fearful subject, which can be pressed upon the American public. There is no people that treat their slaves with so much kindness and so little cruelty."

In almost every address delivered before the Society similar expressions occur.—On the propriety of discussing the evils of slavery, without bitterness and without fear, good men may differ in opinion; though I think the time is fast coming, when they will all agree.—But by assuming the ground implied in the above remarks, the Colonization Society have fallen into the habit of glossing over the enormities of the slave system; at least, it so appears to me. In their constitution they have pledged themselves not to speak, write, or do anything to offend the Southerners; and as there is no possible way of making the truth pleasant to those who do not love it, the Society must perforce keep the truth out of sight. In many of their publications, I have thought I discovered a lurking tendency to palliate slavery; or, at least to make the best of it. They often bring to my mind the words of Hamlet:

> "Forgive me this my virtue;
> For in the fatness of these pursy times,
> Virtue itself of vice must pardon beg;
> Yea, curb and woo, for leave to do him good."

Thus in an Address delivered March, 1833, we are told, "It ought never to be forgotten that the slave-trade between Africa and America, had its origin in a compassionate endeavor to relieve, by the substitution of negro labor, the toils endured by native Indians. It was the *simulated form of mercy* that piloted the first slave-ship across the Atlantic."

I am aware that Las Casas used this argument; but it was less unbecoming in him than it is in a philanthropist of the present day. The speaker does indeed say that "the 'infinite of agonies' and the infinite of crime, since suffered and committed, proves that mercy cannot exist in opposition to justice." I can hardly realize what sort of a conscience it must be, that needed the demonstration.

The plain truth was, the Spaniards were in a hurry for gold; they overworked the native Indians, who were inconsiderate enough to die in very inconvenient numbers; but the gold must be had, and that quickly; and so the Africans were forced to come and die in company with the Indians. And in the nineteenth century, we are told it is our duty not to forget that this was a "simulated form of mercy"! A *dis*simulated form would have been the better expression.

If we may believe slave owners, the whole system, from beginning to end, is a matter of mercy. They have described the Middle Passage, with its gags, fetters, and thumbscrews, as "the happiest period of a negro's life"; they say they do the slaves a great charity in bringing them from barbarous Africa to a civilized and Christian country; and on the plantation, under the whip of the driver, the negroes are so happy, that a West India planter publicly declared he could not look upon them, without wishing to be himself a slave.

In the speech above referred to, we are told, that as to any political interference, "the slave States are *foreign* States. We can alienate their feelings until they become foreign enemies; or, on the other hand, we can conciliate them until they become allies and auxiliaries in the sacred cause of emancipation."

But so long as the South insist that slavery is *unavoidable,* and say they will not tolerate any schemes *tending* to its abolition—and so long as the North take the *necessity* of slavery for an unalterable truth, and put down any discussions, however mild and candid, which tend to show that it *may* be done away with safety—so long as we thus strengthen each other's hands in evil, what remote hope is there of emancipation? If by political interference is meant *hostile* interference, or even a desire to promote insurrection, I should at once pronounce it to be most wicked; but if by political interference is meant the liberty to investigate this subject, as other subjects are investigated—to inquire into what has been done, and what may be done—I say it is our sacred duty to do it. To enlighten public opinion is the best way that has yet been discovered for the removal of national evils; and slavery is certainly a *national* evil.

The Southern States, according to their own evidence, are impoverished by it; a great amount of wretchedness and crime inevitably follows in its train; the prosperity of the North is continually checked by it; it promotes feelings of rivalry between the States; it separates our interests; makes our councils discordant; threatens the destruction of our government; and disgraces us in the eyes of the world. I have often heard Americans who had been abroad, declare that nothing embarrassed them so much as being questioned about our slaves; and that nothing was so mortifying as to have the pictures of runaway negroes pointed at in the newspapers of this republic. La Fayette, with all his admiration for our institutions, can never speak of the subject without regret and shame.

Now a common evil certainly implies a common right to remedy; and where is the remedy to be found, if the South in all their speeches and writings repeat that slavery *must* exist—if the Colonization Society re-echo, in all their Addresses and Reports, that there is no help for the evil, and it is very wicked to hint that there is—and if public opinion here brands every body as a fanatic and madman, who wishes to *inquire* what can be done? The supineness of New England on this subject, reminds me of the man who being asked to work at the pump, because the vessel was going down, answered, "I am only a passenger."

An error often and urgently repeated is apt to receive the sanction of truth; and so it is in this case. The public take it for granted that slavery is a "lamentable *necessity*." Nevertheless there *is* a way to effect its cure, if we all join sincerely, earnestly, and kindly in the work; but if we expend our energies in palliating the evil, or mourning over its hopelessness, or quarreling about who is the most to blame for it, the vessel,—crew, passengers, and all,—will go down together.

I object to the Colonization Society, because it tends to put public opinion asleep, on a subject where it needs to be wide awake.

The address above alluded to, does indeed inform us of one thing which we are at liberty to do: "We must *go* to the master and *adjure* him, by all the sacred rights of humanity, by all the laws of natural justice, by his dread responsibilities,—which in the economy of Providence, are always coëxtensive and commensurate with power,—to *raise the slave* out of his abyss of degradation, to give him a participation in the benefits of mortal existence, and to make him a member of the *intellectual* and moral world, from which he, and his fathers, for so many generations, have been exiled." The practical *utility* of such a plan needs no comment. Slave owners will smile when they read it.

I will for a moment glance at what many suppose is still the intention of the Colonization Society, viz. gradually to remove all the blacks in the United States. The Society has been in operation more than fifteen years, during which it has transported between two and three thousand *free* people of color. There are in the United States two million of slaves, and three hundred thousand free blacks; and their numbers are increasing at the rate of seventy thousand annually. While the Society have removed less than three thousand,—five hundred thousand have been born. While one hundred and fifty *free* blacks have been sent to Africa in a *year*, two hundred *slaves* have been born in a *day*. To keep the evil just where it is, seventy thousand a year must be transported. How many ships, and how many millions of money, would it require to do this? It would cost 3,500,000 dollars a year, to provide for the safety of our Southern brethren in this way!

To use the language of Mr Hayne, it would "bankrupt the treasury of the world" to execute the scheme. And if such a great number could be removed annually, how would the poor fellows subsist? Famines have already been produced, even by the few that have been sent. What would be the result of landing several thousand destitute beings, even on the most fertile of our own cultivated shores?

And why *should* they be removed? Labor is greatly needed, and we are glad to give good wages for it. We encourage emigration from all parts of the world; why is it not good policy, as well as good feeling, to improve the colored people, and pay them for the use of their faculties? For centuries to come, the means of sustenance in this vast country must be much greater than the population; then why should we drive away people, whose services may be most useful? If the moral cultivation of negroes received the attention it ought, thousands and thousands would at the present moment be gladly taken up in families, factories, &c. And, like other men, they ought to be allowed to fit themselves for more important usefulness, as far and as fast as they can.

There will, in all human probability, never be any decrease in the black population of the United States. Here they are, and here they must remain, in very large numbers, do what we will. We may at once agree to live together in mutual good will, and perform a mutual use to each other—or we may go on, increasing tyranny on one side, and jealousy and revenge on the other, until the fearful elements complete their work of destruction, and something better than this sinful republic rises on the ruins. Oh, how earnestly do I wish that we may choose the holier and safer path!

To transport the blacks in such annual numbers as has hitherto been done, cannot have any beneficial effect upon the present state of things. It is Dame Partington with her pail mopping up the rushing waters of the Atlantic! So far as this gradual removal has *any* effect, it tends to keep up the price of slaves in the market, and thus perpetuate the system. A writer in the Kentucky Luminary, speaking of colonization, uses the following argument: "None are obliged to follow our example; and those who do not, *will find the value of their negroes increased by the departure of ours.*"

If the value of slaves is kept up, it will be a strong temptation to smuggle in the commodity; and thus while one vessel carries them out from America, another will be bringing them in from Africa. This would be like dipping up the waters of Chesapeake Bay into barrels, conveying it across the Atlantic, and emptying it into the Mediterranean: the Chesapeake would remain as full as ever, and by the time the vessel returned, wind and waves would have brought the *same* water back again.

Slaves owners have never yet, in any part of the world, been known to favor, as a body, any scheme, which could ultimately *tend* to abolish slavery; yet in this country, they belong to the Colonization Society in large numbers, and agree to pour from their State treasuries into its funds. Individuals object to it, it is true; but the scheme is very generally favored in the slave States.

The following extract from Mr Wood's speech in the Legislature of Virginia, will show upon what ground the owners of slaves are willing to sanction any schemes of benevolence. The "Colonization Society may be a part of the grand system of the Ruler of the Universe, to provide for the transfer of negroes to their *mother* country. Their introduction into this land may have been one of the inscrutable ways of Providence to confer blessings upon that race—it may have been decreed that they shall be the means of conveying to the minds of their benighted countrymen, the blessing of religious and civil liberty. But I fear there is little ground to believe the means have yet been created to effect so glorious a result, or that the present race of slaves are to be benefited by such a removal. *I shall trust that many of them may be carried to the southwestern States as slaves.* Should this door be closed, how can Virginia get rid of so large a number as are now annually deported to the different States and Territories where slaves are wanted? Can the gentlemen show us how from *twelve thousand to twenty thousand* can be *annually* carried to Liberia?"

Yet notwithstanding such numbers of mothers and children are yearly sent from a single State, "separately or in lots," to supply the demands of the internal *slave trade*, Mr Hayne, speaking of *freeing* these people and sending them away, says: "It is wholly irreconcilable with *our* notions of humanity to *tear asunder the tender ties,* which they had formed among us, to gratify the feelings of a false philanthropy"!

As for the *removal* of blacks from this country, the real fact is this; the slave States are very desirous to get rid of their troublesome *surplus* of colored population, and they are willing that we should help to pay for the transportation. A double purpose is served by this; for the active benevolence which is eager to work in the cause, is thus turned into a harmless and convenient channel. Neither the planters

nor the Colonization Society, seem to ask what *right* we have to remove people from the places where they have been born and brought
up,—where they have a home, which, however miserable, is still their
home,—and where their relatives and acquaintances all reside. Africa
is no more their native country than England is ours,*—nay, it is less
so, because there is no community of language or habits;—besides,
we cannot say to them, as Gilpin said to his horse, " 'Twas for *your*
pleasure you came here, you shall go back for mine."

In the Virginia Debate of 1832 it was agreed that very few of the
free colored people would be *willing* to go to Africa; and this is
proved by several petitions from them, praying for leave to remain.
One of the Virginian legislators said, "either *moral* or *physical* force
must be used to compel them to go;" some of them advised immediate coercion; others recommended persuasion first, until their numbers were thinned, and coercion afterward. I believe the resolution
finally passed the House without any proviso of this sort; and I
mention it merely to show that it was generally supposed the colored
people would be unwilling to go.

The planters are resolved to drive the free blacks away; and it is
another evil of the Colonization Society that their funds and their
influence coöperate with them in this project. They do not indeed
thrust the free negroes off, at the point of the bayonet; but they make
their *laws* and *customs* so very unequal and oppressive, that the poor
fellows are surrounded by raging fires on every side, and must leap
into the Atlantic for safety. In slave ethics I suppose this is called
"*moral* force." If the slave population is left to its own natural increase, the crisis will soon come; for labor will be so very cheap that
slavery will not be for the interest of the whites. Why should we
retard this crisis?

In the next place, many of the Colonizationists, (I do not suppose
it applies to all) are averse to giving the blacks a good education; and
they are not friendly to the establishment of schools and colleges for
that purpose. Now I would ask any candid person why colored children should *not* be educated? Some say, it will raise them above their
situation; I answer, it will raise them *in* their situation—not *above* it.

*At the close of the last war, General Jackson issued a proclamation to the colored
people of the South, in which he says: "I knew that you *loved the land of your nativity,*
and that, like ourselves, you had to defend all that is dear to man. But you surpass my
hopes. I have found in you, united to those qualities, that noble enthusiasm which
impels to great deeds."

When a High School for white girls was first talked of in this city, several of the wealthy class objected to it; because, said they, "if everybody is educated, we shall have no servants." This argument is based on selfishness, and therefore cannot stand. If carried into oper-ation, the welfare of many would be sacrificed to the convenience of a few. We might as well protest against the sunlight, for the benefit of lamp-oil merchants. Of all monopolies, a monopoly of *knowledge* is the worst. Let it be as active as the ocean—as free as the wind—as universal as the sun-beams! Lord Brougham said very wisely, "If the higher classes are afraid of being left in the rear, they likewise must hasten onward."

With our firm belief in the natural inferiority of negroes, it is strange we should be so much afraid that knowledge will elevate them quite too high for our convenience. In the march of improvement, we are several centuries in advance; and if, with this obstacle at the very beginning, they can outstrip us, why then, in the name of justice, let them go ahead! Nay, give them three cheers as they pass. If any nation, or any class of men, can obtain intellectual preëminence, it is a sure sign they deserve it; and by this republican rule the condition of the world will be regulated as surely as the waters find their level.

Besides, like all selfish policy, this is not *true* policy. The more useful knowledge a person has, the better he fulfils his duties in *any* station; and there is no kind of knowledge, high or low, which may not be brought into *use*.

But it has been said, that information will make the blacks discon-tented; because, if ever so learned, they will not be allowed to sit at the white man's table, or marry the white man's daughter.

In relation to this question, I would ask, "Is there anybody so high, that they do not see others above them?" The working classes of this country have no social communication with the aristocracy. Every day of my life I see people who can dress better, and live in better houses, than I can afford. There are many individuals who would not choose to make my acquaintance, because I am not of their *caste*—but I should speak a great untruth, if I said this made me discontented. They have their path and I have mine; I am happy in my own way, and am willing they should be happy in theirs. If asked whether what little knowledge I have produces discontent, I should answer, that it made me happier, infinitely happier, than I could be without it.

Under every form of government, there will be distinct classes of society, which have only occasional and transient communication with each other; and the colored people, whether educated or not, will form one of these classes. By giving them means of information, we increase their happiness, and make them better members of society. I have often heard it said that there was a disproportionate number of crimes committed by the colored people in this State. The same thing is true of the first generation of Irish emigrants; but we universally attribute it to their ignorance, and agree that the only remedy is to give their children as good an education as possible. If the policy is wise in one instance, why would it not be so in the other?

As for the possibility of social intercourse between the different colored races, *I* have not the slightest objection to it, provided they were equally virtuous, and equally intelligent; but I do not wish to war with the prejudices of others; I am willing that all, who consult their consciences, should keep them as long as ever they can. One thing is certain, the blacks will never come into your houses, unless you *ask* them; and you need not ask them unless you choose. They are very far from being intrusive in this respect.

With regard to marrying your daughters, I believe the feeling in opposition to such unions is quite as strong among the colored class, as it is among white people.—While the prejudice exists, such instances must be exceedingly rare, because the consequence is degradation in society. Believe me, you may safely trust to anything that depends on the pride and selfishness of unregenerated human nature.

Perhaps, a hundred years hence, some negro Rothschild may come from Hayti, with his seventy *millions* of pounds, and persuade some white woman to *sacrifice* herself to him—Stranger things than this do happen every year.—But before that century has passed away, I apprehend there will be a sufficient number of well-informed and elegant colored women in the world, to meet the demands of colored patricians. Let the sons and daughters of Africa *both* be educated, and then they will be fit for each other. They will not be forced to make war upon their white neighbors for wives; nor will they, if they have intelligent women of their own, see anything so very desirable in the project. Shall we keep this class of people in everlasting degradation, for fear one of their descendants *may* marry our great-great-great-great-grandchild?

While the prejudice exists, such unions cannot take place; and when the prejudice is melted away, they will cease to be a degradation, and of course cease to be an evil.

My third and greatest objection to the Colonization Society is, that its members write and speak, both in public and private, as if the prejudice against skins darker colored than our own, was a fixed and unalterable law of our nature, which cannot possibly be changed. The very *existence* of the Society is owing to this prejudice: for if we could make all the colored people white, or if they could be viewed as impartially as if they were white, what would be left for the Colonization Society to do? Under such circumstances, they would have a fair chance to rise in their moral and intellectual character, and we should be glad to have them remain among us, to give their energies for our money, as the Irish, the Dutch, and people from all parts of the world are now doing.

I am aware that some of the Colonizationists make large professions on this subject; but nevertheless we are constantly told by this Society, that people of color must be removed, not only because they are in our way, but because they *must* always be in a state of degradation here—that they never *can* have all the rights and privileges of citizens—and all this is because the *prejudice* is so great.

"The Managers consider it clear that causes exist and are operating to prevent their (the blacks) improvement and elevation to any considerable extent as a class, in this country, which are fixed, not only beyond the control of the friends of humanity, but of any human power. *Christianity will not* do for them *here,* what it will do for them in *Africa.* This is not the fault of the colored man, nor Christianity; but *an ordination of Providence,* and no more to be changed than the laws of Nature!"—*Last Annual Report of American Colonization Society.*

"The habits, the feelings, all the prejudices of society—prejudices which neither *refinement,* nor *argument,* nor *education,* NOR RELIGION ITSELF, can subdue—mark the people of color, whether bond or free, as the subjects of a degradation *inevitable* and *incurable.* The African *in this country* belongs *by birth* to the very lowest station in society; and from that station HE CAN NEVER RISE, be his *talents, his enterprise, his virtues what they may.* They constitute a class by themselves—a class out of which *no individual can be elevated,* and below which none can be depressed."—*African Repository,* vol. iv. pp. 118, 119.

This is shaking hands with iniquity, and covering sin with a silver veil. Our prejudice against the blacks is founded in sheer pride; and it originates in the circumstance that people of their color only, are universally allowed to be slaves. We made slavery, and slavery makes the prejudice. No Christian, who questions his own conscience, can justify himself in indulging the feeling. The removal of this prejudice is not a matter of opinion—it is a matter of *duty*. We have no right to palliate a feeling, sinful in itself, and highly injurious to a large number of our fellow beings. Let us no longer act upon the narrow-minded idea, that we must always continue to do wrong, because we have so long been in the habit of doing it. That there is no *necessity* for the prejudice is shown by facts. In England, it exists to a much less degree than it does here. If a respectable colored person enters a church there, the pews are readily opened to him; if he appears at an inn, room is made for him at the table, and no laughter, or winking, reminds him that he belongs to an outcast race. A highly respectable English gentleman residing in this country has often remarked that nothing filled him with such utter astonishment as our prejudice with regard to color.—There is now in old England a negro, with whose name, parentage, and history, I am well acquainted, who was sold into West Indian slavery by his New England master; (I know *his* name.) The unfortunate negro became free by the kindness of an individual, and has now a handsome little property, and the command of a vessel. He must take care not to come into the ports of our Southern republics!—The anecdote of Prince Saunders is well known; but it will bear repeating. He called upon an American family, then residing in London.—The fashionable breakfast hour was very late, and the family were still seated at the table. The lady fidgetted between the contending claims of politeness and prejudice. At last, when all but herself had risen from the table, she said, as if struck by a sudden thought, "Mr Saunders, I forgot to ask if you had breakfasted." "I thank you, madam," replied the colored gentleman; "but I have engaged to breakfast with the Prince Regent this morning."

Mr Wilberforce and Mr Brougham have often been seen in the streets of London, walking arm in arm with people of color. The same thing is true of Brissot, La Fayette, and several other distinguished Frenchmen.—In this city, I never but once saw such an instance: When the Philadelphia company were here last summer, I met one of the officers walking arm in arm with a fine looking black musician. The circumstance gave me a good deal of respect for the white man; for I thought he must have kind feelings and correct principles, thus fearlessly to throw off a worse than idle prejudice.

In Brazil, people of color are lawyers, clergymen, merchants and military officers; and in the Portuguese, as well as the Spanish settlements, intermarriages bring no degradation. On the shores of the Levant, some of the wealthiest merchants are black. If we were accustomed to see intelligent and polished negroes, the prejudice would soon disappear. There is certainly no law of our nature which makes a *dark color* repugnant to our feelings. We admire the swarthy beauties of Spain; and the finest forms of statuary are often preferred in bronze. If the whole world were allowed to vote on the question, there would probably be a plurality in favor of complexions decidedly dark. Everybody knows how much the Africans were amused at the sight of Mungo Park, and what an ugly misfortune they considered his pale color, prominent nose, and thin lips.

Ought we to be called Christians, if we allow a prejudice so absurd to prevent the improvement of a large portion of the human race, and interfere with what all civilized nations consider the most common rights of mankind? It cannot be that my enlightened and generous countrymen will sanction anything so narrow-minded and so selfish.

Having found much fault with the Colonization Society, it is pleasant to believe that one portion of their enterprise affords a distant prospect of doing more good than evil. They now principally seek to direct the public attention to the founding of a Colony in Africa; and this may prove beneficial in process of time. If the colored emigrants were *educated* before they went there, such a Colony would tend slowly, but certainly, to enlighten Africa, to raise the character of the negroes, to strengthen the increasing liberality of public opinion, and to check the diabolical slave trade. If the Colonizationists will work zealously and judiciously in this department, pretend to do nothing more, and let others work in another and more efficient way, they will deserve the thanks of the country; but while it is believed that they do all the good which *can* be done in this important cause, they will do more harm in America, than they can atone for in Africa.

Very different pictures are drawn of Liberia; one party represents it as thriving beyond description, the other insists that it will soon fall into ruin. It is but candid to suppose that the colony is going on as well as could possibly be expected, when we consider that the emigrants are almost universally ignorant and vicious, without property, and without habits of industry or enterprise. The colored people in our slave States must, almost without exception, be destitute of information; and in choosing negroes to send away, the masters would be very apt to select the most helpless and the most refractory. Hence the superintendents of Liberia have made reiterated complaints of being flooded with ship-loads of "vagrants." These causes are powerful drawbacks. But the negroes in Liberia have schools and churches, and they have freedom, which, wherever it exists, is always striving to work its upward way.

There is a palpable contradiction in some of the statements of this Society.

"We are told that the Colonization Society is to civilize and evangelize Africa. '*Each emigrant,*' says Henry Clay, the ablest advocate which the Society has yet found, '*is a missionary,* carrying with him *credentials* in the holy cause of civilization, religion and free institutions!!' "

"Who are these emigrants—these *missionaries?*"

"The Free people of color. 'They, and they *only,*' says the African Repository, the Society's organ, 'are QUALIFIED for colonizing Africa.' "

"What are their *qualifications?* Let the Society answer in its own words:

" 'Free blacks are a greater nuisance than even slaves themselves.' "—*African Repository,* vol. ii. p. 328.

" 'A horde of miserable people—the objects of universal suspicion—subsisting by plunder.' "—*C. F. Mercer.*

" 'An anomalous race of beings, the most debased upon earth.' "—*African Repository,* vol. vii. p. 230.

" 'Of all classes of our population the most vicious is that of the free colored.' "—*Tenth Annual Report of Colonization Society.*

An Education Society has been formed in connection with the Colonization Society, and their complaint is principally that they cannot find proper subjects for instruction. Why cannot such subjects be found? Simply because our ferocious prejudices compel the colored children to grow up in ignorance and vicious companionship, and when we seek to educate them, we find their minds closed against the genial influence of knowledge.

When I heard of the Education Society, I did hope to find one instance of *sincere, thorough, disinterested* good will for the blacks. But in the constitution of that Society, I again find the selfish principle predominant. They pledge themselves to educate no colored persons, unless they are solemnly bound to *quit the country.* The abolitionists are told that they must wait till the slaves are more fit for freedom. But if this system is pursued, when are they to be more fit for freedom? Never—never—to the end of time.

Whatever other good the Colonization Society may do, it seems to me evident that they do not produce *any* beneficial effect on the condition of colored people in America; and indirectly they produce much evil.

In a body so numerous as the Colonization Society, there is, of course, a great variety of character and opinions. I presume that many among them believe the ultimate tendency of the Society to be very different from what it really is. Some slave owners encourage it, because they think it cannot decrease slavery, and will keep back the inconvenient crisis when free labor will be cheaper than slave labor; others of the same class join it because they really want to do some act of kindness to the unfortunate African race, and all the country insists upon it that this is the only way; some politicians in the free States countenance it from similar motives, and because less cautious measures might occasion a loss of Southern votes and influence; the time-serving class—so numerous in every community,—who are always ready to flatter existing prejudices, and sail smoothly along the current of popular favor, join it, of course; but I am willing to believe that the largest proportion belong to it, because they have compassionate hearts, are fearful of injuring their Southern brethren, and really think there is no other way of doing so much good to the negroes. With this last mentioned class, I sympathize in feeling, but differ in opinion.

The Anti-Slavery Society was formed in January, 1832. Its objects are distinctly stated in the second Article of their constitution, which is as follows:

"ART. 2. The objects of the Society shall be, to endeavor, by all means sanctioned by law, humanity and religion, to effect the abolition of slavery in the United States; to improve the character and condition of the free people of color, to inform and correct public opinion in relation to their situation and rights, and obtain for them equal civil and political rights and privileges with the whites."

From this it will be seen that they think it a duty to give colored people all possible means of education, and instead of removing them away from the prejudice, to remove the prejudice away from them.

They lay it down as a maxim that immediate emancipation is the only just course, and the only safe policy. They say that slavery is a common evil, and therefore there is a common right to investigate it, and search for modes of relief. They say that New England shares, and ever has shared, in this national sin, and is therefore bound to atone for the mischief, as far as it can be done.

The strongest reason why the Anti-Slavery Society wish for the emancipation of slaves, is because they think no other course can be pursued which does not, in its very nature, involve a constant violation of the laws of God. In the next place, they believe there is no other sure way of providing for the safety of the white population in the slave States. I know that many of the planters affect to laugh at the idea of fearing their slaves; but why are their laws framed with such cautious vigilance? Why must not negroes of different plantations communicate together? Why are they not allowed to be out in the evening, or to carry even a stick to defend themselves, in case of necessity?

In the Virginia Legislature a gentleman said, "It was high time for something to be done when men did not dare to open their own doors without pistols at their belts;" and Mr Randolph has publicly declared that a planter was merely "a sentry at his own door."

Mr Roane of Virginia, asks,—"Is there an intelligent man who does not know that this *excess* of slavery is increasing, and will continue to increase in a ratio which is alarming in the extreme, and must overwhelm our descendants in ruin? Why then should we shut our eyes and turn our backs upon the evil? Will delay render it less gigantic, or give us more Herculean strength to meet and subdue it at a future time? Oh, no—delay breeds danger—procrastination is the thief of time, and the refuge of sluggards."

It is very true that insurrection is perfect madness on the part of the slaves; for they are sure to be overpowered. But such madness has happened; and innocent women and children have fallen victims to it.

A few months ago, I was conversing with a very mild and judicious member of the Anti-Slavery Society, when a gentleman originally from the South came in. As he was an old acquaintance, and had been a long time resident in New England, it was not deemed necessary, as a matter of courtesy, to drop the conversation. He soon became excited. "Whatever you may think, Mrs Child," said he, "the slaves are a great deal happier than either of us; the less people know, the more merry they are." I replied, "I heard you a short time since talking over your plans for educating your son; if knowledge brings wretchedness, why do you not keep him in happy ignorance?" "The fashion of the times requires some information," said he; "but why do you concern yourself about the negroes? Why don't you excite the horses to an insurrection, because they are obliged to work, and are whipped if they do not?" "One *horse* does not whip another," said I; "and besides, I do not wish to promote insurrections. I would, on the contrary, do all I could to prevent them." "Perhaps you do not like the comparison between slaves and horses," rejoined he; "it is true, the horses have the advantage." I made no reply; for where such ground is assumed, what *can* be said; besides, I did not then, and I do not now, believe that he expressed his real feelings. He was piqued, and spoke unadvisedly. This gentleman denied that the lot of the negroes was hard. He said they loved their masters, and their masters loved them; and in any cases of trouble or illness, a man's slaves were his best friends. I mentioned some undoubted instances of cruelty to slaves; he acknowledged that such instances might very rarely happen, but said that in general the masters were much more to be pitied than the negroes. A lady, who had been in South Carolina when an insurrection was apprehended, related several anecdotes concerning the alarm that prevailed there at the time: and added, "I often wish that none of my friends lived in a slave State." "Why should you be anxious?" rejoined the Southern gentleman; "You know that they have built a strong citadel in the heart of the city, to which all the inhabitants can repair, in case of insurrection." "So," said I, "they have built a *citadel* to protect them from their happy, contented servants—a citadel against their *best friends!*" I could not but be amused at the contradictions that occurred during this conversation.

That emancipation has in several instances been effected with safety has been already shown. But allowing that there is some danger in discontinuing slavery, is there not likewise danger in continuing it? In one case, the danger, if there were any, would soon be subdued; in the other, it is continually increasing.

The planter tells us that the slave is very happy, and bids us leave him as he is. If laughter is a sign of happiness, the Irishman, tumbling in the same mire as his pigs, is happy. The merely sensual man is no doubt merry and heedless; but who would call him happy? Is it not a fearful thing to keep immortal beings in a state like beasts? The more the senses are subjected to the moral and intellectual powers, the happier man is,—the more we learn to sacrifice the present to the future, the higher do we rise in the scale of existence. The negro may often enjoy himself, like the dog when he is not beaten, or the hog when he is not starved; but let not this be called *happiness*.

How far the slave laws are conducive to the enjoyment of those they govern, each individual can judge for himself. In the Southern papers, we continually see pictures of runaway negroes, and sometimes the advertisements identify them by scars, or by letters branded upon them. Is it natural for men to run away from comfort and happiness, especially when any one who meets them may shoot them, like a dog? and when whipping nearly unto death is authorized as the punishment? I forbear to describe how much more shocking slave whipping is than anything we are accustomed to see bestowed upon cattle.

But the advocates of slavery tell us, that on the negro's own account, it is best to keep him in slavery; that without a master to guide him and take care of him, he is a wretched being; that freedom is the greatest curse that can be bestowed upon him. Then why do their Legislatures grant it as a reward for "*meritorious services to the State*"? Why do benevolent masters bequeath the legacy of freedom, "in consideration of long and faithful service"? Why did Jefferson so earnestly, and so very humbly request the Legislature of Virginia to ratify the manumission of his five *favorite* slaves?

Notwithstanding the disadvantageous position of free negroes in a community consisting of whites and slaves, it is evident that, even upon these terms, freedom is considered a blessing.

The Anti-Slavery Society agree with Harriet Martineau in saying, "Patience with the *men,* but no patience with the *principles.* As much patience as you please in enlightening those who are unaware of the abuses, but no patience with social crimes"!

The Colonization Society are always reminding us that the *master* has rights as well as the slave: The Anti-Slavery Society urge us to remember that the *slave* has rights as well as the master. I leave it for sober sense to determine which of these claims is in the greatest danger of being forgotten.

The abolitionists think it a duty to maintain at all times, and in all places, that slavery *ought* to be abolished, and that it *can* be abolished. When error is so often repeated it becomes very important to repeat the truth; especially as good men are apt to be quiet, and selfish men are prone to be active. They propose no *plan*—they leave that to the wisdom of Legislatures.—But they never swerve from the *principle* that slavery is both wicked and unnecessary. Their object is to turn the public voice against this evil, by a plain exposition of facts.

Perhaps it may seem of little use for individuals to maintain any particular *principle,* while they do not attempt to prescribe the ways and means by which it can be carried into operation: But the voice of the public is mighty, either for good or evil; and that far sounding echo is composed of single voices.

Schiller makes his Fiesco exclaim, "Spread out the thunder into its *single* tones, and it becomes a lullaby for children; pour it forth in *one* quick peal, and the royal sound shall move the heavens!"

If the work of abolition must necessarily be slow in its progress, so much the more need of beginning soon, and working vigorously. My life upon it, a safe remedy can be found for this evil, whenever we are sincerely desirous of doing justice for its own sake.

The Anti-Slavery Society is loudly accused of being seditious, fanatical, and likely to promote insurrections. It seems to be supposed, that they wish to send fire and sword into the South, and encourage the slaves to hunt down their masters. Slave owners wish to have it viewed in this light, because they know that the subject they have chosen, will not bear discussion; and men here, who give the tone to public opinion, have loudly repeated the charge—some from good motives and some from bad. I once had a very strong prejudice against anti-slavery;—(I am ashamed to think *how* strong—for mere prejudice should never be stubborn,) but a candid examination has convinced me, that I was in an error. I made the common mistake of taking things for granted, without stopping to investigate.

This Society do not wish to see any coercive or dangerous measures pursued. They wish for universal emancipation, because they believe it is the only way to *prevent* insurrections. Almost every individual among them, is a strong friend to Peace Societies. They wish to move the public mind on this subject, in the same manner that it has been moved on other subjects: viz. by open, candid, fearless discussion. This is *all* they want to do; and this they are determined to do, because they believe it to be an important duty. For a long time past, public sympathy has been earnestly directed in the wrong way; if it could be made to turn round, a most happy change would be produced. There are many people at the South who would be glad to have a safe method of emancipation discovered; but instead of encouraging *them,* all our presses, and pulpits, and books, and conversation, have been used to strengthen the hands of those who wish to perpetuate the "costly iniquity." Divine Providence *always* opens the way for the removal of evils, individual or national, whenever man is sincerely willing to have them removed; it may be difficult to do right, but it is never impossible. Yet a majority of my countrymen do, in effect, hold the following language: "We know that this evil *cannot* be cured; and we will speak and publish our opinion on every occasion; but you must not, for your lives, dare to assert that there is a possibility of our being mistaken."

If there were any apparent wish to get rid of this sin and disgrace, I believe the members of the Anti-Slavery Society would most heartily and courageously defend slave owners from any risk they might incur in a sincere effort to do right. They would teach the negro that it is the Christian's duty meekly and patiently to *suffer* wrong; but they dare not excuse the white man for continuing to *inflict* the wrong.

They think it unfair that all arguments on this subject should be founded on the convenience and safety of the master *alone*. They wish to see the white man's claims have their due weight; but they insist that the negro's rights ought not to be thrown out of the balance.

At the time a large reward was offered for the capture of Mr Garrison, on the ground that his paper excited insurrections, it is a fact, that he had never sent or caused to be sent, a single paper south of Mason and Dixon's line. He *afterwards* sent papers to some of the leading politicians there; but they of course were not the ones to promote negro insurrections. "But," it has been answered, "the papers did find their way there." Are we then forbidden to publish our opinions upon an important subject, for fear *somebody* will send them *somewhere?* Is slavery to remain a sealed book in this most communicative of all ages, and this most inquisitive of all countries? If so, we live under an actual censorship of the press. This is like what the Irishman said of our paved cities—tying down the stones, and letting the mad dogs run loose.

If insurrections do occur, they will no doubt be attributed to the Anti-Slavery Society. But we must not forget that there were insurrections in the West Indies long before the English abolitionists began their efforts; and that masters were murdered in this country, before the Anti-Slavery Society was thought of. Neither must we forget that the increased severity of the laws is very likely to goad an oppressed people to madness. The very cruelty of the laws against resistance under any circumstances, would be thought to justify a white man in rebellion, because it gives resistance the character of self-defence. "The law," says Blackstone, "respects the passions of the human mind; and when external violence is offered to a man himself, or those to whom he bears a near connexion, makes it lawful in him to do himself that immediate justice, to which he is prompted by nature, and which no prudential motives are strong enough to restrain."

As it respects promoting insurrections by discussing this subject, it should be remembered that it is very rare for any colored person at the South to know how to read or write.

Furthermore, if there be danger in the discussion, *our* silence cannot arrest it; for the whole world is talking and writing about it;— even children's handkerchiefs seem to be regarded as sparks falling into a powder magazine. How much better it would be not to live in the midst of a powder magazine.

The English abolitionists have labored long and arduously. Every inch of the ground has been contested.—After obtaining the decision that negroes brought into England were freemen, it took them *thirtyfive years* to obtain the abolition of the slave *trade*. But their progress, though slow and difficult, has been certain. [The slaves are now emancipated in every British colony; and in effecting this happy change, not one drop of blood has been spilt, nor any property destroyed, except two sheds called *trash houses,* which were set on fire by some unknown hand.

In Antigua and Bermuda, emancipation was unqualified; that is, the slaves at once received the stimulus of wages. In those Islands, there has not been the slightest difficulty. In the other colonies, the slaves were made apprentices, and obliged to work five years more, before they received their freedom, and magistrates decided what proportion of time should be employed for their own benefit. The planters had been so violent in opposition to abolition, and had prophesied such terrible disasters resulting from it, that they felt some anxiety to have their prophecies fulfilled. The abolition act, by some oversight, did not stipulate that while the apprentices worked without wages, they should have all the privileges to which they had been accustomed as slaves. It had been a universal practice for one slave to cook for all the rest, so that their food was ready the moment they left the field; and the aged female slaves tended the little children, while their mothers were at work. The planters changed this. Every slave was obliged to go to his cabin, whether distant or near, and cook his own dinner; and the time thus lost must be made up to the masters from the hours set apart for the benefit of the apprentices. The aged slaves were likewise sent into the field to work, while mothers were obliged to toil with infants strapped at their backs.

Under these circumstances, the apprentices very naturally refused to work. They said, "We are worse off than when we were slaves; for they have taken away privileges to which we were accustomed in bondage, without paying us the wages of freemen." Still under all these provocations, they offered merely *passive* resistance. The worst enemies of the cause have not been able to discover that a single life has been lost in the West Indies, or a single plantation destroyed in consequence of emancipation! It is a lamentable proof of the corrupt state of the American press, on the subject of slavery, that the irritating conduct of the West Indian planters has been passed over in total silence, while every effort has been made to represent the *passive* resistance of the apprentices as some great "raw-head and bloody-bones story."

While the good work was in progress in England, it was for a long time called by every odious name.]* It was even urged that the abolition of the slave *trade* would encourage the massacre of white men. Clarkson, who seems to have been the meekest and most patient of men, was stigmatized as an insurrectionist.—It was said he wanted to bring all the horrors of the French Revolution into England, merely because he wanted to abolish the slave *trade.*—It was said Liverpool and Bristol would sink, never to rise again, if that traffic were destroyed.

The insurrection at Barbadoes, in 1816, was ascribed to the influence of missionaries infected with the wicked philanthropy of the age; but it was discovered that there was no missionary on the island at the time of that event, nor for a long time previous to it. The insurrection at Demerara, several years after, was publicly and angrily ascribed to the Methodist missionaries; they were taken up and imprisoned; and it was lucky for these innocent men, that, out of their twelve hundred black converts, only *two* had joined the rebellion.

Ridicule and reproach has been abundantly heaped upon the laborers in this righteous cause. Power, wealth, talent, pride, and sophistry, are all in arms against them; but God and truth is on their side.

---

*Bracketed passage substituted in 1836 edition for the following passage in the 1833 edition:

"They are now on the very eve of entire, unqualified emancipation in all their colonies. I take very little interest in politics, unless they bear upon the subject of slavery;—and then I throw my whole soul into them. Hence the permanence of Lord Grey's ministry has become an object of intense interest. But all England is acting as one man on this subject, and she *must* prevail.

"The good work has indeed been called by every odious epithet."—Ed.

The cause of anti-slavery is rapidly gaining ground. Wise heads as well as warm hearts, are joining in its support. In a few years I believe the opinion of New England will be unanimous in its favor. Maine, which enjoys the enviable distinction of never having had a slave upon her soil, has formed an Anti-Slavery Society composed of her best and most distinguished men. Those who are determined to be on the popular side, should be cautious how they move just now: It is a trying time for such characters, when public opinion is on the verge of a great change.

Men who *think* upon the subject, are fast coming to the conclusion that slavery can never be much ameliorated, while it is allowed to exist. What Mr Fox said of the *trade* is true of the *system*—"you may as well try to *regulate* murder." It is a disease as deadly as the cancer; and while one particle of it remains in the constitution, no cure can be effected. The relation is unnatural in itself, and therefore it reverses all the rules which are applied to other human relations. Thus a free government, which in every other point of view is a blessing, is a curse to the slave. The liberty around him is contagious, and therefore the laws must be endowed with a tenfold crushing power, or the captive will break his chains. A despotic monarch can follow the impulses of humanity without scruple. When Vidius Pollio ordered one of his slaves to be cut to pieces and thrown into his fish pond, the Emperor Augustus commanded him to emancipate immediately, not only that slave, but all his slaves. In a free State there is no such power; and there would be none needed, if the laws were equal,—but the slave owners are legislators, and *make* the laws, in which the negro has no voice—the master influences public opinion, but the slave cannot.

Miss Martineau very wisely says; "To attempt to combine freedom and slavery is to put new wine into old skins. Soon may the old skins burst! for we shall never want for better wine than they have ever held."

A work has been lately published, written by Jonathan Dymond, who was a member of the Society of Friends, in England; it is entitled "Essays on the Principles of Morality"—and most excellent Essays they are. Every sentence recognises the principle of sacrificing all selfish considerations to our inward perceptions of duty; and therefore every page shines with the mild but powerful light of true christian philosophy. I rejoice to hear that the book is likely to be re-published in this country. In his remarks on slavery the author says:

"The supporters of the *system* will hereafter be regarded with the same public feelings, as he who was an advocate of the slave *trade* now is. How is it that legislators and public men are so indifferent to their fame? Who would now be willing that biography should record of him,— *This man defended the slave trade?* The time will come when the record,— *This man opposed the abolition of slavery,* will occasion a great deduction from the public estimate of weight of character."

CHAPTER VI.

Intellect of Negroes.

We must not allow negroes to be *men,* lest we ourselves
should be suspected of not being *Christians.*
—Montesquieu.

In order to decide what is our duty concerning the Africans and their
descendants, we must first clearly make up our minds whether they
are, or are not, human beings—whether they have, or have not, the
same capacities for improvement as other men.

The intellectual inferiority of the negroes is a common, though
most absurd apology, for personal prejudice, and the oppressive inequality of the laws; for this reason, I shall take some pains to prove
that the present degraded condition of that unfortunate race is produced by artificial causes, not by the laws of nature.

In the first place, naturalists are universally agreed concerning "the
identity of the *human* type;" by which they mean that all living
creatures, that can, by any process, be enabled to perceive moral and
intellectual truths, are characterized *by similar peculiarities of organization.* They may differ from each other widely, but they still belong
to the same class. An eagle and a wren are very unlike each other; but
no one would hesitate to pronounce that they were both birds: so it is
with the almost endless varieties of the monkey tribe. We all know
that beasts, however sagacious, are incapable of abstract thought, or
moral perception. The most wonderful elephant in the world could
not command an army, or govern a state. An ourang-outang may eat,
and drink, and dress, and move like a man; but he could never write
an ode, or learn to relinquish his own good for the good of his species.
The *human* conformation, however it may be altered by the operation of physical or moral causes, differs from that of all other beings,
and on this ground, the negro's claim to be ranked as a *man,* is universally allowed by the learned.

The condition of this people in ancient times is very far from indicating intellectual or moral inferiority.—Ethiopia held a conspicuous place among the nations.—Her princes were wealthy and powerful, and her people distinguished for integrity and wisdom. Even the proud Grecians evinced respect for Ethiopia, almost amounting to reverence, and derived thence the sublimest portions of their mythology. The popular belief that all the gods made an annual visit to the Ethiopians, shows the high estimation in which they were held; for we are not told that such an honor was bestowed on any other nation. In the first book of the Iliad, Achilles is represented as anxious to appeal at once to the highest authorities; but his mother tells him: "Jupiter set off yesterday, attended by all the gods, on a journey toward the ocean, to feast with the excellent Ethiopians, and is not expected back at Olympus till the twelfth day."

In Ethiopia, was likewise placed the table of the Sun, reported to kindle of its own accord, when exposed to the rays of that great luminary.

In Africa was the early reign of Saturn, under the appellation of Ouranus, or Heaven; there the impious Titans warred with the sky; there Jupiter was born and nursed; there was the celebrated shrine of Ammon, dedicated to Theban Jove, which the Greeks reverenced more highly than the Delphic Oracle; there was the birth-place and oracle of Minerva; and there, Atlas supported both the heavens and the earth upon his shoulders.

It will be said that fables prove nothing.—But there is probably much deeper meaning in these fables than we now understand; there was surely some reason for giving them such a "local habitation." Why did the ancients represent Minerva as born in Africa,—and why are we told that Atlas there sustained the heavens and the earth, unless they meant to imply that Africa was the centre, from which religious and scientific light had been diffused?

Some ancient writers suppose that Egypt derived all the arts and sciences from Ethiopia; while others believe precisely the reverse. Diodorus supported the first opinion,—and asserts that the Ethiopian vulgar spoke the same language as the learned of Egypt.

It is well known that Egypt was the great school of knowledge in the ancient world. It was the birth-place of Astronomy; and we still mark the constellations as they were arranged by Egyptian shepherds. The wisest of the Grecian philosophers, among whom were Solon, Pythagoras and Plato, went there for instruction, as our young men now go to England and Germany. The Eleusinian mysteries were introduced from Egypt; and the important secret which they taught, is supposed to have been the existence of one, invisible God. A large portion of Grecian mythology was thence derived; but in passing from one country to the other, the form of these poetical fables was often preserved, while the original meaning was lost.

Herodotus, the earliest of the Greek historians, informs us that the Egyptians were negroes. This fact has been much doubted, and often contradicted. But Herodotus certainly had the best means of knowing the truth on this subject; for he travelled in Egypt, and obtained his knowledge of the country by personal observation. He declares that the Colchians must be a colony of Egyptians, because, "like them, they have a black skin and frizzled hair."

The statues of the Sphinx have the usual characteristics of the negro race. This opinion is confirmed by Blumenbach, the celebrated German naturalist, and by Volney, who carefully examined the architecture of Egypt.

Concerning the sublimity of the architecture in this ancient negro kingdom, some idea may be conceived from the description of Thebes given by Denon, who accompanied the French army into Egypt: "This city, renowned for numerous kings, who through their wisdom have been elevated to the rank of gods; for laws, which have been revered without being known; for sciences, which have been confided to proud and mysterious inscriptions; for wise and earliest monuments of the arts, which time has respected;—this sanctuary, abandoned, isolated through barbarism, and surrendered to the desert from which it was won; this city, shrouded in the veil of mystery by which even colossi are magnified; this remote city, which imagination has only caught a glimpse of through the darkness of time—was still so gigantic an apparition, that, at the sight of its scattered ruins, the army halted of its own accord, and the soldiers with one spontaneous movement, clapped their hands."

The Honorable Alexander Everett, in his work on America, says: "While Greece and Rome were yet barbarous, we find the light of learning and improvement emanating from the continent of Africa, (supposed to be so degraded and accursed,) out of the midst of this very woolly-haired, flat-nosed, thick-lipped, coal-black race, which some persons are tempted to station at a pretty low intermediate point between men and monkeys. It is to Egypt, if to any nation, that we must look as the real *antiqua mater* of the ancient and modern refinement of Europe. The great lawgiver of the Jews was prepared for his divine mission by a course of instruction in all the wisdom of the Egyptians."

"The great Assyrian empires of Babylon and Nineveh, hardly less illustrious than Egypt in arts and arms, were founded by Ethiopian colonies, and peopled by blacks.

"Palestine, or Canaan, before its conquest by the Jews, is represented in Scripture, as well as in other histories, as peopled by blacks; and hence it follows that Tyre and Carthage, the most industrious, wealthy, and polished states of their time, were of this color."

Another strong argument against the natural inferiority of negroes may be drawn from the present condition of Africa. Major Denham's account of the Sultan of Sackatoo proves that the brain is not necessarily rendered stupid by the color of the face: "The palace as usual in Africa, consisted of a sort of inclosed town, with an open quadrangle in front. On entering the gate, he was conducted through three huts serving as guard-houses, after which he found Sultan Bello seated on a small carpet in a sort of painted and ornamented cottage. Bello had a noble and commanding figure, with a high forehead and large black eyes. He gave the traveller a hearty welcome, and after inquiring the particulars of his journey, proceeded to serious affairs. He produced books belonging to Major Denham, which had been taken in the disastrous battle of Dirkullah; and though he expressed a feeling of dissatisfaction at the Major's presence on that occasion, readily accepted an apology, and restored the volumes. He only asked to have the subject of each explained, and to hear the sound of the language, which he declared to be beautiful. He then began to press his visiter with theological questions, and showed himself not wholly unacquainted with the controversies which have agitated the christian world; indeed, he soon went beyond the depth of his visiter, who was obliged to own he was not versant in the abstruser mysteries of divinity.

"The Sultan now opened a frequent and familiar communication with the English envoy, in which he showed himself possessed of a good deal of information. The astronomical instruments, from which, as from implements of magic, many of his attendants started with horror, were examined by the monarch with an intelligent eye. On being shown the planisphere, he proved his knowledge of the planets and many of the constellations, by repeating their Arabic names. The telescope, which presented objects inverted,—the compass, by which he could always turn to the East when praying,—and the sextant, which he called 'the looking glass of the sun,' excited peculiar interest. He inquired with evident jealousy, into some parts of English history; particularly the conquest of India and the attack upon Algiers."

The same traveller describes the capital of Loggun, beneath whose high walls the river flowed in majestic beauty. "It was a handsome city, with a street as wide as Pall Mall, bordered by large dwellings, having spacious areas in front. Manufacturing industry was honored. The cloths woven here were superior to those of Bornou, being finely dyed with indigo, and beautifully glazed.—There was even a current coin, made of iron, somewhat in the form of a horse-shoe; and rude as this was, none of their neighbors possessed anything similar. The women were handsome, intelligent and lively."

All travellers in Africa agree, that the inhabitants, particularly of the interior, have a good deal of mechanical skill. They tan and dye leather, sometimes thinning it in such a manner that it is as flexible as paper. In Houssa, leather is dressed in the same soft, rich style as in Morocco; they manufacture cordage, handsome cloths, and fine tissue. Though ignorant of the turning machine, they make good pottery ware, and some of their jars are really tasteful. They prepare indigo, and extract ore from minerals. They made agricultural tools, and work skilfully in gold, silver and steel. Dickson, who knew jew-ellers and watch-makers among them, speaks of a very ingenious wooden clock made by a negro. Hornemann says the inhabitants of Haissa give their cutting instruments a keener edge than European artists, and their files are superior to those of France or England. Golberry assures us that some of the African stuffs are extremely fine and beautiful.

Mungo Park says "The industry of the Foulahs, in pasturage and agriculture is everywhere remarkable.—Their herds and flocks are numerous, and they are opulent in a high degree. They enjoy all the necessaries of life in the greatest profusion. They display much skill in the management of their cattle, making them extremely gentle by kindness and familiarity." The same writer remarks that the negroes love instruction, and that they have advocates to defend the slaves brought before their tribunals.

Speaking of Wasiboo he says: "Cultivation is carried on here on a very extensive scale; and, as the natives themselves express it, 'hunger is never known.'"

On Mr Park's arrival at one of the Sego ferries, for the purpose of crossing the Niger to see the king, he says: "We found a great number waiting for a passage; they looked at me with silent wonder. The view of this extensive city; the numerous canoes upon the river; the crowded population, and the cultivated state of the surrounding country, formed altogether a prospect of civilization and magnificence, which I little expected to find in the bosom of Africa."

"The public discussions in Africa, called *palavers,* exhibit a fluent and natural oratory, often accompanied with much good sense and shrewdness. Above all, the passion for poetry is nearly universal. As soon as the evening breeze begins to blow, the song resounds throughout all Africa,—it cheers the despondency of the wanderer through the desert—it enlivens the social meetings—it inspires the dance,—and even the lamentations of the mourners are poured forth in measured accents.

"In these extemporary and spontaneous effusions, the speaker gives utterance to his hopes and fears, his joys and sorrows. All the sovereigns are attended by singing men and women, who like the European minstrels and troubadours celebrate interesting events in verse, which they repeat before the public. Like all, whose business it is to rehearse the virtues of monarchs, they are of course, too much given to flattery. The effusions of the African muse are inspired by nature and animated by national enthusiasm. From the few specimens given, they seem not unlikely to reward the care of a collector. How few among our peasantry could have produced the pathetic lamentation uttered in the little Bambarra cottage over the distresses of Mungo Park! These songs handed down from father to son, evidently contain all that exists among the African nations of traditional history. From the songs of the Jillimen, or minstrels, of Soolimani, Major Laing was enabled to compile the annals of that small kingdom for more than a century."*

In addition to the arguments drawn from the ancient conditions of Africa, and the present character of people in the interior of that country, there are numerous individual examples of spirit, courage, talent, and magnanimity.

History furnishes very few instances of bravery, intelligence, and perseverance, equal to the famous Zhinga, the negro queen of Angola, born in 1582. Like other despotic princes, her character is stained with numerous acts of ferocity and crime; but her great abilities cannot be for a moment doubted.

During her brother's reign, Zhinga was sent as ambassadress to

*English Family Library, No. XVI.

Loanda, to negotiate terms of peace with the Portuguese. A palace was prepared for her reception; and she was received with the honors due to her rank. On entering the audience-chamber, she perceived that a magnificent chair of state was prepared for the Portuguese Viceroy, while in front of it, a rich carpet, and velvet cushions, embroidered with gold, were arranged on the floor for her use. The haughty princess observed this in silent displeasure. She gave a signal with her eyes, and immediately one of her women knelt on the carpet, supporting her weight on her hands. Zhinga gravely seated herself upon her back, and awaited the entrance of the Viceroy. The spirit and dignity with which she fulfilled her mission excited the admiration of the whole court. When an alliance was offered, upon the condition of annual tribute to the king of Portugal, she proudly answered: "Such proposals are for a people subdued by force of arms; they are unworthy of a powerful monarch, who voluntarily seeks the friendship of the Portuguese, and who scorns to be their vassal."

She finally concluded a treaty, upon the single condition of restoring all the Portuguese prisoners. When the audience was ended, the Viceroy, as he conducted her from the room, remarked that the attendant, upon whose back she had been seated, still remained in the same posture. Zhinga replied: "It is not fit that the ambassadress of a great king should be twice served with the same seat. I have no further use for the woman."

Charmed with the politeness of the Europeans, and the evolutions of their troops, the African princess long delayed her departure. Having received instruction in the christian religion, she professed a deep conviction of its truth. Whether this was sincere, or merely assumed from political motives, is uncertain. During her visit, she received baptism, being then forty years old. She returned to Angola loaded with presents and honors.—Her brother, notwithstanding a solemn promise to preserve the treaty she had formed, soon made war upon the Portuguese. He was defeated, and soon after died of poison; some said his death was contrived by Zhinga. She ascended the throne, and having artfully obtained possession of her nephew's person, she strangled him with her own hands. Revenge, as well as ambition, impelled her to this crime; for her brother had, many years before, murdered *her* son, lest he should claim the crown.

The Portuguese increased so fast in numbers, wealth, and power, that the people of Angola became jealous of them, and earnestly desired war. Zhinga, having formed an alliance with the Dutch, and with several neighboring chiefs, began the contest with great vigor. She obtained several victories, at first, but was finally driven from her kingdom with great loss. Her conquerors offered to re-establish her on the throne, if she would consent to pay tribute. She haughtily replied, "If my cowardly *subjects* are willing to bear shameful fetters, *I* cannot endure even the thought of dependence upon any foreign power."

In order to subdue her stubborn spirit, the Portuguese placed a king of their own choosing upon the throne of Angola. This exasperated Zhinga to such a degree, that she vowed everlasting hatred against her enemies, and publicly abjured their religion. At the head of an intrepid and ferocious band, she, during eighteen years, perpetually harassed the Portuguese. She could neither be subdued by force of arms, nor appeased by presents. She demanded complete restitution of her territories, and treated every other proposal with the utmost scorn. Once, when closely besieged in an island, she asked a short time to reflect on the terms of surrender. The request being granted, she silently guided her troops through the river at midnight, and carried fire and sword into another portion of the enemy's country.

The total defeat of the Hollanders, and the death of her sister, who had been taken captive during the wars, softened her spirit. She became filled with remorse for having renounced the christian religion. She treated her prisoners more mercifully, and gave orders that the captive priests should be attended with the utmost reverence. They perceived the change, and lost no opportunity of regaining their convert. The queen was ready to comply with their wishes, but feared a revolt among her subjects and allies, who were strongly attached to the customs of their fathers. The priest, by numerous artifices, worked so powerfully upon the superstitious fears of the people, that they were prepared to hail Zhinga's return to the Catholic faith with joy.

The queen, thus reconciled to the church, signed a treaty of peace; took the Capuchins for her counsellors; dedicated her capital city to the Virgin, under the name of Saint Mary of Matamba; and erected a large church. Idolatry was forbidden, under the most rigorous penalties; and not a few fell martyrs to Zhinga's fiery zeal.

A law prohibiting polygamy excited discontent.—Zhinga, though seventyfive years old, publicly patronized marriage, by espousing one of her courtiers; and her sister was induced to give the same example.

The Portuguese again tried to make her a vassal to the crown; but the priests, notwithstanding their almost unlimited influence, could never obtain her consent to this degradation.

In 1657, one of her tributaries having violated the treaty of peace, she marched at the head of her troops, defeated the rebel, and sent his head to the Portuguese.

In 1658, she made war upon a neighboring king, who had attacked her territories; and returned in triumph, after having compelled him to submit to such conditions as she saw fit to impose. The same year, she abolished the cruel custom of immolating human victims on the tombs of princes; and founded a new city, ornamented with a beautiful church and palace.

She soon after sent an embassage to the Pope, requesting more missionaries among her people. The Pontiff's answer was publicly read in the church, where Zhinga appeared with a numerous and brilliant train. At a festival in honor of this occasion, she and the ladies of her court performed a mimic battle, in the dress and armor of Amazons. Though more than eighty years old, this remarkable woman displayed as much strength, agility, and skill, as she could have done at twentyfive. She died in 1663, aged eightytwo. Arrayed in royal robes, ornamented with precious stones, with a bow and arrow in her hand, the body was shown to her sorrowing subjects. It was then, according to her wish, clothed in the Capuchin habit, with crucifix and rosary.*

The commandant of a Portuguese fort, who expected the arrival of an African envoy, ordered splendid preparations, that he might be dazzled with the idea of European wealth. When the negro entered the richly ornamented saloon, he was not invited to sit down. Like Zhinga, he made a signal to an attendant, who knelt upon the floor, and thus furnished him a seat. The commandant asked, "Is thy king as powerful as the king of Portugal?" The colored envoy replied: "My king has a hundred servants like the king of Portugal; a thousand like thee; and but one like myself." As he said this, he indignantly left the room.

Michaud, the elder, says that in different places on the Persian Gulf, he has seen negroes as heads of great commercial houses, receiv-

*See Biographie Universelle.

ing orders and expediting vessels to various parts of India. Their intelligence in business is well known on the Levant.

The Czar Peter of Russia, during his travels became acquainted with Annibal, an African negro, who was intelligent and well educated. Peter the Great, true to his generous system of rewarding merit wherever he found it, made Annibal Lieutenant General and Director of the Russian Artillery. He was decorated with the riband of the order of St Alexander Nenski. His son, a mulatto, was Lieutenant General of Artillery, and said to be a man of talent. St Pierre and La Harpe were acquainted with him.

Job Ben Solomon, was the son of the Mohammedan king of Bunda, on the Gambia. He was taken in 1730, and sold in Maryland. By a train of singular adventures he was conveyed to England, where his intelligence and dignified manners gained him many friends; among whom was Sir Hans Sloane, for whom he translated several Arabic manuscripts. After being received with distinction at the Court of St James, the African Company became interested in his fate, and carried him back to Bunda, in the year 1734. His uncle embracing him, said, "During sixty years, you are the first slave I have ever seen return from the American isles." At his father's death, Solomon became king, and was much beloved in his states.

The son of the king of Congo, and several of the young people of rank were sent to the Portuguese universities, in the time of King Immanuel. Some of them were distinguished scholars, and several of them promoted to the priesthood.

In 1765, a negro in England was ordained by Doctor Keppell, bishop of Exeter. In Prevot's General History of Voyages, there is an account of a black bishop who studied at Rome.

Antonio Perura Rebouças, who is at the present time Deputy from Bahia, in the Cortes of Brazil, is a distinguished lawyer, and a good man. He is learned in political economy, and has written ably upon the currency of Brazil. I have heard intelligent white men from that country speak of him in terms of high respect and admiration.

Henry Diaz, who is extolled in all the histories of Brazil, was a negro and slave. He became Colonel of a regiment of foot-soldiers, of his own color; and such was his reputation for sagacity and valor, that it was considered a distinction to be under his command. In the contest between the Portuguese and Hollanders, in 1637, Henry Diaz fought bravely against the latter. He compelled them to capitulate at Arecise, and to surrender Fernanbon. In a battle, struggling against the superiority of numbers, and perceiving that some of his soldiers began to give way, he rushed into the midst of them, exclaiming, "Are these the brave companions of Henry Diaz!" His example renewed their courage, and they returned so impetuously to the charge, that the almost victorious army were compelled to retreat hastily.

Having wounded his left hand in battle, he caused it to be struck off, rather than to lose the time necessary to dress it. This regiment, composed of blacks, long existed in Brazil under the popular name of Henry Diaz.

Antony William Amo, born in Guinea was brought to Europe when very young. The Princess of Brunswick, Wolfenbuttle, defrayed the expenses of his education. He pursued his studies at Halle and at Wittenberg, and so distinguished himself by his character and abilities, that the Rector and Council of Wittenberg thought proper to give public testimony of their respect in a letter of congratulation. In this letter they remark that Terence also was an African—that many martyrs, doctors, and fathers of the church were born in the same country, where learning once flourished, and which by losing the christian faith, again fell back into barbarism. Amo delivered private lectures on philosophy, which are highly praised in the same letter. He became a doctor.

Lislet Geoffrroy, a mulatto, was an officer of Artillery and guardian of the Depôt of Maps and Plans of the Isle of France. He was a correspondent of the French Academy of Sciences, to whom he regularly transmitted meteorological observations, and sometimes hydrographical journals. His map of the Isles of France and Reunion is considered the best map of those islands that has appeared. In the archives of the Institute of Paris is an account of Lislet's voyage to the Bay of St Luce. He points out the exchangeable commodities and other resources which it presents; and urges the importance of encouraging industry by the hope of advantageous commerce, instead of exciting the natives to war in order to obtain slaves. Lislet established a scientific society at the Isle of France, to which some white men refused to belong, because its founder had a skin more deeply colored than their own.

James Derham, originally a slave at Philadelphia, was sold to a physician, who employed him in compounding drugs; he was afterward sold to a surgeon, and finally to Doctor Robert Dove, of New Orleans. In 1788, at the age of twentyone, he became the most distinguished physician in that city, and was able to talk with French, Spanish, and English in their own languages. Doctor Rush says, "I conversed with him on medicine, and found him very learned. I thought I could give him information concerning the treatment of diseases, but I learned from him more than he could expect from me."

Thomas Fuller, an African residing in Virginia, did not know how to read or write, but had great facility in arithmetical calculations. He was once asked how many seconds has an individual lived when he is seventy years, seven months, and seven days old? In a minute and a half he answered the question. One of the company took a pen, and after a long calculation, said Fuller had made the sum too large. "No," replied the negro, "the error is on your side. You did not calculate the leap-years." These facts are mentioned in a letter from Doctor Rush, published in the fifth volume of the American Museum.

In 1788, *Othello,* a negro, published at Baltimore an Essay against Slavery. Addressing white men, he says, "Is not your conduct, compared with your principles, a sacrilegious irony? When you dare to talk of civilization and the gospel, you pronounce your own anathema. In you the superiority of power produces nothing but a superiority of brutality and barbarism. Your fine political systems are sullied by the outrages committed against human nature and the divine majesty."

Olandad Equiano, better known by the name of Gustavus Vasa, was stolen in Africa, at twelve years old, together with his sister. They were torn from each other; and the brother, after a horrible passage in a slave ship, was sold at Barbadoes. Being purchased by a lieutenant, he accompanied his new master to England, Guernsey, and the siege of Louisbourg. He afterwards experienced great changes of fortune, and made voyages to various parts of Europe and America. In all his wanderings, he cherished an earnest desire for freedom. He hoped to obtain his liberty by faithfulness and zeal in his master's service; but finding avarice stronger than benevolence, he began trade with a capital of three pence, and by rigid economy was at last able to purchase—*his own body and soul*; this, however, was not effected, until he had endured much oppression and insult. He was several times shipwrecked, and finally, after thirty years of vicissitude and suffering, he settled in London and published his Memoirs. The book is said to be written with all the simplicity, and something of the roughness, of uneducated nature. He gives a *naïve* description of his terror at an earthquake, his surprise when he first saw snow, a picture, a watch, and a quadrant.

He always had an earnest desire to understand navigation, as a probable means of one day escaping from slavery. Having persuaded a sea-captain to give him lessons, he applied himself with great diligence, though obliged to contend with many obstacles, and subject to frequent interruptions. Doctor Irving, with whom he once lived as a servant, taught him to render salt water fresh by distillation. Some time after, when engaged in a northern expedition, he made good use of this knowledge, and furnished the crew with water they could drink.

His sympathies were, very naturally, given to the weak and the despised, wherever he found them. He deplores the fate of modern Greeks, nearly as much degraded by the Turks as the negroes are by their white brethren. In 1789, Vasa presented a petition to the British parliament, for the suppression of the slave trade. His son, named Sancho, was assistant librarian to Sir Joseph Banks, and Secretary to the Committee for Vaccination.

Another negro, named *Ignatius Sancho,* was born on board a Guinea ship, where his parents were both captives, destined for the South American slave market.—Change of climate killed his mother, and his father committed suicide. At two years old the orphan was carried to England, and presented to some ladies residing at Greenwich. Something in his character reminded them of Don Quixote's squire, and they added Sancho to his original name of Ignatius. The Duke of Montague saw him frequently and thought he had a mind worthy of cultivation. He often sent him books, and advised the ladies to give him a chance for education; but they had less liberal views, and often threatened to send the poor boy again into slavery. After the death of his friends, he went into the service of the Duchess of Montague, who at her death left him an annuity of thirty pounds; beside which he had saved seventy pounds out of his earnings.

Something of dissipation mixed with his love of reading, and sullied the better part of his character.—He spent his last shilling at

Drury Lane, to see Garrick, who was extremely friendly to him. At one time he thought of performing African characters on the stage, but was prevented by a bad articulation.

He afterward became very regular in his habits, and married a worthy West Indian girl. After his death, two volumes of his letters were printed, of which a second edition was soon published, with a portrait of the author, designed by Gainsborough, and engraved by Bartolozzi.

Sterne formed an acquaintance with Ignatius Sancho; and in the third volume of his letters, there is an epistle addressed to this African, in which he tells him that varieties in nature do not sunder the bands of brotherhood; and expresses his indignation that certain men wish to class their equals among the brutes, in order to treat them as such with impunity. Jefferson criticises Sancho with some severity, for yielding too much to an eccentric imagination; but he acknowledges that he has an easy style, and a happy choice of expressions.

The letters of Sancho are thought to bear some resemblance to those of Sterne, both in their beauties and defects.

Francis Williams, a negro, was born in Jamaica.—The Duke of Montaigne, governor of the island, thinking him an unusually bright boy, sent him to England to school. He afterward entered the University of Cambridge, and became quite a proficient in mathematics.—During his stay in Europe, he published a song which became quite popular, beginning, "Welcome, welcome, brother debtor." After his return to Jamaica, the Duke tried to obtain a place for him in the council of the government, but did not succeed. He then became a teacher of Latin and mathematics. He wrote a good deal of Latin verse, a species of composition of which he was very fond. This negro is described as having been pedantic and haughty; indulging a profound contempt for men of his own color. Where learning is a rare attainment among any people, or any class of people, this effect is very apt to be produced.

Phillis Wheatly, stolen from Africa when seven or eight years old, was sold to a wealthy merchant in Boston, in 1761. Being an intelligent and winning child, she gained upon the affections of her master's family, and they allowed her uncommon advantages. When she was nineteen years old, a little volume of her poems was published, and passed through several editions, both in England and the United States. Lest the authenticity of the poems should be doubted, her

master, the governor, the lieutenant governor, and fifteen other respectable persons, acquainted with her character and circumstances,
testified that they were really her own productions. Jefferson denies
that these poems have any merit; but I think he would have judged
differently, had he been perfectly unprejudiced. It would indeed be
absurd to put Phillis Wheatly in competition with Mrs Hemans,
Mary Hewitt, Mrs Sigourney, Miss Gould, and other modern writers; but her productions certainly appear very respectable in comparison with most of the poetry of that day.

Phillis Wheatly received her freedom in 1775; and two years after
married a colored man, who, like herself was considered a prodigy.
He was at first a grocer; but afterward became a lawyer, well known
by the name of Doctor Peter. He was in the habit of pleading causes
for his brethren before the tribunals of justice, and gained both
reputation and fortune by his practice. Phillis had been flattered and
indulged from her earliest childhood; and, like many literary women
in old times, she acquired something of contempt for domestic oc-
cupations. This is said to have produced unhappiness between her
and her husband. She died in 1780.

Mr Wilberforce, (on whom may the blessing of God rest forever!)
aided by several benevolent individuals, established a seminary for
colored people at Clapham, a few leagues from London. The first
scholars were twentyone young negroes, sent by the Governor of
Sierra Leone. The Abbé Grégoire says, "I visited this establishment in
1802, to examine the progress of the scholars; and I found there
existed no difference between them and European children, except
that of color. The same observation has been made, first at Paris, in
the ancient college of La Marche, where Coesnon, professor of the
University, taught a number of colored boys.—Many members of the
National Institute, who have carefully examined this college, and
watched the progress of the scholars in their particular classes, and
public exercises, will testify to the truth of my assertion."

Correa de Serra, the learned Secretary of the Academy at Portugal,
informs us that several negroes have been able lawyers, preachers, and
professors.

In the Southern States, the small black children are proverbially
brighter and more forward than white ones of the same age. Rep-
artees, by no means indicative of stupidity, have sometimes been
made by negroes. A slave was suddenly roused with the exclamation,

"Why don't you wake, when your master calls!" The negro answered, "*Sleep has no master.*"

On a public day the New England Museum, in Boston, was thronged with visiters to see the representation of the Salem murder. Some colored women being jostled back by a crowd of white people, expostulated thus: "Don't you know it is always proper to let the *mourners* walk first?" It argues some degree of philosophy to be able to indulge wit at the expense of what is, most unjustly, considered a degradation. Public prejudice shamefully fetters these people; and it has been wisely said, "If we cannot *break* our chains, the next best thing we can do, is to *play* with them."*

Among Bonaparte's officers there was a mulatto General of Division, named Alexander Dumas. In the army of the Alps, with charged bayonet, he ascended St Bernard, defended by a number of redoubts, took possession of the enemy's cannon, and turned their own ammunition against them. He likewise signalized himself in the expedition to Egypt. His troop, composed of blacks and mulattoes, were everywhere formidable. Near Lisle, Alexander Dumas, with only four men, attacked a post of fifty Austrians, killed six, and made sixteen prisoners. Napoleon called him the Horatius Cocles of the Tyrols.

On his return from Egypt, Dumas unluckily fell into the hands of the Neapolitan government, and was two years kept in irons. He died in 1807.

Between 1620 and 1630, some fugitive negroes, united with some Brazilians, formed two free states in South America, called the Great and Little Palmares; so named on account of the abundance of palm trees. The Great Palmares was nearly destroyed by the Hollanders, in 1644; but at the close of the war, the slaves in the neighborhood of Fernanbouc, resolved to form an establishment, which would secure their freedom. Like the old Romans, they obtained wives by making incursions upon their neighbors, and carrying off the women.

They formed a constitution, established tribunals of justice, and adopted a form of worship similar to Christianity. The chiefs chosen for life were elected by the people.

They fortified their principal towns, cultivated their gardens and fields, and reared domestic animals. They lived in prosperity and peace, until 1696, when the Portuguese prepared an expedition against them. The Palmarisians defended themselves with desperate

*In a beautiful little volume called Mary's Journey, by Francis Graeter.

valor, but were overcome by superior numbers. Some rushed upon death, that they might not survive their liberty; others were sold and dispersed by the conquerors. Thus ended this interesting republic. Had it continued to the present time, it might have produced a very material change in the character and condition of the colored race.

In the seventeenth century, when Jamaica was still under the dominion of the Spaniards, a party of slaves under the command of John de Bolas, regained their independence. They increased in numbers, elected the famous Cudjoe as their chief, and became very formidable.—Cudjoe established a confederation among all the Maroon tribes, and by his bravery and skilful management compelled the English to make a treaty, in which they acknowledged the freedom of the blacks, and ceded to them forever a portion of the territory of Jamaica.

The French National Assembly admitted free colored deputies from St Domingo, and promised a perfect equality of rights, without regard to complexion. But, as usual, the white colonists made every possible exertion to set aside the claims of their darker faced brethren.—It was very short-sighted policy; for the planters absolutely needed the friendship of the free mulattoes and negroes, as a defence against the slaves. Oge, one of the colored deputies, an energetic and shrewd man, was in Paris, watching political movements with intense interest,—resolved to maintain the rights of his oppressed companions, "quietly if he could—forcibly if he must." Day after day, a hearing was promised; and day after day, upon some idle pretext or other, it was deferred.—Oge became exasperated. His friends in France recommended the only medicine ever offered by the white man to the heart-sick African,—patience—patience.—But he had long observed the operation of slavery, and he knew that patience, whatever it might do for the white man, brought upon the negro nothing but contempt and accumulated wrong. Discouraged in his efforts to make head against the intrigues of the slave-holders, he could not contain his indignation: "I begin," said he to Clarkson, "not to care whether the National Assembly will hear us or not. But let it beware of the consequences. We will no longer continue to be held in a degraded light. Despatches shall go directly to St Domingo; and we will soon follow them. We can produce as good soldiers on our own estates, as those in France. Our own arms shall make us independent and respectable. If we are forced to desperate measures, it will be in vain that thousands are sent across the Atlantic to bring us back to our former state."

The French government issued orders to prevent the embarkation of negroes and mulattoes; but Oge, by the way of England, contrived to return to St Domingo.—On his arrival, he demanded the execution of decrees made in favor of his brethren, but either resisted or evaded by their white oppressors. His plea, founded in justice, and sanctioned by Divine authority, was rejected. The parties became exasperated, and an attack ensued. The Spanish government basely and wickedly delivered Oge to his enemies. He asked for a defender to plead his cause; but he asked in vain. Thirteen of his companions were condemned to the galleys; more than twenty to the gibbet; and Oge and Chavanne were tortured on the wheel.

Where rests the guilt in this case? Let those blame Oge, who can. My heart and conscience both refuse to do it.

Toussaint L'Ouverture, the celebrated black chieftain, was born a slave, in the year 1745, upon the plantation of Count de Noé. His amiable deportment as a slave, the patience, mildness, and benevolence of his disposition, and the purity of his conduct amid the general laxity of morals which prevailed in the island, gained for him many of those advantages which afterwards gave him such absolute ascendency over his insurgent brethren. His good qualities attracted the attention of M. Bayou de Libertas, the agent on the estate, who taught him reading, writing, and arithmetic,—elements of knowledge, which hardly one in ten thousand of his fellow slaves possessed. M. Bayou made him his postillion, which gave him advantages much above those of the field slaves. When the general rising of the blacks took place, in 1791, much solicitation was used to induce Toussaint to join them; but he declined, until he had procured an opportunity for the escape of M. Bayou and his family to Baltimore, shipping a considerable quantity of sugar for the supply of their immediate wants. In his subsequent prosperity, he availed himself of every occasion to give them new marks of his gratitude. Having thus provided security for his benefactor, he joined a corps of blacks, under the orders of General Biassou; but was soon raised to the principal command, Biassou being degraded on account of his cruelty and ferocity. Indeed, Toussaint was every way so much superior to the other negroes, by reason of his general intelligence and education, his prudence, activity and address, not less than his bravery, that he immediately attained a complete ascendency over all the black chieftains. In 1797, Toussaint received from the French government a commission of General-in-Chief of the armies of St Domingo, and as such

signed the convention with General Maitland for the evacuation of
the island by the British. From 1798 until 1801, the island continued
tranquil under the government of Toussaint, who adopted and enforced the most judicious measures for healing the wounds of his
country, and restoring its commercial and agricultural prosperity. His
efforts would have been attended with much success, but for the ill-
judged expedition, which Bonaparte sent against the island, under
the command of Le Clerc. This expedition, fruitless as it was in
respect of its general object, proved fatal to the negro chieftain.

Toussaint was noted for private virtues; among the rest, warm
affection for his family. Le Clerc brought out from France Toussaint's
two sons, with their preceptor, whose orders were to carry his pupils
to their father, and make use of them to work on his tenderness, and
induce him to abandon his countrymen. If he yielded, he was to be
made second in command to Le Clerc; if he refused, his children
were to be reserved as hostages of his fidelity to the French. Notwithstanding the greatness of the sacrifice demanded of him, Toussaint
remained faithful to his brethren. We pass over the details of the war,
which at length, ended in a treaty of peace concluded by Toussaint,
Dessalines and Christophe, against their better judgment, but in
consequence of the effect of Le Clerc's professions upon their simple followers, who were induced to lay down their arms. Toussaint
retired to his plantation, relying upon the solemn assurances of
Le Clerc, that his person and property should be held sacred. Notwithstanding these assurances, he was treacherously seized in the
night, hurried on board a ship of war, and conveyed to Brest. He was
conducted first to close prison in Chateaux de Joux, and from thence
to Besançon, where he was plunged into a cold, wet, subterranean
prison, which soon proved fatal to a constitution used only to the
warm skies and free air of the West Indies. He languished through the
winter of 1802–1803; and his death, which happened in April, 1803,
raised a cry of indignation against the government, which had chosen
this dastardly method of destroying one of the best and bravest of the
negro race.

Toussaint L'Ouverture is thus spoken of by Vincent, in his Reflections on the state of St Domingo: "Toussaint L'Ouverture is the most
active and indefatigable man, of whom it is possible to form an idea.
He is always present wherever difficulty or danger makes his presence
necessary. His great sobriety,—the power of living without repose,—
the facility with which he resumes the affairs of the cabinet, after the

most tiresome excursions,—of answering daily a hundred letters,—and of habitually tiring five secretaries—render him so superior to all around him, that their respect and submission almost amount to fanaticism. It is certain no man in modern times has obtained such an influence over a mass of ignorant people, as General Toussaint possesses over his brethren of St Domingo. He is endowed with a prodigious memory. He is a good father and a good husband."

Toussaint re-established religious worship in St Domingo; and on account of his zeal in this respect, a certain class of men called him, in derision, the Capuchin.

With the genius and energy of Bonaparte, General Toussaint is said to have possessed the same political duplicity, and far-sighted cunning. These are qualities which almost inevitably grew out of the peculiar circumstances in which they were placed, and the obstacles with which they were obliged to contend.

Wordsworth addressed the following sonnet to Toussaint L'Ouverture:

"Toussaint, thou most unhappy man of men!
Whether the whistling rustic tends his plough
Within thy hearing, or thou liest now
Buried in some deep dungeon's earless den;—
O, miserable chieftain! where and when
Wilt thou find patience? Yet die not; do thou
Wear rather in thy bonds a cheerful brow:
Though fallen thyself, never to rise again,
Live, and take comfort. Thou hast left behind
Powers that will work for thee; air, earth, and skies;
There's not a breathing of the common wind
That will forget thee; thou hast great allies.
Thy friends are exultations, agonies,
And love, and man's unconquerable mind."

Godwin, in his admirable Lectures on Colonial Slavery, says: "Can the West India islands, since their first discovery by Columbus, boast a single name which deserves comparison with that of Toussaint L'Ouverture?"

If we are willing to see and believe, we have full opportunity to convince ourselves that the colored population are highly susceptible of cultivation. St Domingo produces black legislators, scholars, and gentlemen.—The very negroes who had been slaves, formed a constitution that would do credit to paler-faced statesmen—Americans may well blush at its *consistent* republicanism.

The enemies of true freedom were very ready to predict that the government of Hayti could not continue for any length of time; but it has now lasted nearly thirty years, constantly increasing in respectability and wealth. The affairs of Greece have been managed with much less ability and discretion, though all the cabinets of Europe have given assistance and advice. St Domingo achieved her independence alone and unaided—nay, in the very teeth of prejudice and scorn. The Greeks had loans from England, and contributions from America, and sympathy from half the world; the decisive battle of Navarino was gained by the combined fleets of England, France and Russia. Is it asked why Hayti has not produced any examples of splendid genius? In reply let me inquire, how long did the Europeans ridicule *us* for our poverty in literature? When Raynal reproached the United States with not having produced one celebrated man, Jefferson requested him to wait until we had existed "as long as the Greeks before they had a Homer, the Romans a Virgil, and the French a Racine." Half a century elapsed before our republic produced Irving, Cooper, Sedgwick, Halleck, and Bryant. We must not forget that the cruel prejudice, under which colored people labor, makes it extremely difficult for them to gain admission to the best colleges and schools; they are obliged to contend with obstacles, which white men never encounter.

It might seem wonderful that the descendants of wise Ethiopia, and learned Egypt, are now in such a state of degradation, if history did not furnish a remarkable parallel in the condition of the modern Greeks. The land of Homer, Pericles, and Plato, is now inhabited by ignorant, brutal pirates. Freedom made the Grecians great and glorious—tyranny has made them stupid and miserable. Yet their yoke has been light, compared with African bondage. In both cases the wrongs of the oppressed have been converted into an argument against them. We first debase the nature of man by making him a slave, and then very coolly tell him that he must always remain a slave because he does not know how to use freedom. We first crush people to the earth, and then claim the right of trampling on them forever, because they are prostrate. Truly, human selfishness never invented a rule, which worked so charmingly both ways!

No one thinks of doubting the intellect of Indians; yet civilization has certainly advanced much farther in the interior of Africa, than it did among the North American tribes. The Indians have strong untutored eloquence,—so have the Africans. And where will you find an Indian chieftain, whose pride, intellect, and valor, are more than a match for Zhinga's? Both of these classes have been most shamefully wronged; but public prejudice, which bows the negro to the earth, has borne with a far less crushing power upon the energies of the red man; yet they have not produced a Shakspeare or a Newton. But I shall be asked how it is that the nations of Africa, having proceeded so far in the arts of civilization, have made a full stop, and remained century after century without any obvious improvement? I will answer this by another question: How long did the ancient Helvetians, Gauls, and Saxons remain in such a state of barbarism, that what they considered splendor and refinement, would be called poverty and rudeness, by their German, French, and English descendants?— What was it that changed the intellectual and moral character of these people, after ages of ignorance and ferocity? It was the *art of printing*. But, alas, with the introduction of printing, modern slavery was introduced! While commerce has carried books and maps to other portions of the globe, she has sent kidnappers, with guns and cutlasses into Africa. We have not preached the Gospel of peace to her princes; we have incited them to make war upon each other, to fill our markets with slaves. While knowledge, like a mighty pillar of fire, has guided the European nations still onward, and onward, a dark cloud has settled more and more gloomily over benighted Africa. The lessons of time, the experience of ages, from which we have learned so much, are entirely lost to this vast continent.

I have heard it asserted that the Indians were evidently superior to the negroes, because it was impossible to enslave *them*. Our slave laws prove that there are some exceptions to this remark; and it must be remembered that the Indians have been fairly met in battle, contending with but one nation at a time; while the whole world have combined against the Africans—sending emissaries to lurk for them in secret places, or steal them at midnight from their homes. The Indian will seek freedom in the arms of death—and so will the negro. By thousands and thousands, these poor people have died for freedom. They have stabbed themselves for freedom—jumped into the waves for freedom—starved for freedom—fought like very tigers for freedom! But they have been hung, and burned, and shot—and their tyrants have been their historians! When the Africans have writers of their own, we shall hear their efforts for liberty called by the true title of heroism in a glorious cause. We are told in the fable that a lion, looking at the picture of one of his own species, conquered and trampled on by man, calmly said, "We lions have no painters."

I shall be told that in the preceding examples I have shown only the bright side of the picture. I readily grant it; but I have deemed it important to show that the picture *has* a bright side. I am well aware that most of the negro authors are remarkable, principally because they are negroes. With considerable talent, they generally evince bad taste. I do not pretend that they are Scotts or Miltons; but I wish to prove that they are *men,* capable of producing their proportion of Scotts and Miltons, if they could be allowed to live in a state of physical and intellectual freedom. But where, at the present time, *can* they live in perfect freedom, cheered by the hopes and excited by the rewards, which stimulate white men to exertion? Every avenue to distinction is closed to them. Even where the body is suffered to be free, a hateful prejudice keeps the soul in fetters. I think every candid mind must admit that it is more wonderful they have done so much, than that they have done no more.

As a class, I am aware that the negroes, with many honorable exceptions, are ignorant, and show little disposition to be otherwise; but this ceases to be the case just in proportion as they are free. The fault is in their unnatural situation, not in themselves. Tyranny always dwarfs the intellect. Homer tells us, that when Jupiter condemns a man to slavery, he takes from him half his mind. A family of children treated with habitual violence or contempt, become stupid and sluggish, and are called fools by the very parents or guardians who have crushed their mental energies. It was remarked by M. Dupuis, the British Consul at Mogadore, that the generality of Europeans, after a long captivity and severe treatment among the Arabs, seemed at first exceedingly dull and insensible. "If they had been any considerable time in slavery," says he, "they appeared lost to reason and feeling; their spirits broken; and their faculties sunk in a species of stupor, which I am unable adequately to describe. They appeared degraded even below the negro slave. The succession of hardships, without any protecting law to which they can appeal for alleviation, or redress, seems to destroy every spring of exertion, or hope in their minds. They appear indifferent to everything around them; abject, servile, and brutish."

Lieutenant Hall, in his Travels in the United States, makes the following just remark: "Cut off hope for the future, and freedom for the present; superadd a due pressure of bodily suffering, and personal degradation; and you have a slave, who, (of whatever zone, nation or complexion,) will be what the poor African is, torpid, debased, and lowered beneath the standard of humanity."

The great Virginian, Patrick Henry, who certainly had a fair chance to observe the effects of slavery, says, "If a man be in chains, he droops and bows to the earth, because his spirits are broken; but let him twist the fetters off his legs and he will stand erect."

The following is the testimony of the Rev. R. Walsh, on the same subject; he is describing his first arrival at Rio Janeiro:

"The whole labor of bearing and moving burdens is performed by these people, and the state in which they appear is revolting to humanity. Here was a number of beings entirely naked, with the exception of a covering of dirty rags tied about their waists. Their skins, from constant exposure to the weather, had become hard, crusty, and seamed, resembling the coarse black covering of some beast, or like that of an elephant, a wrinkled hide scattered with scanty hairs. On contemplating their persons you saw them with a physical organization resembling beings of a grade below the rank of man; long projecting heels, the gastronymic muscle wanting, and no calves to their legs; their mouths and chins protruded, their noses flat, their foreheads retiring, having exactly the head and legs of the baboon tribe. Some of these beings were yoked to drays, on which they dragged heavy burdens. Some were chained by the necks and legs, and moved with loads thus encumbered. Some followed each other in ranks, with heavy weights on their heads, chattering the most inarticulate and dismal cadence as they moved along. Some were munching young sugar-canes, like beasts of burden eating green provender; and some were seen near the water, lying on the bare ground among filth and offal, coiled up like dogs, and seeming to expect or require no more comfort or accommodation, exhibiting a state and conformation so unhuman, that they not only seemed, but actually were, far below the inferior animals around them. Horses and mules were not employed in this way; they were used only for pleasure, and not labor. They were seen in the same streets, pampered, spirited, and richly caparisoned, enjoying a state far superior to the negroes, and appearing to look down on the fettered and burdened wretches they were passing, as on beings of an inferior rank in the creation. Some of the negroes actually seemed to envy the caparisons of their fellow brutes, and eyed with jealousy their glittering harness. In imitation of this finery, they were fond of thrums of many colored threads; and I saw one creature, who supported the squalid rag that wrapped his waist by a suspender of gaudy worsted, which he turned every moment to look at, on his naked shoulder. The greater number, however, were as unconscious of any covering for use or ornament, as a pig or an ass.

"The first impression of all this on my mind, was to shake the conviction I had always felt, of the wrong and hardship inflicted on our black fellow-creatures, and that they were only in that state which God and nature had assigned them; that they were the lowest grade of human existence, and the link that connected it with the brute; and that the gradation was so insensible, and their natures so intermingled, that it was impossible to tell where one had terminated and the other commenced; and that it was not surprising that people who contemplated them every day, so formed, so employed, and so degraded, should forget their claims to that rank in the scale of being in which modern philanthropists are so anxious to place them. I did not at the moment myself recollect, that the white man, made a slave on the coast of Africa, suffers not only a similar mental but physical deterioration from hardships and emaciation, and becomes in time the dull and deformed beast I now saw yoked to a burden.

"A few hours only were necessary to correct my first impressions of the negro population, by seeing them under a different aspect. We were attracted by the sound of military music, and found it proceeded from a regiment drawn up in one of the streets. Their colonel had just died, and they attended to form a procession to celebrate his obsequies. They were all of different shades of black, but the majority were negroes. Their equipment was excellent; they wore dark jackets, white pantaloons, and black leather caps and belts, all which, with their arms, were in high order. Their band produced sweet and agreeable music, of the leader's own composition, and the men went through some evolutions with regularity and dexterity. They were only a militia regiment, yet were as well appointed and disciplined as one of our regiments of the line. Here then was the first step in that gradation by which the black population of this country ascend in the scale of humanity; he advances from the state below that of a beast of burden into a military rank, and he shows himself as capable of discipline and improvement as a human being of any other color.

"Our attention was next attracted by negro men and women bearing about a variety of articles for sale; some in baskets, some on boards and cases carried on their heads. They belonged to a class of small shopkeepers, many of whom vend their wares at home, but the greater number send them about in this way, as in itinerant shops. A few of these people were still in a state of bondage, and brought a certain sum every evening to their owners, as the produce of their daily labor. But a large proportion, I was informed, were free, and exercised this little calling on their own account. They were all very neat and clean in their persons, and had a decorum and sense of respectability about them, superior to whites of the same class and calling. All their articles were good in their kind and neatly kept, and they sold them with simplicity and confidence, neither wishing to take advantage of others, nor suspecting that it would be taken of themselves. I bought some confectionary from one of the females, and I was struck with the modesty and propriety of her manner; she was a young mother, and had with her a neatly dressed child, of which she seemed very fond. I gave it a little comfit, and it turned up its dusky countenance to her and then to me, taking my sweetmeat and at the same time kissing my hand. As yet unacquainted with the coin of the country, I had none that was current about me, and was leaving the articles; but the poor young woman pressed them on me with a ready confidence, repeating in broken Portuguese, *outo tempo*. I am sorry to say, the 'other time' never came, for I could not recognise her person afterwards to discharge her little debt, though I went to the same place for the purpose.

"It soon began to grow dark, and I was attracted by a number of persons bearing large lighted wax tapers, like torches, gathering before a house. As I passed by, one was put into my hand by a man who seemed in some authority, and I was requested to fall into a procession that was forming. It was the preparation for a funeral, and on such occasions, I learned that they always request the attendance of a passing stranger, and feel hurt if they are refused. I joined the party, and proceeded with them to a neighboring church. When we entered we ranged ourselves on each side of a platform which stood near the choir, on which was laid an open coffin, covered with pink silk and gold borders. The funeral service was chanted by a choir of priests, one of whom was a negro, a large comely man, whose jet black visage formed a strong and striking contrast to his white vestments.—He seemed to perform his part with a decorum and sense of solemnity, which I did not observe in his brethren.—After scattering flowers on the coffin, and fumigating it with incense, they retired, the procession dispersed, and we returned on board.

"I had been but a few hours on shore for the first time, and I saw an African negro under four aspects of society; and it appeared to me, that in every one his character depended on the state in which he was placed, and the estimation in which he was held. As a despised slave, he was far lower than other animals of burthen that surrounded him; more miserable in his look, more revolting in his nakedness, more distorted in his person, and apparently more deficient in intellect, than the horses and mules that passed him by. Advanced to the grade of a soldier, he was clean and neat in his person, amenable to discipline, expert at his exercises, and showed the port and being of a white man similarly placed. As a citizen, he was remarkable for the respectability of his appearance, and the decorum of his manners in the rank assigned him; and as a priest, standing in the house of God, appointed to instruct society on their most important interests, and in a grade in which moral and intellectual fitness is required, and a certain degree of superiority is expected, he seemed even more devout in his impressions, and more correct in his manners, than his white associates. I came, therefore, to the irresistible conclusion in my mind, that color was an accident affecting the surface of a man, and having no more to do with his qualities than his clothes—that God had equally created an African in the image of his person, and equally given him an immortal soul; and that a European had no pretext but his own cupidity, for impiously thrusting his fellow-man from that rank in the creation which the Almighty had assigned him, and degrading him below the lot of the brute beasts that perish."

The Hon. A. H. Everett, in his able work on the political situation of America, says, "Nations, and races, like individuals, have their day, and seldom have a second. The blacks had a long and glorious one; and after what they have been and done, it argues not so much a mistaken theory, as sheer ignorance of the most notorious historical facts, to pretend that they are naturally inferior to the whites. It would seem indeed, that if any race have a right claim to a sort of preëminence over others, on the fair and honorable ground of talents displayed, and benefits conferred, it is precisely this very one, which we take upon us, in the pride of a temporary superiority, to stamp with the brand of essential degradation. It is hardly necessary to add, that while the blacks were the leading race in civilization and political power, there was no prejudice among the whites against their color. On the contrary, we find that the early Greeks regarded them as a superior variety of the human species, not only in intellectual and moral qualities, but in outward appearance. 'The Ethiopians,' says Herodotus, 'surpass all other men in longevity, stature, and personal beauty.' "

Then let the slave-holder no longer apologize for himself by urging the stupidity and sensuality of negroes. It is upon the *system,* which thus transforms men into beasts, that the reproach rests in all its strength and bitterness. And even if the negroes were, beyond all doubt, our inferiors in intellect, this would form no excuse for oppression, or contempt. The use of law and public opinion is to protect the weak against the strong; and the government, which perverts these blessings into means of tyranny, resembles the priest, who administered poison with the Holy Sacrament.

Is there an American willing that the intellectual and the learned should bear despotic sway over the simple and the ignorant? If there be such a one, *he* may consistently vindicate our treatment of the Africans.

CHAPTER VII.

MORAL CHARACTER OF NEGROES.

"Fleecy locks and black complexion
Cannot forfeit Nature's claim;
Skins may differ, but affection
Dwells in black and white the same.

"Slaves of gold! whose sordid dealings
Tarnish all your boasted powers,
Prove that *you* have human feelings,
Ere you proudly question ours."
—THE NEGRO'S COMPLAINT; BY COWPER.

THE opinion that negroes are naturally inferior in intellect is almost universal among white men; but the belief that they are worse than other people, is, I believe, much less extensive: indeed, I have heard some, who were by no means admirers of the colored race, maintain that they were very remarkable for kind feelings, and strong affections. Homer calls the ancient Ethiopians "the most honest of men;" and modern travellers have given innumerable instances of domestic tenderness, and generous hospitality in the interior of Africa. Mungo Park informs us that he found many schools in his progress through the country, and observed with pleasure the great docility and submissive deportment of the children, and heartily wished they had better instructers and a purer religion.

The following is an account of his arrival at Jumbo, in company with a native of that place, who had been absent several years: "The meeting between the blacksmith and his relations was very tender; for these rude children of nature, free from restraint, display their emotions in the strongest and most expressive manner.—Amidst these transports, the aged mother was led forth, leaning upon a staff. Every one made way for her, and she stretched out her hand to bid her son welcome. Being totally blind, she stroked his hands, arms, and face, with great care, and seemed highly delighted that her latter days were blessed by his return, and that her ears once more heard the music of his voice. From this interview, I was fully convinced, that whatever difference there is between the negro and the European, in the conformation of the nose, and the color of the skin, there is none in the genuine sympathies and characteristic feelings of our common nature."

At a small town in the interior, called Wawra, he says, "In the course of the day, several women, hearing that I was going to Sego, came and begged me to inquire of Mansong, the king, what was become of their children. One woman, in particular, told me that her son's name was Mamadee; that he was no heathen; but prayed to God morning and evening; that he had been taken from her about three years ago by Mansong's army, since which she had never heard from him. She said she often dreamed about him, and begged me, if I should see him in Bambarra, or in my own country, to tell him that his mother and sister were still alive."

At Sego, in Bambarra, the king, being jealous of Mr Park's intentions, forbade him to cross the river. Under these discouraging circumstances, he was advised to lodge at a distant village; but there the same distrust of the white man's purposes prevailed, and no person would allow him to enter his house. He says, "I was regarded with astonishment and fear, and was obliged to sit all day without food, under the shade of a tree. The wind rose, and there was great appearance of a heavy rain, and the wild beasts are so very numerous in the neighborhood, that I should have been under the necessity of resting among the branches of the tree. About sunset, however, as I was preparing to pass the night in this manner, and had turned my horse loose, that he might graze at liberty, a woman, returning from the labors of the field, stopped to observe me. Perceiving that I was weary and dejected, she inquired into my situation, which I briefly explained to her; whereupon, with looks of great compassion, she took up my saddle and bridle and told me to follow her. Having conducted me into her hut, she lighted a lamp, spread a mat on the floor, and told me I might remain there for the night. Finding that I was hungry, she went out, and soon returned with a very fine fish, which being broiled upon some embers, she gave me for supper. The women then resumed their task of spinning cotton, and lightened their labor with songs, one of which must have been composed extempore, for I was myself, the subject of it. It was sung by one of

the young women, the rest joining in a kind of chorus. The air was sweet and plaintive, and the words, literally translated, were these:

> "The winds roar'd, and the rains fell;
> The poor white man, faint and weary,
> Came and sat under our tree.—
> He has no mother to bring him milk;
> No wife to grind his corn.

> CHORUS.
> "Let us pity the white man;
> No mother has he to bring him milk,
> No wife to grind his corn."

The reader can fully sympathize with this intelligent and liberal minded traveller, when he observes, "Trifling as this recital may appear, the circumstance was highly affecting to a person in my situation. I was oppressed with such unexpected kindness, and sleep fled from my eyes. In the morning, I presented my compassionate landlady with two of the four brass buttons remaining on my waistcoat; the only recompense I could make her."

The Duchess of Devonshire, whose beauty and talent gained such extensive celebrity, was so much pleased with this African song, and the kind feelings in which it originated, that she put it into English verse, and employed an eminent composer to set it to music:

> The loud wind roar'd, the rain fell fast;
> The white man yielded to the blast;
> He sat him down beneath our tree,
> For weary, faint, and sad was he;
> And ah, no wife or mother's care,
> For him the milk or corn prepare.

> CHORUS.
> The white man shall our pity share;
> Alas, no wife, or mother's care,
> For him the milk or corn prepare.

> The storm is o'er, the tempest past,
> And mercy's voice has hush'd the blast;
> The wind is heard in whispers low;
> The white man far away must go;—
> But ever in his heart will bear
> Remembrance of the negro's care.

CHORUS.
Go, white man, go—but with thee bear
The negro's wish, the negro's prayer,
Remembrance of the negro's care.

At another time, Mr Park thus continues his narrative: "A little before sunset, I descended on the northwest side of a ridge of hills, and as I was looking about for a convenient tree, under which to pass the night, (for I had no hopes of reaching any town) I descended into a delightful valley, and soon afterward arrived at a romantic village called Kooma. I was immediately surrounded by a circle of the harmless villagers. They asked me a thousand questions about my country, and in return for my information brought corn and milk for myself, and grass for my horse; kindled a fire in the hut where I was to sleep, and appeared very anxious to serve me."

Afterward, being robbed and stripped by banditti in the wilderness, he informs us that the robbers stood considering whether they should leave him quite destitute; even in *their* minds, humanity partially prevailed over avarice; they returned the worst of two shirts, and a pair of trowsers; and as they went away, one of them threw back his hat. At the next village, Mr Park entered a complaint to the Dooty, or chief man, who continued very calmly smoking while he listened to the narration; but when he had heard all the particulars, he took the pipe from his mouth, and tossing up the sleeve of his cloak with an indignant air, he said, "You shall have everything restored to you—I have sworn it." Then, turning to an attendant, he added, "Give the white man a draught of water; and with the first light of morning go over the hills, and inform the Dooty of Bammakoo, that a poor white man, the king of Bambarra's stranger, has been robbed by the king of Foolodoo's people." He then invited the traveller to remain with him, and share his provisions, until the messenger returned. Mr Park accepted the kind offer most gratefully: and in a few days his horse and clothes were restored to him.

At the village of Nemacoo, where corn was so scarce that the people were actually in a state of starvation, a negro pitied his distress and brought him food.

At Kamalia, Mr Park was earnestly dissuaded by an African named Karfa, from attempting to cross the Jalonka wilderness during the rainy season; to which he replied that there was no alternative—for he was so poor, that he must either beg his subsistence from place to place, or perish with hunger. Karfa eagerly inquired if he could eat the food of the country, adding that, if he would stay with him, he should have plenty of victuals, and a hut to sleep in; and that after he had been safely conducted to the Gambia, he might make what return he thought proper. He was accordingly provided with a mat to sleep on, an earthen jar for holding water, a small calabash for a drinking cup, and two meals a day, with a supply of wood and water, from Karfa's own dwelling. Here he recovered from a fever, which had tormented him several weeks. His benevolent landlord came daily to inquire after his health, and see that he had everything for his comfort. Mr Park assures us that the simple and affectionate manner of those around him contributed not a little to his recovery. He adds, "Thus was I delivered, by the friendly care of this benevolent negro, from a situation truly deplorable. Distress and famine pressed hard upon me; I had before me the gloomy wilderness of Jallonkadoo, where the traveller sees no habitation for five successive days. I had observed, at a distance, the rapid course of the river Kokaro, and had almost marked out the place where I thought I was doomed to perish, when this friendly negro stretched out his hospitable hand for my relief." Mr Park having travelled in company with a coffle of thirty-five slaves, thus describes his feelings as they came near the coast: "Although I was now approaching the end of my tedious and toil-some journey, and expected in another day to meet with countrymen and friends, I could not part with my unfortunate fellow travellers,—doomed as I knew most of them to be, to a life of slavery in a foreign land,—without great emotion. During a peregrination of more than five hundred miles, exposed to the burning rays of a tropical sun, these poor slaves, amidst their own infinitely greater sufferings, would commiserate mine, and frequently, of their own accord, bring water to quench my thirst, and at night collect branches and leaves to prepare me a bed in the wilderness. We parted with mutual regret and blessings.—My good wishes and prayers were all I could bestow upon them, and it afforded me some consolation to be told that they were sensible I had no more to give."

The same enlightened traveller remarks, "All the negro nations that fell under my observation, though divided into a number of petty, independent states, subsist chiefly by the same means, live nearly in the same temperature, and possess a wonderful similarity of disposition. The Mandingoes, in particular, are a very gentle race, cheerful, inquisitive, credulous, simple, and fond of flattery. Perhaps the most prominent defect in their character, was that insurmountable propensity, which the reader must have observed to prevail in all classes, to steal from me the few effects I was possessed of. No complete justification can be offered for this conduct, because theft is a crime in their own estimation; and it must be observed that they are not habitually and generally guilty of it towards each other. But before we pronounce them a more depraved people than any other, it were well to consider, whether the lower class of people in any part of Europe, would have acted, under similar circumstances, with greater honesty towards a stranger. It must be remembered that the laws of the country afforded me no protection; that every one was permitted to rob me with impunity; and that some part of my effects were of as great value in the estimation of the negroes, as pearls and diamonds would have been in the eyes of a European. Let us suppose a black merchant of Hindostan had found his way into England, with a box of jewels at his back, and the laws of the kingdom afforded him no security—in such a case, the wonder would be, not that the stranger was robbed of any part of his riches, but that any part was left for a second depredator.* Such, on sober reflection, is the judgment I have formed concerning the pilfering disposition of the Mandingo negroes toward me.

"On the other hand, it is impossible for me to forget the disinterested charity, and tender solicitude, with which many of these poor heathens, from the sovereign of Sego, to the poor women, who at different times received me into their cottages, sympathized with my sufferings, relieved my distress, and contributed to my safety. Perhaps this acknowledgment is more particularly due to the female part of the nation. Among the men, as the reader must have seen, my reception, though generally kind, was sometimes otherwise. It varied according to the tempers of those to whom I made application. Avarice in some, and bigotry in others, had closed up the avenues to compassion; but I do not recollect a single instance of hardheartedness towards me in the women. In all my wanderings and wretchedness, I found them uniformly kind and compassionate; and I can truly say, as Mr Ledyard has eloquently said before me—'To a woman, I never addressed myself in the language of decency and friendship, without receiving a decent and friendly answer. If I was

---

*Or suppose a colored pedler with valuable goods travelling in slave states, where the laws afford little or no protection to negro property, what would probably be his fate?

hungry, or thirsty, wet, or ill, they did not hesitate, like the men, to perform a generous action. In so free and so kind a manner, did they contribute to my relief, that if I were dry, I drank the sweeter draught; and if I were hungry, I ate the coarsest meal with a double relish.'

"It is surely reasonable to suppose that the soft and amiable sympathy of nature, thus spontaneously manifested to me in my distress, is displayed by these poor people as occasion requires, much more strongly toward those of their own nation and neighborhood. Maternal affection, neither suppressed by the restraints, nor diverted by the solicitudes of civilized life, is everywhere conspicuous among them, and creates reciprocal tenderness in the child. 'Strike me,' said a negro to his master, who spoke disrespectfully of his parent, 'but do not curse my mother.' The same sentiment I found to prevail universally."

"I perceived, with great satisfaction, that the maternal solicitude extended not only to growth and security of the person, but also, in a certain degree, to the improvement of the character; for one of the first lessons, which the Mandingo women teach their children is the practice of truth. A poor unhappy mother, whose son had been murdered by Moorish banditti, found consolation in her deepest distress from the reflection that her boy, in the whole course of his blameless life, had never told a lie."

Adanson, who visited Senegal, in 1754, describes the negroes as sociable, obliging, humane, and hospitable. "Their amiable simplicity," says he, "in this enchanting country, recalled to me the idea of the primitive race of man; I thought I saw the world in its infancy. They are distinguished by tenderness for their parents, and great respect for the aged." Robin speaks of a slave at Martinico, who having gained money sufficient for his own ransom, preferred to purchase his mother's freedom.

Proyart, in his history of Loango, acknowledges that the negroes on the coast, who associate with Europeans, are inclined to licentiousness and fraud; but he says those of the interior are humane, obliging, and hospitable. Golberry repeats the same praise, and rebukes the presumption of white men in despising "nations improperly called savage, among whom we find men of integrity, models of filial, conjugal, and paternal affection, who know all the energies and refinements of virtue; among whom sentimental impressions are more deep, because they observe, more than we, the dictates of nature, and know how to sacrifice personal interest to the ties of friendship."

Joseph Rachel, a free negro of Barbadoes, having become rich by commerce, consecrated all his fortune to acts of charity and benefi-cence. The unfortunate of all colors, shared his kindness. He gave to the needy, lent without hope of return, visited prisoners, and endeav-ored to reform the guilty. He died in 1758. The philanthropists of England speak of him with the utmost respect.

Jasmin Thoumazeau was born in Africa, 1714, and sold at St Do-mingo, 1736. Having obtained his freedom, he returned to his native country, and married a negro girl of the Gold Coast. In 1756, he established a hospital for poor negroes and mulattoes. During more than forty years, he and his wife devoted their time and fortune to the comfort of such invalids as sought their protection. The Phila-delphian Society, at the Cape, and the Agricultural Society of Paris, decreed medals to this worthy and benevolent man.

Louis Desrouleaux was the slave of M. Pinsum, *a captain in the negro trade,* who resided at St Domingo. The master having amassed great riches, went to reside in France, where circumstances combined to ruin him. Depressed in fortune and spirits, he returned to St Do-mingo; but those who had formerly been proud of his friendship, now avoided him. Louis heard of his misfortunes and immediately went to see him. The scales were now turned; the negro was rich, and the white man poor. The generous fellow offered every assistance, but advised M. Pinsum by all means to return to France, where he would not be pained by the sight of ungrateful men. "But I cannot gain a living there," replied the white man. "Will the annual revenue of fifteen thousand francs be sufficient?" asked Louis. The Frenchman's eyes filled with tears. The negro signed the contract, and the pension was regularly paid, till the death of Louis Desrouleaux, in 1774.

Benoit of Palermo, also named Benoit of Santo Fratello, some-times called *The Holy Black,* was a negro, and the son of a female slave. Roccho Pirro, author of the *Sicilia Sacra,* eulogizes him thus: "Nigro quidem corpore sed candore animi proeclarisimus quem mi-raculis Deus contestatum esse voluit." "His body was black, but it pleased God to testify by miracles the whiteness of his soul." He died at Palermo, in 1589, where his tomb and memory are much revered. A few years ago, it was said the Pope was about to authorize his canoniz-ation. Whether he is yet registered as a saint in the Calendar, I know not; but many writers agree that he was a saint indeed—eminent for his virtues, which he practised in meekness and silence, desiring no witness but his God.

The moral character of Toussaint L'Ouverture is even more worthy of admiration than his intellectual acuteness. What can be more beautiful than his unchanging gratitude to his benefactor, his warm attachment to his family, his high-minded sacrifice of personal feeling to the public good! He was a hero in the sublimest sense of the word. Yet he had no white blood in his veins—he was all negro.

The following description of a slave-market at Brazil is from the pen of Doctor Walsh: "The men were generally less interesting objects than the women; their countenances and hues were very varied, according to the part of the African coast from which they came; some were soot black, having a certain ferocity of aspect that indicated strong and fierce passions, like men who were darkly brooding over some deep-felt wrongs, and meditating revenge. When any one was ordered, he came forward with a sullen indifference, threw his arms over his head, stamped with his feet, shouted to show the soundness of his lungs, ran up and down the room, and was treated exactly like a horse put through his paces at a repository; and when done, he was whipped to his stall.

"Many of them were lying stretched on the bare boards; and among the rest, mothers with young children at their breasts, of which they seemed passionately fond. They were all doomed to remain on the spot, like sheep in a pen, till they were sold; they have no apartment to retire to, no bed to repose on, no covering to protect them; they sit naked all day, and lie naked all night, on the bare boards, or benches, where we saw them exhibited.

"Among the objects that attracted my attention in this place were some young boys, who seemed to have formed a society together. I observed several times in passing by, that the same little group was collected near a barred window; they seemed very fond of each other, and their kindly feelings were never interrupted by peevishness; indeed, the temperament of a negro child is generally so sound, that he is not affected by those little morbid sensations, which are the frequent cause of crossness and ill-temper in our children. I do not remember, that I ever saw a young black fretful, or out of humor; certainly never displaying those ferocious fits of petty passion, in which the superior nature of infant whites indulges. I sometimes brought cakes and fruit in my pocket, and handed them in to the group. It was quite delightful to observe the generous and disinterested manner in which they distributed them. There was no scrambling with one another; no selfish reservation to themselves. The child to whom I happened to give them, took them so gently, looked so thankfully, and distributed them so generously, that I could not help thinking that God had compensated their dusky hue, by a more than usual human portion of amiable qualities."

Several negroes in Jamaica were to be hung. One of them was offered his life, if he would hang the others; he preferred death. A negro slave who was ordered to do it, asked time to prepare; he went into his cabin, chopped off his right hand with an axe, and then came back, saying he was ready.

Sutcliff in his Travels, speaks of meeting a coffle of slaves in Maryland, one of whom had voluntarily gone into slavery, in hopes of meeting her husband, who was a free black and had been stolen by kidnappers. The poor creature was in treacherous hands, and it is a great chance whether she ever saw her husband again.

An affecting instance of negro friendship may be found in 1 Bay's Report, 260–3. A female slave in South Carolina was allowed to work out in the town, on condition that she paid her master a certain sum of money, per month. Being strong and industrious, her wages amounted to more than had been demanded in their agreement. After a time she earned enough to buy her freedom; but she preferred to devote the sum to the emancipation of a negro girl, named Sally, for whom she had conceived a strong affection. For a long time the master pretended to have no property in his slave's manumitted friend, never paid taxes for her, and often spoke of her as a free negro. But, from some motive or other, he afterward claimed Sally as his slave, on the ground that no slave could make any purchase on his own account, or possess anything which did not legally belong to his master. It is an honor to Chief Justice Rutledge that his charge was given in a spirit better than the laws. He concluded by saying, "If the wench chose to appropriate the savings of her extra labor to the purchase of this girl, in order to set her free, will a jury of the country say, No? I trust not. I hope they are too upright and humane, to do such manifest violence to such an extraordinary act of benevolence." By the prompt decision of the jury, Sally was declared free.*

In speaking of the character of negroes, it ought not to be omitted that many of them were brave and faithful soldiers during our Revolution. Some are now receiving pensions for their services. At New

---

*Stroud says of the above, "This is an isolated case, of pretty early date; it deserves to be noticed because it is in opposition to the spirit of the laws, and to *later* decisions of the courts.

Orleans, likewise, the conduct of the colored troops was deserving of the highest praise.

It is common to speak of the negroes as a very unfeeling race; and no doubt the charge has considerable truth when applied to those in a state of bondage; for slavery blunts the feelings, as well as stupifies the intellect. The poor negro is considered as having no right in his wife and children. They may be suddenly torn from him to be sold in a distant market; but he cannot prevent the wrong. He may see them exposed to every species of insult and indignity; but the law, which stretches forth her broad shield to guard the white man's rights, excludes the negro from her protection. They may be tied to the whipping post and *die* under *moderate* punishment; but he dares not complain. If he murmur, there is the tormenting lash; if he resist, it is death.—And the injustice extends even beyond the grave; for the story of the slave is told by his oppressor, and the manly spirit which the poor creature shows, when stung to the very heart's core, is represented as diabolical revenge. A short time ago, I read in a Georgia paper, what was called a horrid transaction, on the part of the negro. A slave stood by and saw his wife whipped, as long as he could possibly endure the sight; he then called out to the overseer, who was applying the lash, that he would kill him if he did not use more mercy. This probably made matters worse; at all events the lashing continued. The husband, goaded to frenzy, rushed upon the overseer, and stabbed him three times. White men! what would *you* do, if the laws admitted that your wives might "*die*" of "*moderate punishment*," administered by your employers? The overseer died, and his murderer was either burned or shot,—I forget which. The Georgia editor viewed the subject only on one side—viz.—the monstrous outrage against the white man—the negro's wrongs passed for nothing! It was very gravely added to the account (probably to increase the odiousness of the slave's offence,) that the overseer belonged to the Presbyterian church! I smiled,—because it made me think of a man, whom I once heard described as "a most excellent Christian, that would steal timber to build a church."

This instance shows that even slaves are not quite destitute of feeling—yet we could not wonder at it, if they were. Who could expect the kindly affections to expand in such an atmosphere! Where there is no hope, the heart becomes paralyzed: it is a merciful arrangement of Divine Providence, by which the acuteness of sensibility is lessened when it becomes merely a source of suffering.

But there are exceptions to this general rule; instances of very strong and deep affection are sometimes found in a state of hopeless bondage. Godwin, in his eloquent Lectures on Colonial Slavery, quotes the following anecdote, as related by Mr T. Pennock, at a public meeting in England:

"A few years ago it was enacted, that it should not be legal to transport once established slaves from one island to another; and a gentleman owner, finding it advisable to do so before the act came in force, the removal of a great part of his *live stock* was the consequence. He had a female slave, a Methodist, and highly valuable to him (not the less so for being the mother of eight or nine children), whose husband, also of our connexion, was the property of another resident on the island, where I happened to be at the time. Their masters not agreeing on a sale, separation ensued, and I went to the beach to be an eye witness of their behaviour in the greatest pang of all. One by one, the man kissed his children, with the firmness of a hero, and blessing them, gave as his last words—(oh! will it be believed, and have no influence upon our veneration for the negro?) 'Farewell! *Be honest, and obedient to your master!'* At length he had to take leave of his wife: there he stood (I have him in my mind's eye at this moment), five or six yards from the mother of his children, unable to move, speak, or do anything but gaze, and still to gaze, on the object of his long affection, soon to cross the blue waves forever from his aching sight. The fire of his eyes alone gave indication of the passion within, until after some minutes standing thus, he fell senseless on the sand, as if suddenly struck down by the hand of the Almighty. Nature could do no more; the blood gushed from his nostrils and mouth, as if rushing from the terrors of the conflict within; and amid the confusion occasioned by the circumstance, the vessel bore off his family forever from the island! After some days he recovered, and came to ask advice of me. What *could* an Englishman do in such a case? I felt the blood boiling within me; but I conquered. I browbeat my own manhood, and gave him the humblest advice I could."

The following account is given by Mr Gilgrass, one of the Methodist missionaries at Jamaica: "A master of slaves, who lived near us in Kingston, exercised his barbarities on a Sabbath morning while we were worshiping God in the Chapel; and the cries of the female sufferers have frequently interrupted us in our devotions. But there was no redress for them, or for us. This man wanted money; and one of the female slaves having two fine children, he sold one of them, and the child was torn from her maternal affection. In the agony of her feelings, she made a hideous howling; and for that crime she was flogged. Soon after he sold her other child. This 'turned her heart within her,' and impelled her into a kind of madness. She howled night and day in the yard; tore her hair; ran up and down the streets and the parade, rending the heavens with her cries, and literally watering the earth with her tears. Her constant cry was, *'Da wicked massa, he sell me children.—Will no buckra master pity nega? What me do! Me have no child!'* As she stood before my window, she said, lifting her hands towards heaven, *'Do, me master minister, pity me! Me heart do so,* (shaking herself violently,) *me heart do so, because me have no child. Me go a massa house, in massa yard, and in me hut, and me no see em;'* and then her cry went up to God. I durst not be seen looking at her."

A similar instance of strong affection happened in the city of Washington, December, 1815. A negro woman, with her two children, was sold, near Bladensburgh, to Georgia traders; but the master refused to sell her husband. When the coffle reached Washington, on their way to Georgia, the poor creature attempted to escape, by jumping from the garret window of a three-story brick tavern. Her arms and back were dreadfully broken. When asked why she had done such a desperate act, she replied, *"They brought me away, and would n't let me see my husband; and I did n't want to go. I was so distracted that I did not know what I was about: but I did n't want to go—and I jumped out of the window."* The unfortunate woman was given to the landlord as a compensation for having her taken care of at his house; her children were sold in Carolina; and thus was this poor forlorn being left alone in her misery. In all this wide land of benevolence and freedom, there was no one who could protect her: for in such cases, the *laws* come in, with iron grasp, to check the stirrings of human sympathy.

Another complaint is that slaves have most inveterate habits of laziness. No doubt this is true—it would be strange indeed if it were otherwise. Where is the human being, who will work from a disinterested love of toil, when his labor brings no improvement to himself, no increase of comfort to his wife and children?

Pelletan, in his Memoirs of the French Colony of Senegal, says, "The negroes work with ardor, because they are now unmolested in their possessions and enjoyments. Since the suppression of slavery, the Moors make no more inroads upon them, and their villages are rebuilt and re-peopled." Bosman, who was by no means very friendly to colored people, says: "The negroes of Cabomonte and Juido, are indefatigable cultivators, economical of their soil, they scarcely leave a foot-path to form a communication between the different possessions; they reap one day, and the next they sow the same earth, without allowing it time for repose."

It is needless to multiply quotations; for the concurrent testimony of all travellers proves that industry is a common virtue in the interior of Africa.

Again, it is said that the negroes are treacherous, cunning, dishonest, and profligate. Let me ask you, candid reader, what you would be, if you labored under the same unnatural circumstances? The daily earnings of the slave, nay, his very wife and children, are constantly wrested from him, under the sanction of the laws; is this the way to teach a scrupulous regard to the property of others? How can purity be expected from him, who sees almost universal licentiousness prevail among those whom he is taught to regard as his superiors? Besides, we must remember how entirely unprotected the negro is in his domestic relations, and how very frequently husband and wife are separated by the caprice, or avarice, of the white man. I have no doubt that slaves are artful; for they *must* be so. Cunning is always the resort of the weak against the strong; children, who have violent and unreasonable parents, become deceitful in self-defence. The only way to make young people sincere and frank, is to treat them with mildness and perfect justice.

The negro often pretends to be ill in order to avoid labor; and if you were situated as he is, you would do the same. But it is said that the blacks are malignant and revengeful. Granting it to be true,—is it their fault, or is it owing to the cruel circumstances in which they are placed? Surely there are proofs enough that they are naturally a kind and gentle people. True, they do sometimes murder their masters and overseers; but where there is utter hopelessness, can we wonder at occasional desperation? I do not believe that any class of people subject to the same influences, would commit fewer crimes. Dickson, in his letters on slavery, informs us that among one hundred and twenty thousand negroes and creoles of Barbadoes, only three murders have been known to be committed by them in the course of thirty years; although often provoked by the cruelty of the planters.

In estimating the vices of slaves, there are several items to be taken into the account. In the first place, we hear a great deal of the negroes'

crimes, while we hear very little of their provocations. If they murder
their masters, newspapers and almanacs blazon it all over the country; but if their masters murder *them,* a trifling fine is paid, and
nobody thinks of mentioning the matter. I believe there are twenty
negroes killed by white men, where there is one white man killed by a
black. If you believe this to be mere conjecture, I pray you examine
the Judicial Reports of the Southern States. The voice of *humanity,*
concerning this subject, is weak and stifled; and when a master kills
his own slave we are not likely to hear the tidings—but the voice of
avarice is loud and strong; and it sometimes happens that negroes
"die" "under a moderate punishment" administered by other hands:
then prosecutions ensue, in order to recover the price of the slave; and
in *this* way we are enabled to form a tolerable conjecture concerning
the frequency of such crimes.

I have said that we seldom hear of the grievous wrongs which
provoke the vengeance of the slave; I will tell an anecdote, which I
know to be true, as a proof in point. Within the last two years, a
gentleman residing in Boston, was summoned to the West Indies in
consequence of troubles on his plantation. His overseer had been
killed by the slaves. This fact was soon made public; and more than
one exclaimed, "what diabolical passions these negroes have!" To
which I replied that I only wondered they were half as good as they
were. It was not long, however, before I discovered the particulars of
the case; and I took some pains that the public should likewise be
informed of them. The overseer was a bad, licentious man. How long
and how much the slaves endured under his power I know not, but at
last, he took a fancy to two of the negroes' wives, ordered them to be
brought to his house, and in spite of their entreaties and resistance,
compelled them to remain as long as he thought proper. The husbands found their little huts deserted, and knew very well where the
blame rested. In such a case, *you* would have gone to law; but the law
does not recognise a negro's rights—he is the *property* of his master,
and subject to the will of his agent. If a slave should talk of being
protected in his domestic relations, it would cause great merriment in
a slave-holding State; the proposition would be deemed equally inconvenient and absurd. Under such circumstances, the negro husbands took justice into their own hands. They murdered the overseer.
Four innocent slaves were taken up, and upon very slight circumstan-
tial evidence were condemned to be shot; but the real actors in this
scene passed unsuspected. When the unhappy men found their com-

panions were condemned to die, they avowed the fact, and exculpated all others from any share in the deed. Was not this true magnanimity? Can you help respecting those negroes? If you can, I pity you.

Since the condition of slaves is such as I have described, are you surprised at occasional insurrections? You may *regret* it most deeply; but *can* you wonder at it. The famous Captain Smith, when he was a slave in Tartary, killed his overseer and made his escape. I never heard him blamed for it—it seems to be universally considered a simple act of self-defence. The same thing has often occurred with regard to white men taken by the Algerines.

The Poles have shed Russian "blood enough to float our navy;" and we admire and praise them, because they did it in resistance of oppression. Yet they have suffered less than black slaves, all the world over, are suffering. We honor our forefathers because they rebelled against certain principles dangerous to political freedom; yet from actual, personal tyranny, they suffered nothing: the negro, on the contrary, is suffering all that oppression *can* make human nature suffer. Why do we execrate in one set of men, what we laud so highly in another? I shall be reminded that insurrections and murders are totally at variance with the precepts of our religion; and this is most true. But according to this rule, the Americans, Poles, Parisians, Belgians, and all who have shed blood for the sake of liberty, are more to blame than the negroes; for the former are more enlightened, and can always have access to the fountain of religion; while the latter are kept in a state of brutal ignorance—not allowed to read their Bibles—knowing nothing of Christianity, except the examples of their masters, who profess to be governed by its maxims.

I hope I shall not be misunderstood on this point. I am not vindicating insurrections and murders; the very thought makes my blood run cold. I believe revenge is *always* wicked; but I say, what the laws of every country acknowledge, that great provocations are a palliation of great crimes. When a man steals food because he is starving, we are more disposed to pity, than to blame him. And what *can* human nature do, subject to continual and oppressive wrong—hopeless of change—not only unprotected by law, but the law itself changed into an enemy—and to complete the whole, shut out from the instructions and consolations of the Gospel! No wonder the West Indian missionaries found it very difficult to decide what they ought to say to the poor, suffering negroes! They could indeed tell them it was very impolitic to be rash and violent, because it could not, under existing circumstances, make their situation better, and would be very likely to make it worse; but if they urged the maxims of religion, the slaves might ask the embarrassing question, is not our treatment in direct opposition to the precepts of the gospel? Our masters can read the Bible—they have a chance to know better. Why do not Christians deal justly by us, before they require us to deal mercifully with them?

Think of all these things, kind-hearted reader. Try to judge the negro by the same rules you judge other men; and while you condemn his faults, do not forget his manifold provocations.

CHAPTER VIII.

Prejudices against People of Color, and Our Duties in Relation to This Subject.

"A negro has a *soul,* an' please your honor," said the Corporal, *(doubtingly.)*

"I am not much versed, Corporal," quoth my Uncle Toby, "in things of that kind; but I suppose God would not leave him without one, any more than thee or me."

"It would be putting one sadly over the head of the other," quoth the Corporal.

"It would so," said my Uncle Toby.

"Why then, an' please your honor, is a black man to be used worse than a white one?"

"I can give no reason," said my Uncle Toby.

"Only," cried the Corporal, shaking his head, "because he has no one to stand up for him."

"It is that very thing, Trim," quoth my Uncle Toby, "which recommends him to protection."

WHILE we bestow our earnest disapprobation on the system of slavery, let us not flatter ourselves that we are in reality any better than our brethren of the South. Thanks to our soil and climate, and the early exertions of the Quakers, the *form* of slavery does not exist among us; but the very *spirit* of the hateful and mischievous thing is here in all its strength. The manner in which we use what power we have, gives us ample reason to be grateful that the nature of our institutions does not intrust us with more. Our prejudice against colored people is even more inveterate than it is at the South. The planter is often attached to his negroes, and lavishes caresses and kind words upon them, as he would on a favorite hound: but our cold-hearted, ignoble prejudice admits of no exception—no intermission.

The Southerners have long continued habit, apparent interest and dreaded danger, to palliate the wrong they do; but we stand without excuse. They tell us that Northern ships and Northern capital have been engaged in this wicked business; and the reproach is true. Several fortunes in this city have been made by the sale of negro blood. If these criminal transactions are still carried on, they are done in silence and secrecy, because public opinion has made them disgraceful. But if the free States wished to cherish the system of slavery forever, they could not take a more direct course than they now do. Those who are kind and liberal on all other subjects, unite with the selfish and the proud in their unrelenting efforts to keep the colored population in the lowest state of degradation; and the influence they unconsciously exert over children early infuses into their innocent minds the same strong feelings of contempt.

The intelligent and well informed have the least share of this prejudice; and when their minds can be brought to reflect upon it, I have generally observed that they soon cease to have any at all. But such a general apathy prevails and the subject is so seldom brought into view, that few are really aware how oppressively the influence of society is made to bear upon this injured class of the community. When I have related facts, that came under my own observation, I have often been listened to with surprise, which gradually increased to indignation. In order that my readers may not be ignorant of the extent of this tyrannical prejudice, I will as briefly as possible state the evidence, and leave them to judge of it, as their hearts and consciences may dictate.

In the first place, an unjust law exists in this Commonwealth, by which marriages between persons of different color is pronounced illegal. I am perfectly aware of the gross ridicule to which I may subject myself by alluding to this particular; but I have lived too long, and observed too much, to be disturbed by the world's mockery. In the first place, the government ought not to be invested with power to control the affections, any more than the consciences of citizens. A man has at least as good a right to choose his wife, as he has to choose his religion. His taste may not suit his neighbors; but so long as his deportment is correct, they have no right to interfere with his concerns. In the second place, this law is a *useless* disgrace to Massachusetts. Under existing circumstances, none but those whose condition in life is too low to be much affected by public opinion, will form such alliances; and they, when they choose to do so, *will* make

such marriages, in spite of the law. I know two or three instances
where women of the laboring class have been united to reputable,
industrious colored men. These husbands regularly bring home their
wages, and are kind to their families. If by some of the odd chances,
which not unfrequently occur in the world, their wives should become heirs to any property, the children may be wronged out of it,
because the law pronounces them illegitimate. And while this injustice exists with regard to *honest,* industrious individuals, who are
merely guilty of differing from us in a matter of taste, neither the
legislation nor customs of slave-holding States exert their influence
against *immoral* connexions.

In one portion of our country this fact is shown in a very peculiar
and striking manner. There is a numerous class at New Orleans,
called Quateroons, or Quadroons, because their colored blood has
for several successive generations been intermingled with the white.
The women are much distinguished for personal beauty and grace-
fulness of motion; and their parents frequently send them to France
for the advantages of an elegant education. White gentlemen of the
first rank are desirous of being invited to their parties, and often
become seriously in love with these fascinating but unfortunate beings. Prejudice forbids matrimony, but universal custom sanctions
temporary connexions, to which a certain degree of respectability is
allowed, on account of the peculiar situation of the parties. These
attachments often continue for years—sometimes for life—and instances are not unfrequent of exemplary constancy and great propriety of deportment.

What eloquent vituperations we should pour forth, if the contending claims of nature and pride produced such a tissue of contradictions in some other country, and not in our own!

There is another Massachusetts law, which an enlightened community would not probably suffer to be carried into execution under
any circumstances; but it still remains to disgrace the statutes of this
Commonwealth.—It is as follows:

"No African or Negro, other than a subject of the Emperor of
Morocco, or a citizen of the United States, (proved so by a certificate
of the Secretary of the State of which he is a citizen,) shall tarry within
this Commonwealth longer than two months; and on complaint a
justice shall order him to depart in ten days; and if he do not then, the
justice may commit such African or Negro to the House of Correction, there to be kept at hard labor; and at the next term of the Court

of C. P., he shall be tried, and if convicted of remaining as aforesaid, shall be whipped not exceeding ten lashes; and if he or she shall not *then* depart such process shall be repeated and punishment inflicted *toties quoties.*" Stat. 1788, Ch. 54.

An honorable Haytian or Brazilian, who visited this country for business or information, might come under this law, unless public opinion rendered it a mere dead letter.

There is among the colored people an increasing desire for information, and a laudable ambition to be respectable in manners and appearance. Are we not foolish as well as sinful, in trying to repress a tendency so salutary to themselves, and so beneficial to the community? Several individuals of this class are very desirous to have persons of their own color qualified to teach something more than mere reading and writing. But in the public schools, colored children are subject to many discouragements and difficulties; and into the private schools they cannot gain admission. A very sensible and well-informed colored woman in a neighboring town, whose family have been brought up in a manner that excited universal remark and approbation, has been extremely desirous to obtain for her eldest daughter the advantages of a private school; but she has been resolutely repulsed, on account of her complexion. The girl is a very light mulatto, with great modesty and propriety of manners; perhaps no young person in the Commonwealth was less likely to have a bad influence on her associates. The clergyman respected the family, and he remonstrated with the instructer; but while the latter admitted the injustice of the thing, he excused himself by saying such a step would occasion the loss of all his white scholars.

In a town adjoining Boston, a well-behaved colored boy was kept out of the public school more than a year, by vote of the trustees. His mother, having some information herself, knew the importance of knowledge, and was anxious to obtain it for her family. She wrote repeatedly and urgently; and the school-master himself told me that the correctness of her spelling, and the neatness of her hand-writing formed a curious contrast with the notes he received from many white parents. At last, this spirited woman appeared before the committee, and reminded them that her husband, having for many years paid taxes as a citizen, had a right to the privileges of a citizen; and if her claim were refused, or longer postponed, she declared her determination to seek justice from a higher source. The trustees were, of course, obliged to yield to the equality of the laws, with the best

grace they could. The boy was admitted, and made good progress in
his studies. Had his mother been too ignorant to know her rights, or
too abject to demand them, the lad would have had a fair chance to
get a living out of the State as the occupant of a workhouse, or
penitentiary.

The attempt to establish a school for African girls at Canterbury,
Connecticut, has made too much noise to need a detailed account in
this volume. I do not know the lady who first formed the project, but
I am told that she is a benevolent and religious woman. It certainly
is difficult to imagine any other motives than good ones, for an
undertaking so arduous and unpopular. Yet had the Pope himself
attempted to establish his supremacy over that commonwealth, he
could hardly have been repelled with more determined and angry
resistance.—Town meetings were held, the records of which are not
highly creditable to the parties concerned. Petitions were sent to the
Legislature, beseeching that no African school might be allowed to
admit individuals not residing in the town where said school was
established; and strange to relate, this law, which makes it impossible
to collect a sufficient number of pupils, was sanctioned by the State.
A colored girl, who availed herself of this opportunity to gain instruction, was warned out of town, and fined for not complying; and the
instructress was imprisoned for persevering in her benevolent plan.

It is said, in excuse, that Canterbury will be inundated with vicious
characters, who will corrupt the morals of the young men; that such a
school will break down the distinctions between black and white; and
that marriages between people of different colors will be the probable
result. Yet they seem to assume the ground that colored people *must*
always be an inferior and degraded class—that the prejudice against
them *must* be eternal; being deeply founded in the laws of God and
nature.—Finally, they endeavored to represent the school as one of
the *incendiary* proceedings of the Anti-Slavery Society; and they appeal to the Colonization Society, as an aggrieved child is wont to
appeal to its parent.

The objection with regard to the introduction of vicious characters
into a village, certainly has some force; but are such persons likely to
leave cities for a quiet country town, in search of moral and intellectual improvement? Is it not obvious that the *best* portion of the
colored class are the very ones to prize such an opportunity for
instruction? Grant that a large proportion of these unfortunate people *are* vicious—is it not our duty, and of course our wisest policy, to

try to make them otherwise? And what will so effectually elevate their character and condition, as knowledge? I beseech you, my countrymen, think of these things wisely, and in season.

As for intermarriages, if there be such a repugnance between the two races, founded in the laws of *nature,* methinks there is small reason to dread their frequency.

The breaking down of distinctions in society, by means of extended information, is an objection which appropriately belongs to the Emperor of Austria, or the Sultan of Egypt.

I do not know how the affair at Canterbury is *generally* considered; but I have heard individuals of all parties and all opinions speak of it—and never without merriment or indignation. Fifty years hence, the *black* laws of Connecticut will be a greater source of amusement to the antiquarian, than her famous *blue* laws.

A similar, though less violent opposition arose in consequence of the attempt to establish a college for colored people at New Haven. A young colored man, who tried to obtain education at the Wesleyan college in Middletown, was obliged to relinquish the attempt on account of the persecution of his fellow students. Some collegians from the South objected to a colored associate in their recitations; and those from New England promptly and zealously joined in the hue and cry. A small but firm party were in favor of giving the colored man a chance to pursue his studies without insult or interruption; and I am told that this manly and disinterested band were all Southerners. As for those individuals, who exerted their influence to exclude an unoffending fellow-citizen from privileges which ought to be equally open to all, it is to be hoped that age will make them wiser—and that they will learn, before they die, to be ashamed of a step attended with more important results than usually belong to youthful follies.

It happens that these experiments have all been made in Connecticut; but it is no more than justice to that State to remark that a similar spirit would probably have been manifested in Massachusetts, under like circumstances. At our debating clubs and other places of public discussion, the demon of prejudice girds himself for the battle, the moment negro colleges and high schools are alluded to. Alas, while we carry on our lips that religion which teaches us to "love our neighbor as ourselves," how little do we cherish its blessed influence within our hearts! How much republicanism we have to *speak of,* and how little do we practise!

Let us seriously consider what injury a negro college could possibly do us. It is certainly a fair presumption that the scholars would be from the better portion of the colored population; and it is an equally fair presumption that knowledge would improve their characters. There are already many hundreds of colored people in the city of Boston.—In the street they generally appear neat and respectable; and in our houses they do not "come between the wind and our nobility." Would the addition of one or two hundred more even be perceived? As for giving offence to the Southerners by allowing such establishments—they have no right to interfere with our internal concerns, any more than we have with theirs.—Why should they not give up slavery to please us, by the same rule that we must refrain from educating the negroes to please them? If they are at liberty to do wrong, we certainly ought to be at liberty to do right. They may talk and publish as much about us as they please; and we ask for no other influence over them.

It is a fact not generally known that the brave Kosciusko left a fund for the establishment of a negro college in the United States. Little did he think he had been fighting for a people, who would not grant one rood of their vast territory for the benevolent purpose!

According to present appearances, a college for colored persons will be established in Canada; and thus, by means of our foolish and wicked pride, the credit of this philanthropic enterprise will be transferred to our mother country.

The preceding chapters show that it has been no uncommon thing for colored men to be educated at English, German, Portuguese and Spanish Universities.

In Boston there is an Infant School, three Primary Schools, and a Grammar School. The two last, are I believe supported by the public; and this fact is highly creditable. [A building for the colored Grammar School is not supplied by the city, though such provision is always made for similar institutions for white boys.—The apartment is close and uncomfortable, and many pupils stay away, who would gladly attend under more convenient circumstances. There ought likewise to be a colored teacher instead of a white one. Under the dominion of existing prejudices, it is difficult to find a white man, well qualified to teach such a school, who feels the interest he ought to feel, in these Pariahs* of our republic. The parents would repose

---

*The Pariahs are the lowest and most degraded caste in Hindostan. The laws prevent them from ever rising in their condition, or mingling with other castes.

more confidence in a colored instructer; and he, both from sympathy and pride, would be better fitted for his task.

It is peculiarly incumbent on the city authorities to supply a commodious building for the colored grammar school, because public prejudice excludes these oppressed people from all lucrative employments, and they cannot therefore be supposed to have ample funds of their own.]*

I was much pleased with the late resolution awarding Franklin medals to the colored pupils of the grammar school; and I was still more pleased with the laudable project, originated by Josiah Holbrook, Esq. for the establishment of a colored Lyceum. Surely a better spirit *is* beginning to work in this cause; and when once begun, the good sense and good feeling of the community will bid it go on and prosper. How much this spirit will have to contend with is illustrated by the following fact. When President Jackson entered this city, the white children of all the schools were sent out in uniform, to do him honor. A member of the Committee proposed that the pupils of the African schools should be invited likewise; but he was the only one who voted for it. He then proposed that the yeas and nays should be recorded; upon which, most of the gentlemen walked off, to prevent the question from being taken. Perhaps they felt an awkward consciousness of the incongeniality of such proceedings with our republican institutions. By order of the Committee the vacation of the African schools did not commence until the day after the procession of the white pupils; and a note to the instructer intimated that the pupils were not expected to appear on the Common. The reason given was because "their numbers were so few;" but in private conversation, fears were expressed lest their sable faces should give offence to our slave-holding President. In all probability the sight of the colored children would have been agreeable to General Jackson, and seemed more like home, than anything he witnessed.

In the theatre, it is not possible for respectable colored people to obtain a decent seat. They must either be excluded, or herd with the vicious.

A fierce excitement prevailed, not long since, because a colored man had bought a pew in one of our churches. I heard a very kind-hearted and zealous democrat declare his opinion that "the fellow ought to be turned out by constables, if he dared to occupy the pew

*Bracketed passage omitted from the 1836 edition.—Ed.

he had purchased." Even at the communion-table, the mockery of human pride is mingled with the worship of Jehovah. Again and again have I seen a solitary negro come up to the altar, meekly and timidly, after all the white communicants had retired. One Episcopal clergyman of this city, forms an honorable exception to this remark. When there is room at the altar, Mr —— often makes a signal to the colored members of his church to kneel beside their white brethren; and once, when two white infants and one colored one were to be baptized, and the parents of the latter bashfully lingered far behind the others, he silently rebuked the unchristian spirit of pride, by first administering the holy ordinance to the little dark-skinned child of God.

An instance of prejudice lately occurred, which I should find it hard to believe, did I not positively know it to be a fact. A gallery pew was purchased in one of our churches for two hundred dollars. A few Sabbaths after, an address was delivered at that church, in favor of the Africans. Some colored people, who very naturally wished to hear the discourse, went into the gallery; probably because they thought they should be deemed less intrusive there than elsewhere. The man who had recently bought a pew, found it occupied by colored people, and indignantly retired with his family. The next day, he purchased a pew in another meeting-house, protesting that nothing would tempt him again to make use of seats, that had been occupied by negroes.

A well known country representative, who makes a very loud noise about his democracy, once attended the Catholic church. A pious negro requested him to take off his hat, while he stood in the presence of the Virgin Mary. The white man rudely shoved him aside, saying, "You son of an Ethiopian, do you dare to speak to me!" I more than once heard the hero repeat this story; and he seemed to take peculiar satisfaction in telling it. Had he been less ignorant, he would not have chosen "son of an *Ethiopian*" as an *ignoble* epithet; to have called the African his own equal would have been abundantly more sarcastic. The same republican dismissed a strong, industrious colored man, who had been employed on the farm during his absence. "I am too great a democrat," quoth he, "to have any body in my house, who don't sit at my table; and I'll be hanged, if I ever eat with the son of an Ethiopian."

Men whose education leaves them less excuse for such illiberality, are yet vulgar enough to join in this ridiculous prejudice. The colored woman, whose daughter has been mentioned as excluded from a private school, was once smuggled into a stage, upon the supposition that she was a white woman, with a sallow complexion. Her manners were modest and prepossessing, and the gentlemen were very polite to her. But when she stopped at her own door, and was handed out by her curly-headed husband, they were at once surprised and angry to find they had been riding with a mulatto—and had, in their ignorance, been really civil to her!

A worthy colored woman, belonging to an adjoining town, wished to come into Boston to attend upon a son, who was ill. She had a trunk with her, and was too feeble to walk. She begged permission to ride in the stage. But the passengers with *noble* indignation, declared they would get out, if she were allowed to get in. After much entreaty, the driver suffered her to sit by him upon the box. When he entered the city, his comrades began to point and sneer. Not having sufficient moral courage to endure this, he left the poor woman, with her trunk, in the middle of the street, far from the place of her destination; telling her, with an oath, that he would not carry her a step further.

A friend of mine lately wished to have a colored girl admitted into the stage with her, to take care of her babe. The girl was very lightly tinged with the sable hue, had handsome Indian features, and very pleasing manners. It was, however, evident that she was not white; and therefore the passengers objected to her company. This of course, produced a good deal of inconvenience on one side, and mortification on the other. My friend repeated the circumstance to a lady, who, as the daughter and wife of a clergyman, might be supposed to have imbibed some liberality. The lady seemed to think the experiment was very preposterous; but when my friend alluded to the mixed parentage of the girl, she exclaimed, with generous enthusiasm, "Oh, that alters the case, *Indians* certainly *have* their rights."

Every year a colored gentleman and scholar is becoming less and less of a rarity—thanks to the existence of the Haytian Republic, and the increasing liberality of the world! Yet if a person of refinement from Hayti, Brazil, or other countries, which we deem less enlightened than our own, should visit us, the very boys of this republic would dog his footsteps with the vulgar outcry of "Nigger! Nigger!" I have known this to be done, from no other provocation than the sight of a colored man with the dress and deportment of a gentleman. Were it not that republicanism, like Christianity, is often perverted from its true spirit by the bad passions of mankind, such things as these would make every honest mind disgusted with the very name of republics.

I am acquainted with a gentleman from Brazil who is shrewd, enterprising, noble-spirited, and highly respectable in character and manners; yet he has experienced almost every species of indignity on account of his color. Not long since, it became necessary for him to visit the southern shores of Massachusetts, to settle certain accounts connected with his business. His wife was in a feeble state of health, and the physicians had recommended a voyage. For this reason, he took passage for her with himself in the steam-boat; and the captain, as it appears, made no objection to a colored gentleman's money. After remaining on deck some time, Mrs —— attempted to pass into the cabin; but the captain prevented her; saying, "You must go down forward."—The Brazilian urged that he had paid the customary price, and therefore his wife and infant had a right to a place in the ladies' cabin. The captain answered, "Your wife a'n't a lady; she is a nigger." The forward cabin was occupied by sailors; was entirely without accommodations for women, and admitted the seawater, so that a person could not sit in it comfortably without keeping the feet raised in a chair. The husband stated that his wife's health would not admit of such exposure; to which the captain still replied, "I don't allow any niggers in my cabin." With natural and honest indignation, the Brazilian exclaimed, "You Americans talk about the Poles! You are a great deal more Russian than the Russians." The affair was concluded by placing the colored gentleman and his invalid wife on the shore, and leaving them to provide for themselves as they could. Had the cabin been full, there would have been some excuse; but it was occupied only by two sailors' wives. The same individual sent for a relative in a distant town on account of illness in his family. After staying several weeks, it became necessary for her to return; and he procured a seat for her in the stage. The same ridiculous scene occurred; the passengers were afraid of losing their dignity by riding with a neat, respectable person, whose face was darker than their own. No public vehicle could be obtained, by which a colored citizen could be conveyed to her home; it therefore became absolutely necessary for the gentleman to leave his business and hire a chaise at great expense. Such proceedings are really inexcusable. No authority can be found for them in religion, reason, or the laws.

The Bible informs us that "a man of Ethiopia, a eunuch of great authority under Candace, Queen of the Ethiopians, who had charge of all her treasure, came to Jerusalem to worship." Returning in his chariot, he read Esaias, the Prophet; and at his request Philip went up into the chariot and sat with him, explaining the Scriptures. Where should we now find an apostle, who would ride in the same chariot with an Ethiopian!

Will any candid person tell me why respectable colored people should not be allowed to make use of public conveyances, open to all who are able and willing to pay for the privilege? Those who enter a vessel, or a stagecoach, cannot expect to select their companions. If they can afford to take a carriage or boat for themselves, then, and then only, they have a right to be exclusive. I was lately talking with a young gentleman on this subject, who professed to have no prejudice against colored people, except so far as they were ignorant and vulgar; but still he could not tolerate the idea of allowing them to enter stages and steam-boats. "Yet, you allow the same privilege to vulgar and ignorant white men, without a murmur," I replied; "Pray give a good republican reason why a respectable colored citizen should be less favored." For want of a better argument, he said—(pardon me, fastidious reader)—he implied that the presence of colored persons was less agreeable than Otto of Rose, or Eau de Cologne; and this distinction, he urged was made by God himself. I answered, "Whoever takes his chance in a public vehicle, is liable to meet with uncleanly white passengers, whose breath may be redolent with the fumes of American cigars, or American gin. Neither of these articles have a fragrance peculiarly agreeable to nerves of delicate organization. Allowing your argument double the weight it deserves, it is utter nonsense to pretend that the inconvenience in the case I have supposed is not infinitely greater. But what is more to the point, do you dine in a fashionable hotel, do you sail in a fashionable steam-boat, do you sup at a fashionable house, without having negro servants behind your chair. Would they be any more disagreeable, as *passengers* seated in the corner of a stage, or a steam-boat, than as *waiters* in such immediate attendance upon your person?"

Stage-drivers are very much perplexed when they attempt to vindicate the present tyrannical customs; and they usually give up the point, by saying they themselves have no prejudice against colored people—they are merely afraid of the public. But stage-drivers should remember that in a popular government, they, in common with every other citizen, form a part and portion of the dreaded public.

The gold was never coined for which I would barter my individual freedom of acting and thinking upon any subject, or knowingly interfere with the rights of the meanest human being. The only true courage is that which impels us to do right without regard to consequences. To fear a populace is as servile as to fear an emperor. The only salutary restraint is the fear of doing wrong.

Our representatives to Congress have repeatedly rode in a stage with colored servants at the request of their masters. Whether this is because New Englanders are willing to do out of courtesy to a Southern gentleman, what they object to doing from justice to a colored citizen,—or whether those representatives, being educated men, were more than usually divested of this absurd prejudice,—I will not pretend to say.

The state of public feeling not only makes it difficult for the Africans to obtain information, but it prevents them from making profitable use of what knowledge they have. A colored man, however intelligent, is not allowed to pursue any business more lucrative than that of a barber, a shoe-black, or a waiter. These, and all other employments, are truly respectable, whenever the duties connected with them are faithfully performed; but it is unjust that a man should, on account of his complexion, be prevented from performing more elevated uses in society. Every citizen ought to have a fair chance to try his fortune in any line of business, which he thinks he has ability to transact. Why should not colored men be employed in the manufactories of various kinds? If their ignorance is an objection, let them be enlightened, as speedily as possible. If their moral character is not sufficiently pure, remove the pressure of public scorn, and thus supply them with motives for being respectable. All this can be done. It merely requires an earnest wish to overcome a prejudice, which has "grown with our growth and strengthened with our strength," but which is in fact opposed to the spirit of our religion, and contrary to the instinctive good feelings of our nature. When examined by the clear light of reason, it disappears. Prejudices of all kinds have their strongest holds in the minds of the vulgar and the ignorant. In a community so enlightened as our own, they must gradually melt away under the influence of public discussion. There is no want of kind feelings and liberal sentiments in the American people; the simple fact is, they have not *thought* upon this subject.—An active and enterprising community are not apt to concern themselves about laws and customs, which do not obviously interfere with their interests or convenience; and various political and prudential motives have combined to fetter free inquiry in this direction. Thus we have gone on, year after year, thoughtlessly sanctioning, by our silence and indifference, evils which our hearts and consciences are far enough from approving.

It has been shown that no other people on earth indulge so strong a prejudice with regard to color, as we do. It is urged that negroes are civilly treated in England, because their numbers are so few. I could never discover any great force in this argument. Colored people are certainly not sufficiently rare in that country to be regarded as a great show, like a giraffe, or a Sandwich Island king; and on the other hand, it would seem natural that those who were more accustomed to the sight of dark faces would find their aversion diminished, rather than increased.

The absence of prejudice in the Portuguese and Spanish settlements is accounted for, by saying that the white people are very little superior to the negroes in knowledge and refinement. But Doctor Walsh's book certainly gives us no reason to think meanly of the Brazilians; and it has been my good fortune to be acquainted with many highly intelligent South Americans, who were divested of this prejudice, and much surprised at its existence here.

If the South Americans are really in such a low state as the argument implies, it is a still greater disgrace to us to be outdone in liberality and consistent republicanism by men so much less enlightened than ourselves.

Pride will doubtless hold out with strength and adroitness against the besiegers of its fortress; but it is an obvious truth that the condition of the world is rapidly improving, and that our laws and customs must change with it.

Neither ancient nor modern history furnishes a page more glorious than the last twenty years in England; for at every step, free principles, after a long and arduous struggle, have conquered selfishness and tyranny. Almost all great evils are resisted by individuals who directly suffer injustice or inconvenience from them; but it is a peculiar beauty of the abolition cause that its defenders enter the lists against wealth, and power, and talent, not to defend their own rights, but to protect weak and injured neighbors, who are not allowed to speak for themselves.

Those, who become interested in a cause laboring so heavily under the pressure of present unpopularity, must expect to be assailed by every form of bitterness and sophistry. At times, discouraged and heart-sick, they will perhaps begin to doubt whether there are in reality any unalterable principles of right and wrong. But let them cast aside the fear of man, and keep their minds fixed on a few of the simple, unchangeable laws of God, and they will certainly receive strength to contend with the adversary.

Paragraphs in the Southern papers already begin to imply that the United States will not look tamely on, while England emancipates her slaves; and they inform us that the inspection of the naval stations has become a subject of great importance since the recent measures of the British Parliament. A republic declaring war with a monarchy, because she gave freedom to her slaves, would indeed form a beautiful moral picture for the admiration of the world!

Mr Garrison was the first person who dared to edit a newspaper, in which slavery was spoken of as altogether wicked and inexcusable. For this crime the Legislature of Georgia have offered five thousand dollars to any one who will "arrest and prosecute him to conviction *under the laws of that State."* An association of gentlemen in South Carolina have likewise offered a large reward for the same object. It is, to say the least, a very remarkable step for one State in this Union to promulgate such a law concerning a citizen of another State, merely for publishing his opinions boldly. The disciples of Fanny Wright promulgate the most zealous and virulent attacks upon Christianity, without any hindrance from the civil authorities; and this is done upon the truly rational ground that individual freedom of opinion ought to be respected—that what is false cannot stand, and what is true cannot be overthrown. We leave Christianity to take care of itself; but slavery is a "delicate subject,"—and whoever attacks that must be punished. Mr Garrison is a disinterested, intelligent, and remarkably pure-minded man, whose only fault is that he cannot be moderate on a subject which it is exceedingly difficult for an honest mind to examine with calmness. Many, who highly respect his character, and motives, regret his tendency to use wholesale and un-qualified expressions; but it is something to have the truth told, even if it be not in the most judicious way. Where an evil is powerfully supported by the self-interest and prejudice of the community, none but an ardent individual will venture to meddle with it. Luther was deemed indiscreet even by those who liked him best; yet a more prudent man would never have given an impetus sufficiently powerful to heave the great mass of corruption under which the church was buried. Mr Garrison has certainly the merit of having first called public attention to a neglected and very important subject.* I believe whoever fairly and dispassionately examines the question, will be more than disposed to forgive the occasional faults of an ardent temperament, in consideration of the difficulty of the undertaking, and the violence with which it has been opposed.

The palliator of slavery assures the abolitionists that their benevolence is perfectly quixotic—that the negroes are happy and contented, and have no desire to change their lot. An answer to this may, as I have already said, be found in the Judicial Reports of slaveholding States, in the vigilance of their laws, in advertisements for runaway slaves, and in the details of their own newspapers. The West India planters make the same protestations concerning the happiness of their slaves; yet the cruelties proved by undoubted and unanswerable testimony are enough to break a compassionate heart. It is said that slavery is a great deal worse in the West Indies than in the United States; but I believe precisely the reverse of this proposition has been true within late years; for the English government have been earnestly trying to atone for their guilt, by the introduction of laws expressly framed to guard the weak and defenceless. A gentleman who has been a great deal among the planters of both countries, and who is by no means favorable to anti-slavery, gives it as his decided opinion that the slaves are better off in the West Indies, than they are in the United States. It is true we *hear* a great deal more about West Indian cruelty than we do about our own.—English books and periodicals are continually full of the subject; and even in the colonies, newspapers openly denounce the hateful system, and take every opportunity to prove the amount of wretchedness it produces. In this country, we have not, until very recently, dared to publish anything upon the subject. Our books, our reviews, our newspapers, our almanacs, have all been silent, or exerted their influence on the wrong side. The negro's crimes are repeated, but his sufferings are never told. Even in our geographies it is taught that the colored race *must* always be degraded. Now and then anecdotes of cruelties committed in the slave-holding States are told by individuals who witnessed them; but they are almost always afraid to give their names to the public, be-

*This remark is not intended to indicate want of respect for the early exertions of the Friends, in their numerous manumission societies; or for the efforts of that staunch, fearless, self-sacrificing friend of freedom—Benjamin Lundy; but Mr. Garrison was the first that boldly attacked slavery as a sin, and Colonization as it twin sister. [Note added to 1836 edition.—Ed.]

cause the Southerners will call them "a disgrace to the soil," and the Northerners will echo the sentiment.—The promptitude and earnestness with which New England has aided the slave-holders in repressing all discussions which they were desirous to avoid, has called forth many expressions of gratitude in their public speeches, and private conversation; and truly we have well earned Randolph's favorite appellation, "the white slaves of the North," by our tameness and servility with regard to a subject where good feeling and good principle alike demanded a firm and independent spirit.

We are told that the Southerners will of themselves do away slavery, and they alone understand how to do it.—But it is an obvious fact that all their measures have tended to perpetuate the system; and even if we have the fullest faith that they mean to do their duty, the belief by no means absolves us from doing ours. The evil is gigantic; and its removal requires every heart and head in the community.

It is said that our sympathies ought to be given to the masters, who are abundantly more to be pitied than the slaves. If this be the case, the planters are singularly disinterested not to change places with their bondmen. Our sympathies *have* been given to the masters—and to those masters who seemed most desirous to remain forever in their pitiable condition. There are hearts at the South sincerely desirous of doing right in this cause; but their generous impulses are checked by the laws of their respective States, and the strong disapprobation of their neighbors. I know a lady in Georgia, who would, I believe, make any personal sacrifice to instruct her slaves, and give them freedom; but if she were found guilty of teaching the alphabet, or manumitting her slaves, fines and imprisonment would be the consequence; if she sold them, they would be likely to fall into hands less merciful than her own. Of such slave-owners we cannot speak with too much respect and tenderness. They are comparatively few in number, and stand in a most perplexing situation; it is a duty to give all our sympathy to *them.* It is mere mockery to say, what is so often said, that the Southerners, as a body, really wish to abolish slavery. If they wished it, they certainly would make the attempt. When the majority heartily desire a change, it is effected, be the difficulties what they may. The Americans are peculiarly responsible for the example they give; for in no other country does the unchecked voice of the people constitute the whole of government.

We must not be induced to excuse slavery by the plausible argument that England introduced it among us.—The wickedness of beginning such a work unquestionably belongs to her; the sin of continuing it is certainly our own. It is true that Virginia, while a province, did petition the British government to check the introduction of slaves into the colonies; and their refusal to do so was afterward enumerated among the public reasons for separating from the mother country: but it is equally true that when we became independent, the Southern States stipulated that the slave trade should not be abolished by law until 1808.

The strongest and best reason that can be given for our supineness on the subject of slavery, is the fear of dissolving the Union. The Constitution of the United States demands our highest reverence. Those who approve, and those who disapprove of particular portions, are equally bound to yield implicit obedience to its authority. But we must not forget that the Constitution provides for any change that may be required for the general good. The great machine is constructed with a safety valve, by which any rapidly increasing evil may be expelled whenever the people desire it.

If the Southern politicians are determined to make a Siamese question of this also—if they insist that the Union shall not exist without slavery—it can only be said that they join two things, which have no affinity with each other, and which cannot permanently exist together.—They chain the living and vigorous to the diseased and dying; and the former will assuredly perish in the infected neighborhood.

The universal introduction of free labor is the surest way to consolidate the Union, and enable us to live together in harmony and peace. If a history is ever written entitled "The Decay and Dissolution of the North American Republic," its author will distinctly trace our downfall to the existence of slavery among us.

There is hardly anything bad, in politics or religion, that has not been sanctioned or tolerated by a suffering community, because certain powerful individuals were able to identify the evil with some other principle long consecrated to the hearts and consciences of men.

Under all circumstances, there is but one honest course; and that is to do right, and trust the consequences to Divine Providence. "Duties are ours; events are God's." Policy, with all her cunning, can devise no rule so safe, salutary, and effective, as this simple maxim.

We cannot too cautiously examine arguments and excuses brought forward by those whose interest or convenience is connected with keeping their fellow creatures in a state of ignorance and brutality; and such we shall find in abundance, at the North as well as the South. I have heard the abolition of slavery condemned on the ground that New England vessels would not be employed to export the produce of the South, if they had free laborers of their own. This objection is so utterly bad in its spirit, that it hardly deserves an answer. Assuredly it is a righteous plan to retard the progress of liberal principles, and "keep human nature forever in the stocks" that some individuals may make a few hundred dollars more per annum! Besides, the experience of the world abundantly proves that all such forced expedients are unwise. The increased prosperity of one country, or of one section of a country, always contributes, in some form or other, to the prosperity of other states.—To "love our neighbor as ourselves" is, after all, the shrewdest way of doing business.

In England, the abolition of the *traffic* was long and stoutly resisted, in the same spirit, and by the same arguments, that characterize the defence of the *system* here; but it would now be difficult to find a man so reckless, that he would not be ashamed of being called a slave dealer. Public opinion has nearly conquered one evil, and if rightly directed, it will ultimately subdue the other.

Is it asked what can be done? I answer, much, very much, can be effected, if each individual will try to deserve the commendation bestowed by our Saviour on the woman of old—"She hath done what she could."

The Friends,—always remarkable for fearless obedience to the inward light of conscience,—early gave an example worthy of being followed. At their annual meeting in Pennsylvania, in 1688, many individuals urged the incompatibility of slavery and Christianity; and their zeal continued until, in 1776, all Quakers who bought or sold a slave, or refused to emancipate those they already owned, were excluded from communion with the society. Had it not been for the early exertions of these excellent people, the fair and flourishing State of Pennsylvania might now, perchance, be withering under the effects of slavery. To this day, the Society of Friends, both in England and America, omit no opportunity, public or private, of discountenancing this bad system; and the Methodists (at least in England) have earnestly labored in the same glorious cause.

The famous Anthony Benezet, a Quaker in Philadelphia, has left us a noble example of what may be done for conscience' sake. Being a teacher, he took effectual care that his scholars should have ample

knowledge and christian impressions concerning the nature of slavery; he caused articles to be inserted in the almanacs likely to arrest
public attention upon the subject; he talked about it, and wrote
letters about it; he published and distributed tracts at his own expense; if any person was going a journey, his first thought was how he
could make him instrumental in favor of his benevolent purposes; he
addressed a petition to the Queen for the suppression of the slave-
trade; and another to the good Countess of Huntingdon beseeching
that the rice and indigo plantations belonging to the orphan-house,
which she had endowed near Savannah, in Georgia, might not be
cultivated by those who encouraged the slave trade; he took care to
increase the comforts and elevate the character of the colored people
within his influence; he zealously promoted the establishment of an
African school, and devoted much of the two last years of his life to
personal attendance upon his pupils. By fifty years of constant industry he had amassed a small fortune; and this was left, after the decease
of his widow, to the support of the African school.

Similar exertions, though on a less extensive scale, were made by
the late excellent John Kenrick, of Newton, Mass. For more than
thirty years the constant object of his thoughts, and the chief purpose
of his life, was the abolition of slavery. His earnest conversation
aroused many other minds to think and act upon the subject. He
wrote letters, inserted articles in the newspapers, gave liberal dona-
tions, and circulated pamphlets at his own expense.

Cowper contributed much to the cause when he wrote the "Negro's Complaint," and thus excited the compassion of his numerous
readers. Wedgewood aided the work, when he caused cameos to be
struck, representing a kneeling African in chains, and thus made even
capricious fashion an avenue to the heart. Clarkson assisted by patient investigation of evidence; and Fox and Wilberforce by eloquent
speeches. Mungo Park gave his powerful influence by the kind and
liberal manner in which he always represented the Africans. The
Duchess of Devonshire wrote verses and caused them to be set to
music; and wherever those lines were sung, some hearts were touched
in favor of the oppressed. This fascinating woman made even her far-
famed beauty serve in the cause of benevolence. Fox was returned for
Parliament through her influence, and she is said to have procured
more than one vote, by allowing the yeomanry of England to kiss her
beautiful cheek.

All are not able to do so much as Anthony Benezet and John

Kenrick have done; but we can all do something. We can speak kindly and respectfully of colored people upon all occasions; we can repeat to our children such traits as are honorable in their character and history; we can avoid making odious caricatures of negroes; we can teach boys that it is unmanly and contemptible to insult an unfortunate class of people by the vulgar outcry of "Nigger!—Nigger!"—Even Mahmoud of Turkey rivals us in liberality—for he long ago ordered a fine to be levied upon those who called a Christian a dog; and in his dominions the *prejudice* is so great that a Christian must be a degraded being. A residence in Turkey might be profitable to those Christians who patronize the eternity of prejudice; it would afford an opportunity of testing the goodness of the rule, by showing how it works both ways.

If we are not able to contribute to African schools, or do not choose to do so, we can at least refrain from opposing them. If it be disagreeable to allow colored people the same rights and privileges as other citizens, we can do with our prejudice, what most of us often do with better feelings—we can conceal it.

Our almanacs and newspapers can fairly show both sides of the question; and if they lean to either party, let it not be to the strongest. Our preachers can speak of slavery, as they do of other evils. Our poets can find in this subject abundant room for sentiment and pathos. Our orators (provided they do not want office) may venture an allusion to our *in-*"glorious institutions."

The union of individual influence produces a vast amount of moral force, which is not the less powerful because it is often unperceived. A mere change in the *direction* of our efforts, without any increased exertion, would in the course of a few years, produce an entire revolution of public feeling. This slow but sure way of doing good is almost the only means by which benevolence can effect its purpose.

Sixty thousand petitions have been addressed to the English parliament on the subject of slavery, and a large number of them were signed by women. The same steps here would be, with one exception, useless and injudicious; because the general government has no control over the legislatures of individual States. But the District of Columbia forms an exception to this rule.—*There* the United States have power to abolish slavery; and it is the duty of the citizens to petition year after year, until a reformation is effected. But who will present remonstrances against slavery? The Hon. John Q. Adams was intrusted with fifteen petitions for the abolition of slavery in the District of Columbia; yet, clearly as that gentleman sees and defines the pernicious effects of the system, he offered the petitions only to protest against them! Another petition to the same effect, intrusted to another Massachusetts representative, was never noticed at all. "Brutus is an honorable man:—So are they all—all honorable men." Nevertheless, there is, in this popular government, a subject on which it is *impossible* for the people to make themselves heard.

By publishing this book I have put my mite into the treasury. The expectation of displeasing all classes has not been unaccompanied with pain. But it has been strongly impressed upon my mind that it was a duty to fulfil this task; and earthly considerations should never stifle the voice of conscience.